Public Administration in Perspective

Public Administration in Perspective

Theory and Practice Through Multiple Lenses

David John Farmer

M.E.Sharpe
Armonk, New York
London, England

Library of Congress Cataloging-in-Publication Data

Farmer, David John, 1935–
  Public administration in perspective : theory and practice through multiple lenses /
by David John Farmer.
    p. cm.
  Includes bibliographical references and index.
  ISBN 978-0-7656-2345-4 (cloth : alk. paper)
  1. Public administration. I. Title.

JF1351.F372 2010
351—dc22   2009030628

Printed in the United States of America

The paper used in this publication meets the minimum requirements of
American National Standard for Information Sciences
Permanence of Paper for Printed Library Materials,
ANSI Z 39.48-1984.

IBT (c)   10   9   8   7   6   5   4   3   2   1

TO: Grace
Ashton
David
Tyler

AND TO: Rosemary

Contents

Preface

There are many ways of looking at public administration thinking and practice. Through its history, the public administration discipline has used a number of different perspectives, and mainstream and other lenses have produced valuable insights and prescriptions. Each of these perspectives can be enriching. At the same time, by itself and in isolation from the others, an individual way of looking can be misleading. A solitary lens can miss critical aspects; it can give only part of the picture.

Looking at public administration through a variety of perspectives, taken together and synthesized, can deepen understanding. Such analysis from a multiplicity of different angles can stimulate fresh ideas in planning, managing, and other areas. It can illuminate underlying and constitutive features of public administration, and shed additional light on the scope of the field. It can trigger imaginative creativity in theorizing and practice. A substantial variety of lenses, analyzed together, can give new life to public administration theory and practice.

The first chapter opens with a practical example of this use of a multiplicity of lenses. It asks the reader to consider planning or managing in, for example, homeland security. It points to valuable insights provided by mainstream analyses. It then adds insights, available from other perspectives, to what is described in such terms as "bloat." These perspectives include more familiar lenses like the business perspective, which point to such techniques—now considered too scarce in the public sector—as supply chain management. They include others like the economic and the political, adding understandings about, say, money and politics. They also include the more unfamiliar—for example, neuroscience—which adds scientific explanations from the neurobiology of fear. Deeper understanding comes from synthesizing a totality of such differing perspectives.

The idea of a multiplicity of robust lenses—an approach called epistemic pluralism—is not new in parts of mainstream American public administration. The first chapter points to advocacy of multiple perspectives by thinkers like Dwight Waldo. Nor is it new to apply one or a few outside perspectives to public administration.

What is fresh is that this book attempts such an approach on a large scale. It is a scale that aims to put public administration theory and practice into perspective.

This book serves as a resource and a catalyst in prompting readers' own reflections about public administration. It is divided into three main parts, following the Introduction. The first part (chapters 2–12) discusses implications for public administration theory and practice of each of the selected perspectives. It does not offer comprehensive accounts of each perspective and implication, but instead aims to suggest what is most salient to public administration. The second part (chapters 13–17) offers an interpretation, synthesizing the implications noted in the first part. The third part (chapter 18) analyzes together all the syntheses. Reflection exercises are added, especially for students.

Sincere thanks to my graduate students, who have studied public administration thinking and practice through a multiplicity of lenses. Thanks also to public administration theorists and practitioners, who helped inform my thinking over the decades.

Public Administration in Perspective

1
Introduction:
Public Administration in Perspective

*Administrative thought must establish a working relationship
with every major province in the realm of human learning.*
—Dwight Waldo

Let's begin a journey to put public administration in perspective. Dwight Waldo, just quoted, is making an important claim. There are multiple lenses and working relationships for looking at the administrative. It bears repeating that mainstream and other perspectives have produced valuable results. Yet single perspectives, or too few of them, can be misleading. They can offer understandings that lack needed perspective.

We can start with ten questions, and with three reflection exercises. Five of these questions are about the book's method—the nature and relative advantages of using multiple lenses:

1. What is an example of multiple lenses (of epistemic pluralism) in action?
2. What are some aims of epistemic pluralism?
3. Isn't epistemic pluralism just another name for relativism?
4. Which kind of epistemic pluralism is the best?
5. Does epistemic pluralism really have antecedents in public administration?

This book analyzes and synthesizes the implications, for public administration theory and practice, of a variety of perspectives. The remaining questions provide preliminary sketches of five elements of public administration that are vehicles, as it were, in this book for examining these implications.

6. What does "planning" mean? And are there different kinds?
7. What does "management" mean? And are there alternatives?
8. What does "underlying public administration" mean?

3

9. What does "scope of the public administration field" mean? And are there options?
10. What is "imaginative creativity"? And what is special about it in administration?

The book is divided into three parts. Part I discusses eleven perspectives or lenses, one perspective (usually a discipline) per chapter. Each chapter (2–12) provides a description of the selected perspective and indicates that perspective's implications for public administration theory and practice. Part II summarizes and synthesizes the implications for public administration theory and practice in terms of the five "representative" public administration elements. One public administration element is treated per chapter (13–17). Part III (chapter 18) describes approaches for contemplating these syntheses as a whole.

Multiple Lenses: Epistemic Pluralism

Looking at both public administration theory and practice through multiple lenses is what can be called epistemic pluralism. Epistemic refers to knowing; pluralism refers to a strategy of more than one way. So theory and practice are examined from a variety of perspectives.

What Is an Example of Multiple Lenses (or Epistemic Pluralism) in Action?

Consider planning or managing a program—basic public administration functions. Consider such planning in the field of, say, homeland security or (if you prefer) policing, both public administration areas of practical concern and contemporary relevance. Feel free to substitute another public administration example.

Start with a former insider on practice and add an academic. First, the insider. Imagine that Richard Clarke (2008, p. 2), former national coordinator for security and counterterrorism, is right in his observation that since 9/11 the national government "has ceased to work well, not just in the well-known failures but almost across the board, in national security." On homeland security, for example, Clarke writes about the problem of "bloat." He observes that most administrators have not resisted bloat. His account of the problem struck me because it is clearly relevant not only to planning and managing homeland security but also to other program areas (e.g., any program area with a budget-maximizing bureaucrat). Clarke (2008, p. 322) claims that every "imaginable agency has asked for and received funds" for the Global War on Terror, and all the agencies have large centers, large staffs, and even more staff through outsourcing. Clarke explains that bloating is a problem not only of money but also effectiveness. "The terrorism bureaucracy has become so enormous that it is filled with many inexperienced staff who must spend large amounts of time dealing with one another" (Clarke 2008, p. 323). He adds that it will take an unusually courageous bureaucrat to "suggest that this new behemoth be pared, because who will want to be blamed after the next attack that his downsizing proposal cost lives?"

For an academic, turn to Donald Kettl (2004) and his earlier case study of a "system under stress." Let's emphasize only one of his observations. This is the catch-22 problem of administrators leveling (telling the truth) about program possibilities (in this case, about the possibility of providing total protection against terrorism)—the administratively fatal difficulty for administrators in telling it like it is. It struck me because it relates not only to planning and managing in homeland security but also to planning and managing in other administrative areas, such as police administration (where serial murder and organized crime do not seem to "require" complete protection—or do they? and why not? and why do some think that homeland security is fundamentally "different?"). Kettl (2004, pp. 36–40) comments, among many other things, on the drive for bureaucratic autonomy, mission conflicts, and different cultural norms in agencies lumped together in the then-new Department of Homeland Security. He includes valuable administrative comments like that indicating the asymmetry between traditional bureaucratic hierarchy and the distinctly nonbureaucratic operating fashion of terrorists—structured organizations versus networked threats (Kettl 2004, pp. 43–44). (By the way, is this the same for police administration, or not?) Kettl's comments on the problem of coordination include references to some famous old-time public administration thinkers like Gulick and Simon (Kettl 2004, pp. 66–69). And his comments on the political costs of managing risks include the catch-22 situations that administrators face. Among these is the observation mentioned above—that while no official "could long survive the furor" of reducing risks as much as possible, no "official wants to suggest publicly that full protection is impossible . . ." (Kettl 2004, p. 76).

There is a significant literature encouraging reflection about homeland security planning and managing. In reflecting, it will be hard for readers (even if they want to do so) to exclude their own administrative sense, probably based on functional areas other than homeland security. It will be hard to exclude thinking about shoes, nail clippers, duct tape, and color-coded alarms (see Kettl 2004, pp. 83–89).

Do you think that homeland security planning and managing (or planning and managing for any other program) can benefit from mainstream or traditional public administration? I myself do. But here is a different question: Do you think that mainstream or traditional public administration has the final answer, the complete answer? I myself do not.

Regardless of your estimate of the utility of traditional public administration (or public administration plus politics), couldn't a feminist perspective add additional insights? Dialogue with ideas from this discipline—an outlier discipline in the sense that it lies outside traditional public administration. Let's pick up on one writer and assume (for the purpose of this example) that Susan Faludi (2007) is right. Faludi claims that, in our post-9/11 political culture and media, there was a shift toward attitudes characterized as John Wayne manhood and Doris Day womanhood—a

Rocky/Rambo comeback. Why a return to what is described as "traditional" manhood, marriage, and maternity? Faludi's answer is a historical analysis that claims that the nation has retreated into myth. What she characterizes as "our central (historical) drama" is our inability to repel invasions of non-Christian, nonwhite "barbarians" from the homestead door. Against this, she describes a counter myth of cowboy swagger and feminine frailty, along the lines of the movie *The Searcher*: "Rumstud"-like public policy; NYFD firemen in the media as hot, hot, hot. Does this contribute insight about the underlying features of the bureaucratic aversions to recommending de-bloating or to telling-it-like-it-is? Does it add insight about societal unconsciousness and the way that, without countervailing arrangements, this unconsciousness can shape administrative and other things? Does it add support for programmatic adjustments?

Doesn't a business perspective add additional insights for homeland security planning and managing? Think about supply chain management, mentioned in the Preface. This has clear relevance to public agencies, like homeland security and the military. Supply chain management (to which we will return in chapter 3) is described as the "combination of art and science that goes into improving the way your company finds the raw components it needs to make a product or service, manufactures that product or service and delivers it to customers" (Koch 2005, p. 1). Supply chain management is taught in business schools and in departments of supply chain management—including the Sam H. Walton College of Business at the University of Arkansas. Indeed, Wal-Mart is prominent in supply chain management.

Don't other outlying perspectives—like the economic, post-structural, and New Rhetoric—each deepen our observations, our insights, and our imaginative creativity about homeland security planning and managing? Consider the economic. Reflect on the implications for planning and management in homeland security of the logic of the claim that economic interests are shaping government policies, warping the administration of policies, buying contracts, and even buying government jobs. The amount of money spent is large and growing.

Consider the post-structural or postmodern. Including the idea that some events and images are "more real than merely real," the concept of hyperreality is illustrated by the current hyper-emphasis on homeland security. To what extent do television or think tank or Internet chat, or forgetfulness or dullness, shape what counts as the really real thing? Consider New Rhetoric. What is the symbolism, amid the vicissitudes of our globalizing world, of "homeland" in homeland security? Kettl (2004, p. 7) describes the surface basis for the choice of the term "homeland." He quotes William Safire, for instance, and he refers to the use of the term by military planners in 1997. But New Rhetoric would seek to deepen the description, delving into what might lie beneath the surface. And think about other words (despite recent attempts to switch to a term like Overseas Contingency Operation and to move away from the "war" metaphor) like War on Terrorism—as in War on Crime, or War on Poverty, or War on Cancer. What is being suggested is not conspiracy;

rather, what is suggested is adding a consciousness in public administration about the power of symbolism, about the grip of language.

Add another outlying perspective. Can't neuroscience add understanding about the way the societal unconsciousness constrains and shapes administrative and other things? Doesn't it add explanations about how what underlies can be adjusted? Think about the neurobiology of fear. Neuroscience recognizes the workings of a neuroscientific unconscious in shaping feelings and actions. Faced with fear situations, for instance, the amygdala in the brain is involved in immediate feelings and action below the level of consciousness—until modified by later signals from the cerebral cortex. François Ansermet and Pierre Magistretti (2007) describe, for instance, how traces (physical modifications in the brain) that result from experience have a homeostatic function. There is what is called the somatic marker hypothesis. To repeat, decisions have a strong bodily component. To the extent that planning and managing homeland security are done by people, for people, and in response to people, the neurobiology of people can add insights.

And add another perspective.

What Are Some Aims of Epistemic Pluralism?

The aims of epistemic pluralism center on putting public administration in perspective, along the lines indicated in the opening paragraph and in the Preface. They include enriching public administration theory and practice with fresh and better ideas—with ideas that are not partial and misleading. Others would go further and say that public administration in perspective is an attempt to answer, for one thing, a complaint written (rightly or not) by Herbert Simon: "But my actual research career started in an academic backwater: public administration" (1991, p. 114).

Another aim of epistemic pluralism is to give new life to public administration theory and practice. In the days of the orthodox period from Woodrow Wilson until World War II and perhaps later, traditional public administration did have a belief that it was on the cutting edge and that its contribution to the life of the country was vital. The claim here is not that the belief was justified, but that it existed. It is the kind of confidence—again, justified or not—that currently emanates from many business schools. The aim is to provide the intellectual basis for a justified rebirth of public administration confidence.

Isn't Epistemic Pluralism Just Another Name for Relativism?

No. It is unclear why pluralism should mean relativism, just as it is unclear why it should imply that each and any perspective is equally significant—or why it should imply abandoning either science or hermeneutics. Epistemic pluralism is not ontological pluralism. The fact that there are (if there were) two roads to New York doesn't imply that there are two New Yorks.

Relativism is an especially empty worry for public administration when it comes to matters of discovery (including developing insights, generating deeper meanings, etc.), as contrasted with justification. The distinction between the logic of discovery and the logic of justification is a commonplace in philosophy of science. (Archimedes is an example. He sits in the bath and, "eureka," he discovers the universal truth about a body displacing an equal volume of water. Justifying his discovery has its own logic.) This distinction can be used to explain Milton Friedman's famous comment that the truth or falsity of a model's premise is irrelevant. As he wrote, the "only relevant test of the validity of a hypothesis is comparison of its predictions with experience" (Friedman 1953, p. 15). Friedman holds that what counts is whether the conclusion is true. The point is that a thinker can use a perspective she considers to be false in order to stimulate insights, and I would call that a kind of play of the imagination. For the purpose of discovery, it is not true that one has to be an X in order to take X seriously or to believe that X is true. For example, it is not true that one has to be feminist (or a womanist, or a critical theorist, or a critical legal theorist, or a Freudian, or a post-structuralist, or a post-traditionalist) in order to learn from and to celebrate feminism (or womanism, or critical theory, or critical legal theory, or Freudianism, or post-structuralism or post-traditionalism). But I don't suppose that a false premise—or a totally false perspective—will be useful as a component of justification.

The relativism worry for public administration is also empty when it is recalled that public administration also deals in making judgments where definite knowledge is unavailable. The ability to make good decisions without definite knowledge (or scientific knowledge) was called euboulia by the ancient Greeks. Paul Woodruff notes that, as no one knows the future, "any government is government by ignorance." As he explains, euboulia is not the same as folk wisdom—or common sense. Such good judgment, such euboulia, involves evaluating "shaky arguments when shaky argument is all we have, being open to adversary debate, and being willing to heed the wisdom of ordinary people" (Woodruff 2005, p. 154). Shall we adopt this or that policy? Shall we administer in this way or that? Public administration is in the euboulia business, and that recognition is not a back road to relativism.

Which Kind of Epistemic Pluralism Is the Best?

How many lenses is best? Choice of an optimal number of perspectives to analyze X could well depend on such factors as purpose, the nature of X, and the importance of X. That is, the number depends on circumstances. Recall the distinction between discovery and justification. If the aim is the discovery of fresh insights or facts or meanings, there is no minimum best (nor the required minimum) number. If the aim is justification of generalizations or facts, there is no need for more than one proof, if one is available. One size does not fit all.

Here are three examples of purposive sets of lenses: the first two are more than minimal, and the third is as expansive (as grand) as can be. First, note Arnold Modell's contention that studying the biology of meaning requires an interdisciplinary effort "that includes the philosophy of language, linguistics, cognitive science, neurobiology, and psychoanalysis" (Modell 2003, p. 1). Second, see Herbert Marcuse's analyses—for particular purposes—that include materials from philosophy, psychoanalysis, politics, economics, and other disciplines. Third, and speaking of the most expansive set of lenses, see chapter 16 and the reference to E.O. Wilson about consilience and the unity of knowledge (uniting the sciences, and ultimately with the humanities).

In an ideal world of gods, I suppose that all lenses are wanted. But in the less-than-optimal world of theorists and practitioners, selection is unavoidable. I suggest that we should do our best—and treat our conclusions with the modesty or hesitancy that they correspondingly deserve. Making choice necessary are factors like the large pool of candidate perspectives and the substantial difficulty in learning enough about outlying perspectives. On the large size of the candidate pool, others may well have selected lenses other than those in this book. Other volumes might take cultural or subcultural or yet other perspectives. Even within the perspectives actually selected, I have had to make further choices. With the political, for instance, consider the number of ideologies—and recall the number of important varieties within each ideology. On the substantial difficulty in learning enough outlying perspectives, it does take time to be at home with a subject like post-structuralism, critical theory, economics, or neuroscience. It takes even longer to be at ease with using them together.

The lenses chosen in this book are those I consider robust. They are fields of study that are rigorous in intellectual terms; for example, neuroscience is shaped by the best standards of science, and critical theory is shaped by an acute literature thought through with the highest of hermeneutic standards. But my individual choices could be supplemented, for example, Waldo (1956, pp. 77–106) might have added the perspective of literature, and I (Farmer 2005a) might have added postcolonialism or evolutionary biology. There are always opportunities for more perspectives.

Is a grand strategy preferable for epistemic pluralism? The strategy for achieving the aims of epistemic pluralism could be minimal (i.e., limited to one or two perspectives) or grand (i.e., the more expansive form). By grand, I mean the seeking of a larger number of perspectives—including what may turn out to be dry holes. I hope that this book serves as a resource for both of these strategies. After all, looking at public administration through a postmodern perspective, my 1995 book was an example of a publication with a minimal strategy. I now advocate the grand strategy. While some public administration educational programs tend to cover in a general way a number of perspectives, I do not know of a successful grand strategy.

Does Epistemic Pluralism Really Have Antecedents in Public Administration?

No, it's not a mere fad. There are antecedents through the history of public administration, including—much less importantly—in my own writing. However, openness to other voices in the history of public administration has been too limited.

Dwight Waldo concluded both editions of his *Administrative State* with the claim, quoted at the head of this chapter, that "administrative thought must establish a working relationship with every major province in the realm of human learning" (Waldo 1984, p. 203). And he published a series of lectures on *Perspectives on Administration* (Waldo 1956). For Waldo, administrative choices ultimately expressed philosophical preferences and values, and he held that administrative philosophy could not be separated from its "material and ideological background." The material background included items like the importance of business and the modern corporation, and the constitutional system. The ideological background includes belief in democracy, a desire to spread it, faith in science, and the "gospel of efficiency" (Waldo 1984, p. 21). As just indicated, Waldo wanted to go to every major province of learning to understand how these preferences arose and how they could meet "the demands of present world civilization" (1984, p. 203). For him, the doctrines of public administration constituted a political philosophy.

Following the end of the orthodox period, relationships between public administration and other disciplines have been commonplace! Aaron Wildavsky's description of himself can serve to symbolize this. In *Speaking Truth to Power: The Art and Craft and Policy Analysis*, Wildavsky (1987, p. 1) writes: "That I came to analysis via the study of budgeting, in which politics and economics are intertwined, may account for my refusal to dissolve one into the other and my preference for trying to keep them together as political economy. . . ." In later chapters, we will notice other examples. For instance, there has been significant work done by Michael Diamond and others in linking public administration with the unconscious. There have been publications on public administration and philosophy. And the lengthy list goes on.

Epistemic pluralism is the second cousin, in more recent times, of deterritorialization and anti-administration. Deterritorialization (discussed in 1995) is removal of the sets of disciplinary boundaries from the study of issues and situations. Anti-administrative consciousness (discussed in 1995 and in 1998) is one that exhibits radical openness in public administration thinking and action.

Yet the public administration record is, at best, mixed. Surely, time and circumstances can change the degree of openness, and this may well explain the relative openness that resulted from the 1968 conference that Dwight Waldo organized at Minnowbrook. Surely, and with exceptions, there has been a general willingness to lap up, albeit with delay, whatever is in style.

The sad fact is that public administration, with the exception of public administration at its edge, has been barely open to the more distant outlying voices. Also it is questionable whether all the perspectives that have been tasted have been thoroughly ingested. Examples are provided by the late and ham-handedly dull reception— perhaps hostility is a better description—public administration exhibited toward postmodernism, postcolonialism, and New Rhetoric. Deconstruction, to give one example, was introduced to the United States by Jacques Derrida in a 1966 seminar at the Johns Hopkins University. Despite its influence in the 1980s and the early 1990s on social sciences like political science, it was not until the mid-'90s that deconstruction found its way into public administration. The utility of deconstruction remains to be adequately recognized. Public administration shortchanges itself to the extent that it has given the outlying disciplines such short shrift.

Getting Public Administration in Perspective: The Pattern of the Book

The three-part pattern of this book was sketched earlier. Recall that each of the chapters (2–12) in the first part discusses a perspective and its implications for public administration. The second part (chapters 13–17) summarizes and synthesizes five elements or functions of public administration theory and practice chosen as the "vehicles" for reflecting on the implications of the various perspectives, with the understanding that the reader can choose to extend identification of implications to yet other targets. The third part (chapter 18) speaks of contemplating the syntheses.

To discuss the implications for public administration, the five public administration elements or functions—the vehicles—are treated repeatedly in the following chapters. These are:

1. planning,
2. management,
3. underlying public administration,
4. the nature of the public administration field, and
5. imaginative creativity in administration.

Each of these five elements includes a variety of descriptions, and it should be re-emphasized that the coverage is not narrow in scope. Planning is implicated (among other things) in policy analysis and policy studies and budgeting, for instance; and management includes directing, coordinating, controlling, and citizen participation. Practical epistemic pluralism can be helped by preliminary comments on each of these five elements. But only a first cut can be expected, because any account might change in important respects when viewed through subsequent lenses.

Think of the relevance of the Buddhist story of how the King of Savatti asks blind men to touch different parts of the elephant. When asked what an elephant is like, the blind men give different answers according to which part they have touched. Isn't it parallel for public administration described through perspective A versus perspective B?

What Does "Planning" Mean? And Are There Different Kinds?

For three reasons, it is misleading to say that planning is planning is planning. It is suggested that it is a mistake to treat planning as a single term. We should avoid painting the details of the picture of planning before we start considering the various perspectives.

First, cannot planning of one kind (e.g., administrative planning) be considered central in public administration, while another kind (e.g., policy studies and policy analysis) is considered to be on the circumference? Here I am borrowing a distinction made by Waldo (1956, p. 157) between activities in the center and at the circumference of public administration, where he indicated his view that a "healthy discipline has a solid center as well as an active circumference." Straddling the circumference of public administration are the various policy studies and policy analyses. The discourse (or world) of the policy analyst is distinctive and important. For example, Spiker (2006, p. 1) speaks of policy analysis in practice as encompassing policy formation, public sector management, and policy analysis and review. Others write of the policy analysis field as "committed to science and its methods" (e.g., Heineman et al. 2002, p. 1), and yet others point out that the "study of public policy is now a well-established component of several academic disciplines, as well as having a literature, professional associations, and theories of its own" (Peters and Pierre 2006, p. 8). And there are developments like New Institutionalism (e.g., see Lecours 2005). We can expect to reencounter policy studies and analysis when we come to perspectives like the political, and perhaps the economic. Yet we should not begin by allowing a particular discourse of planning to dominate our reflection on the implications of perspectives on public administration planning.

Second, does making a choice for, say, planning mean that function is distinct from other public administration functions? No. Planning, managing, organizing, staffing, directing, coordinating, reporting, budgeting, policy making, efficiency, privatizing, creating, managing symbolization, anti-corruption management, bureaucratic-speak, citizen participation in bureaucratic decisions, stereotyping, and human capital management are practices that are abstracted and analyzed in public administration. All of these are implicated in planning. Some of these items are themselves terms for planning in specified areas or ways—for example, modern budgeting. At a minimum, there is planning for managing, for organizing, for staffing, for directing, for coordinating, and for each of the other functions. There is even planning for planning.

Third, aren't there different levels in public administration planning (as in public administration management or any other function)? In other words, cannot the meaning of planning change between levels? For instance, there is a difference between someone responsible for planning nuclear war and someone planning for highway construction. Even for the same agency, civil service systems recognize levels of job responsibility such as, in the U.S. government, the difference between those classified as GS-11s and those classified as GS-15s. Yes, there are different meanings for the term "planning" between different levels. Is it satisfactory to be limited by a meaning that planning has on a single level, such as for the mid-level official, the target of much public administration teaching?

Let's avoid becoming entrapped in the large and important specialist literatures of the particular choice (on such varied topics as strategic planning and particular areas like disaster recovery planning, human resources planning, facilities planning) and thus being constrained within the categories of such literatures. We don't have to commit to dealing with planning according to a particular definition, for example, even Luther Gulick's general definition as "working out in broad outline the things that need to be done and the methods for doing them to accomplish the purpose of the enterprise" (Gulick and Urwick 1937, p. 13). At least at the start, I want to leave the planning canvass as open as possible.

What Does "Management" Mean? And Are There Alternatives?

Ditto for managing. It is no less misleading to say that managing is managing is managing. Managing also overlaps with other public administration functions—as in managing the planning, managing the organizing, managing the staffing, managing the directing, managing the coordinating, managing the reporting, managing the budgeting, managing the policy making, managing the privatizing, managing the symbolization, managing anti-corruption management, managing bureaucratic-speak, managing citizen participation in bureaucratic decisions, managing fear, managing stereotyping, managing public administration facts, and managing human capital management. There is also managing the managing.

Is the managing of a secretary of defense the same as the managing of a stock-room manager? Clearly not.

The meanings of managing (as for planning) also change as the boundaries of managing vary. By "boundaries," I mean the area of public administration practice that is considered relevant for public administration management theorizing or study. In terms of terrain, such boundaries for understanding managing can be drawn more or less narrowly. For instance, a boundary for the domain of public managing could be drawn that includes—or excludes—nonprofit administration. As another example, the boundary could be drawn to include—or to exclude—the military. Public administration traditionally has excluded the military. Luther Gulick advised that public administration should learn from the experiences of the military, but apparently he did not think of the learning as a two-way street. Excluding the military terrain, it will be recognized, excludes certain issues from public administration management. For instance, among the military-related issues described by Turse (2008, p. 15) are the changing face of the military-industrial complex—as it extends to academia, think tanks, entertainment, homeland security, and other components.

For now and for such reasons, let's leave as open as possible the meaning of managing.

What Does "Underlying Public Administration" Mean?

Our participation in the world is not merely through rational calculation but also through such underlying and dynamic features as individual and societal consciousness and unconsciousness. Such features as ideology, language, and symbols impact and shape the administrative (and much else) in areas like planning and management. To suggest what this means, let's anticipate some items that later chapters can be expected to include.

Ideologies, like liberalism and conservatism, shape administrative and other judgments. Ideology refers to "a structure of interrelated values, ideas and beliefs about the nature of people and society. It includes a set of ideas about the best way to live and about the most appropriate institutional arrangements for society" (Cochran and Malone 1999, p. 90). But the roots go deeper. Language and symbols, as well as history, shape the forms and choice of ideologies; they shape the world we see and want. It is "a truism that the problems that get on the agenda and the viable policy options will be determined by the culture and institutions of the society" (p. 90).

Each of us is shaped by the dynamics of our individual unconscious, as is explained in both psychoanalysis and neuroscience. For one account, see Carl Jung, who speaks of the collective unconscious and the archetypes. For example, there is the hero, whom we may mistake as part of the leadership identity required for a manager.

Each of us, as noted above, is shaped by our societal unconscious. For example, see Cornelius Castoriadis, who speaks of the webs of meaning—the magma of social imaginary significations—"that are carried by and embodied in the institution of a given society and that, so to speak animate it" (Castoriadis 1995, p. 7). So, for example, a "Roman man and a Roman woman were and are something totally different from today's American man and woman" (pp. 7–8).

What Does "Scope of the Public Administration Field" Mean? And Are There Options?

The scope of the field of public administration theory and public administration practice will also be a recurring theme in the following chapters. Explored will be such issues as (first) whether existing boundaries of public administration theory and practice are dysfunctional, (second) whether current boundary lines are arbitrary, and (third) whether the efforts to reverse the fragmentation of the social sciences can be achieved through epistemic pluralism. The boundaries refer not only to content (e.g., whether to include or exclude particular functional and programmatic areas) but also to aims (e.g., shorter- or longer-term aims).

What Is "Imaginative Creativity?" And What Is Special About It in Administration?

It is false also that imaginative creativity is imaginative creativity is imaginative creativity. Again and for now, let's leave the meaning as open as possible.

Take the adjective. Let's recognize that the meaning of imaginative (as of most words) has changed over time; probably it will change more in the future: and there is no right meaning. In Shakespeare's time, for instance, imagination had sinister undertones. "The word was juridically associated with treasonable plotting, or even with just thinking about such plotting, against the monarch's life" (Kermode 2004, p. 53). Coleridge shifted the meaning later.

The 9/11 National Commission on Terrorist Attacks upon the United States adopted a relatively narrow view of imagination as "connecting the dots." By imagination, shouldn't public administration mean more than thinking outside of the box? Imagination can mean more than being imaginative in rationalizing. What these and other alternatives are, we should hope to learn from the multiple perspectives. Should (or shouldn't) public administration be more imaginative than the 9/11 Commission?

Getting Public Administration in Perspective: Reflection Exercises

Getting public administration in perspective can be facilitated by reflection and dialogue exercises. Three are indicated here. Reflection Exercise 1 aims to help the reader in identifying implications from each of the selected perspectives, and it refers to the contents of chapters 3–12. Reflection Exercise 2 aims to help attempts to effect a grand syntheses of the implications of the entire range of perspectives, and so it refers to chapters 13–17. Reflection Exercise 3 focuses on making meaning of the grand synthesis, and it refers to chapter 18. The exercises are intended to be helpful to all readers. For students who want to write analytical papers, suggestions are made in the text.

Reflection Exercise 1: Seeking Implications

What insight(s) or implication(s) about public administration theory or practice interest the reader from the selected perspective? Exercise 1 (referring to chapters 3–12) consists in answering this question. The aim is for the reader to delve into the perspective in order to generate insights and identify what she judges to be the meaning of that perspective for the public administration element.

Reflection and discussion will help. Both include analysis in assessing claims of explanations and interpretations from the selected perspective. Inside her head or in discussion, the reader may wish to develop pro arguments and con arguments and further arguments, and then make judgments with reasons. For a book on analysis, see Weston (2001). Weston writes about "exploring the issue." He discusses the need to explore the argument on all sides of the issue, to question and to defend each argument's premises, and to revise and rethink arguments as they emerge.

(For students, instructors may well ask that they write down the implications and then discuss them in groups. For instructors, it is recognized that they may choose to limit class attention to selected perspectives—those in which they have a special interest.)

Reflection Exercise 2: Effecting a Grand Synthesis

The aim of a grand synthesis is to reflect on how all of the perspectives, taken together, relate to each of the five selected public administration elements—to planning, to management, to what underlies public administration, to the nature of the public administration field, and to imaginative creativity. There are two steps. Step 1 is to summarize the implications for the selected perspective. Step 2 is to synthesize implications. How do the implications from all the selected perspectives relate to each of the five public administration elements?

My own views are offered in chapters 13–17. The reader should use these views as points of departure. It would be surprising if the reader agreed with me completely.

The approach is what is called hermeneutics, interpreting the meaning of the set of implications listed for the selected public administration elements. Hermeneutics is not as formidable as the word suggests. It refers to the interpretation of a text, elucidating the underlying meaning. The text in this case is the long list of implications (or insights) that the reader has developed. Chapter 13 will indicate the hermeneutic circle approach that I prefer. The circle approach tries various interpretations until (considering all components) the "best-fit" understanding is reached about the meaning. For a masterful account of hermeneutics in general, see Diesing (1991, pp. 104–145). Two caveats: First, the reader is not at all obligated to follow the form of hermeneutics that I prefer. Second, a chief impediment to good interpretations is to forget to reflect.

Reflection (or Contemplation) Exercise 3: Public Administration on a Treadmill?

Exercise 3, explained in chapter 18, uses exercises from neuroscientist Nancy Andreasen (2005) to permit answering four sets of questions. My own suggestions in each case are intended to serve as a springboard for the reader's own reflections. Supplemental written versions are suggested for students.

The first set asks the public administration participant to reflect on the meaning of single items from the list of syntheses. What do each grand synthesis mean? The second set invites reflection on the selected synthesis in terms of understandings and emotions that readers have absorbed from their own examined work and lived experience. The third question asks how a selected synthesis could be implemented or applied to this or that practice, program, or situation. The fourth set suggests spending some time each day exploring the relevance to public administration of an unfamiliar, or less familiar, area of knowledge.

Epilogue

Chapter 1 has had the aims of sketching the pattern, and of indicating the flavor, of the book. Let's turn now to the second chapter and to traditional public administration.

Suggested Readings

Diesing, Paul. 1991. *How Does Social Science Work? Reflections on Practice.* Pittsburgh, PA: University of Pittsburgh.
Weston, Anthony. 2001. *A Rulebook for Arguments.* Indianapolis, IN: Hackett.

Part I

Public Administration from Multiple Perspectives

2

Public Administration from a Traditional Perspective

A traditional perspective is what is regarded as established or mainstream in ways of thinking, of believing, of assuming, of interpreting, and of doing. It also includes ways of not thinking, not believing, not assuming, not interpreting, and not doing. A traditional perspective includes, but it is not limited to, the varieties of and emphases on what is customary or what is handed down by predecessors. Approximately, the traditional perspective(s) includes what is recognized in established or mainstream public administration (PA) literature—books, journals, and reports. It includes what is considered acceptable, with exceptions, in established or mainstream public administration professional organizations like the American Society for Public Administration (ASPA, which runs the major annual public administration conference) and the National Association of Schools of Public Affairs and Administration (NASPAA, which accredits and therefore shapes the curricular content of master's of public administration university degree programs).

From this starting point, the first part of this chapter sketches the general pattern of traditional public administration thinking. The objective is to capture what is critically significant for public administration practice and theorizing. Five questions are discussed, starting with the surface:

1. What is traditional public administration? On the surface, isn't it a profusion of paradigms?
2. What is traditional public administration? How does it make sense of the profusion?
3. What is traditional public administration? Does it recognize surface challenges?
4. What is traditional public administration? How does it echo administrative things?
5. What is traditional public administration? Is it the whole or part of the story?

The second part of this chapter goes on to discuss implications (some advantages and others disadvantages) of the traditional perspective(s). The five questions discussed are as follows:

6. Implication for planning. Isn't there help enough from traditional public administration?
7. Implication for management. Isn't there help for short-run managing?
8. Implication for the underlying. What underlies surface systems and problems?
9. Implication for the public administration field. Isn't the coping strategy all it can be?
10. Implication for creativity. Aren't public administration insights imaginative enough?

Discussed are each of the five PA elements noted in Chapter 1—planning, management, underlying the administrative, nature of the PA discipline, and imaginative creativity of PA. Note the question and the readings at the chapter's end.

Sketching Traditional Public Administration

Traditional public administration is mainstream American public administration. Yet we shouldn't be content with such a simple but true dictionary-type description. Dwight Waldo (1955, p. 2) was right to claim that the "immediate effect of all one-sentence or one-paragraph definitions of public administration is mental paralysis rather than enlightenment and stimulation." He objected that such definitions inevitably contain abstractions that require further explanation in terms of other abstractions. Nor should we insist, with dichotomous blinders, that traditional public administration must be either completely right or completely wrong.

Instead, to sketch traditional public administration thinking or theorizing, start with striking surface features. Among these features, a first is that the history of American public administration is a profusion of "paradigms," as listed later. A second is that ways of classifying these paradigms are often over-orderly. A third feature is that there are well-recognized surface challenges, like those about contraries and identity. A fourth is that traditional public administration aims to echo and celebrate a constricted view of administrative practice. A fifth is that traditional public administration is truncated in such terms as geography and time.

What Is Traditional Public Administration? On the Surface, Isn't It a Profusion of Paradigms?

On the surface at least, traditional public administration thinking or theorizing is a confusion of paradigms. It is a multiparadigm world. "Paradigms" is the term public administration specialists use in the literature. Consistent with philosophy of science, it would be more accurate to say "pre-paradigms." Or, again, shouldn't they be called low-codified paradigms?

For Thomas Kuhn, the well-known philosopher of science, all the social sciences are in a pre-paradigm state. This pre-paradigm state is where many theories and paradigms coexist within the selected discipline. Kuhn made no specific reference to public administration, as far as I know; but he would say that it is pre-paradigm, with all that entails for the coexistence of paradigms (e.g., Kuhn 1970, p. viii). At one point, Kuhn described the natural sciences as proceeding by means of a revolution—a paradigm shift, a gestalt change, a change in conceptual framework—that set a new agenda for normal science as it continued to work out the details of that revolution. Examples of revolutions in physics are the Newtonian and the Einsteinian. Traditional public administration worries about the paradigms that coexist within the field, and many traditional public administration thinkers aspire to be able to declare one paradigm true.

The paradigms of traditional public administration are low codified; the content in this sense is low paradigm. Highly codified are disciplines like physics; low codified are disciplines like sociology (Klein 1990, pp. 104–105). Highly paradigmatic are subjects like mathematics and low paradigm are subjects like social sciences. Within the social sciences, an action subject like traditional public administration is lower codified and lower paradigm than, say, economics. Within economics, there is no doubt about identifying traditional or mainstream economics—and its twists and turns can be traced. There is no doubt about identifying nonmainstream schools of economics. In public administration, the contrast between traditional and nontraditional is more blurred and overlapping. Consider the difference between public administration being what is regarded as valuably traditional by, say, ASPA (just mentioned) and public administration being what is regarded as valuably nontraditional by, say, PATNet (the Public Administration Theory Network). Despite the blurring and ambiguity, the difference is still meaningful.

Are there yet other striking surface features of traditional public administration? Yes! Beyond those discussed in the following four questions, others will be suggested from the perspectives in other chapters. Within traditional public administration, for example, a start could have been made by stressing the horde of topics that are shaped and stretched by the paradigms. Look at any well-known textbook. Shafritz and colleagues' *Classics of Public Administration*, for example, contains materials on twelve topics (Shafritz et al. 2004)—the discipline of PA, the political content of PA, bureaucracy, organization theory, human resources management, the budgetary process, public management, public policy and analysis, implementation, program evaluation, intergovernmental relations, and public service ethics. Rabin's *Handbook of Public Administration*, for another example, discusses fifteen topics (Rabin 2007)—PA history, organization theory, public budgeting and financial management, decision making, public personnel management, federalism and intergovernmental relations, public policy, comparative and international relations, public law, PA pedagogy, information technology, conduct of inquiry, judicial administration, political economy, PA as a profession.

What Is Traditional Public Administration? How Does It Make Sense of the Profusion?

How does traditional PA thinking or theorizing make surface sense of its profusion of paradigms? Let's offer a partial account of PA history. This account sketches some of the groupings, drawing on some scholars that I admire, like Richard Stillman (1991) and adding others for inspiration like Orion and Cynthia McSwite. This account raises points about the following seven groupings:

1. Before World War II
2. Human relations
3. Post–World War II challenge to POSDCORB
4. Heterodoxy
5. Oppositional emphasis in 1960s and 1970s
6. New Public Management
7. Pluralist or disconnect

Yet first let's explain what it means to suggest that readers should guard against accounts that describe the history of public administration as more orderly than it was (and is). That is, beware of accounts that present too prettified (too beautiful, too clean, too orderly) a picture as if the history of the field could be seen as an onward and upward, a purely forward movement. This is even more understandable if you agree with Sigmund Freud that order is one of the marks of civilization. The danger in such over-orderly accounts is that public administration does contain pockets of disconnected and semi-disconnected nontraditional thinking, such as (two examples) the significant literature on "PA and the unconscious" and on "PA and narrative storytelling." Any account that does not emphasize a buzzing confusion of pre-paradigms, sometimes connected and sometimes not, is itself a misleading confusion.

Let's give a couple of illustrations of what it means to speak of an over-orderly account, and suggest the possibility of paths for the field other than straight-line progress. Whether the subject is public administration or the history of the world, history writing is more than picking out "objective facts," as if it were like picking up rocks lying on the ground of a landscape. The interpretive quality in writing any history is suggested by the historian John Lewis Gaddis when he remarks that "if you think of the past as a landscape, then history is the way we represent it, and it's that act of representation that lifts us above the familiar to let us experience vicariously what we can't experience directly: a wider view" (Gaddis 2005, p. 5). Guard against my account, for example.

Guard against any account. Is the order in the following account or categorization of paradigms—an account of public administration history—an example of prettifying, presumably undertaken for pedagogical purposes? This account speaks of paradigms in five time periods (e.g., McCurdy 1972 and Nigro and Nigro 1973):

Administrative Reform Movement	1870–1926
Orthodox Period: Administrative Science Movement	1906–1952
Politics Period	1936–1967
Human Relations and Behavioral Science	1933–present
Program Effectiveness	1964–present

Holzer, Gabrielyan, and Yang (2007, p. 51) explain that "Although the history of insights into public administration is neatly divided into discrete periods, that neatness can be unnecessarily arbitrary. . . . Hard and fast divisions are also misleading if students then presume that each successive school displaced its predecessor based on the correct core idea of an emerging new school."

Is the neatness (orderliness) in the following account or categorization an example of showing more of a unified and onward pattern than is justified? This account gives a decade-by-decade account, each decade with its own subtitle (Keller 2007). The subtitles are:

1880s	Intimations and foundations;
1890s	Prelude continued;
1900s	Transformations in practice;
1910s	Reform continued and intensified;
1920s	Maturation of the public interest model;
1930s	The rise of the administrative state;
1940s	Reflection on the administrative state;
1950s	The beginnings of self-awareness;
1960s	Beyond political science;
1970s	Identity revisited, new currents and curriculum;
1980s	Crosscurrents and return to basics;
1990s	Reshaping management, searching for macro legitimacy; and
2000s	PA and the search for governance in a global security state.

To the extent that the set of decade-by-decade titles can be read (or misread) as suggesting a single and concerted movement, caution is justified.

So, as promised, here is an account, consisting of a listing of the seven groupings noted above. But, to repeat, guard against "this" account, as against any other.

Grouping 1

Stillman and others describe a first stage that leads to a synthesis encapsulated in 1926 in public administrations's first introductory textbook (Leonard D. White's

Study of Public Administration). The synthesis culminated in the ideas associated with POSDCORB. Published in 1937 in *Papers on the Science of Administration*, POSDCORB is Luther Gulick's acronym for what he thought should be the functions of all public administration managers on earth—planning, organizing, staffing, directing, coordinating, reporting, and budgeting. In more detail, Stillman emphasizes five associated themes in the synthesis. The first is the politics-administration dichotomy (helpful for reforms like those in planning and budgeting). The second is scientific processes (in the form of scientifically grounded principles). The third is economy and efficiency (encouraged by Taylor's scientific management and by the Taft Commission on Economy and Efficiency, 1910–1912). The fourth is top-down hierarchy (emphasizing the manager as like a business CEO). The fifth is expert administrators (helped by civil service reform and encouraged, for instance, by the Brownlow Commission, 1937). The synthesis was also contained, according to Stillman, in the 1924 establishment of the first public administration school (the Maxwell School of Citizenship and Public Affairs), and in the creation in 1940 of *Public Administration Review*. The development of the synthesis had begun with Woodrow Wilson (his 1887 *Study of Administration*) and the 1883 Pendleton Civil Service Act. This was Wilson, arguing for administrative neutrality and for efficiency. He argued for a politics-administration dichotomy (a dichotomy between policy making and administration) and implementation through nonpolitical administration. The Pendleton Act was a seminal, albeit limited, "beginning" in developing qualified personnel capability.

Grouping 2

Slip in an overlapping human relations movement. This would extend from the experiments beginning in the 1920s on the relationship between working conditions and productivity at the Western Electric Company's Hawthorne Works. It would include thinkers like Chris Argyris, Abraham Maslow, Douglas McGregor and organizational development—aiming to "integrate" individuals and organizations. (Michael Harmon and Richard Meir (1986) speak of divisions of organization theory such as baseline, neoclassical, systems, later human relations, market, interpretive and critical, and emergence theories.)

Grouping 3

This is a post–World War II "Challenge to POSDCORB" theme or synthesis. Stillman speaks of attacks on the POSDCORB synthesis coming from Herbert Simon, Dwight Waldo, and Paul Appleby. Simon (1976, p. 1) challenged the orthodox theme in arguing that "it has not commonly been recognized that a theory of administration should be concerned with the processes of decision as well as the processes of action." Waldo's challenge, including a plea for heterodoxy, was reflected in the subtitle of his 1948 book as "The study of the political theory of American public administration." Appleby's claim revolved around his contention that "Public administration is policymaking" (Appleby 1949, p. 170). On opposition to POSDCORB principles, Simon criticized the principles as contradictory and unscientific. Waldo denied that the neutral POSDCORB principles were value free. Appleby denied that administration is limited to execution of policies.

Grouping 4

This is heterodoxy. Stillman describes the public administration field as having moved from its grand POSDCORB synthesis to parts of professional technocracy. As he put it, "the field itself became captive to its own specialization, subspecializations and professionalization, fashioning a conceptual heterodoxy fed by diverse university disciplines" (Stillman 1991, p. 126). He includes six contributing disciplines and their heterodox contributions.

- From political science, e.g., policy science
- From sociology, e.g., systems theory and organization theory
- From history, e.g., case studies
- From business, e.g., decision sciences
- From economics, e.g., fiscal policy
- From social psychology disciplines, e.g., the individual in organizations

Grouping 5

This concerns an oppositional emphasis in American public administration in the 1960s and 1970s. Stillman calls this emphasis antistate; but some may want to distinguish between a transformed state and antistate. Prominent in this phase was "New Public Administration," resulting from the 1968 Minnowbrook Conference at Syracuse University. Michael Harmon and Richard Mayer (1986, pp. 228–229) describe the overall sentiment of the Minnowbrook Conference to be expressed in Todd LaPorte's argument that "our primary normative premise should be that *the purpose of public organization is the reduction of economic, social, and psychic suffering and the enhancement of life opportunities for those inside and outside the organization*" (LaPorte 1971, p. 32, emphasis in original). They summarize the five themes that Frank Marini (1971) described. One of the themes was concern about the relevance of public administration to events like the reaction to the Vietnam War, the civil rights movement, and the War on Poverty. Another was opposition to the idea of value-free social science. The other themes were called adapting to turbulence in the environment, new organizational forms, and client-centered organization. These included opposition to the kind of bureaucracy that Weber described (but did not endorse, some would say). They also embraced the idea of citizen participation and an emphasis on social justice.

Grouping 6

Now we come to a New Public Management (or Market Fundamentalist) stage, extending into the present. Public Choice Economics surely signals an attitude toward public management. Vincent Ostrom (1973) took up this attitude to propose a market turn in public administration. He opposed what he called the Wilsonian-Weberian paradigm, characterized as single-centered administrative power, hierarchical administration, and separation of politics and administration. In its place, he advocated what he called democratic administration. He favored decentralized and fragmented authority, diverse and overlapping jurisdictions, and competition between delivery systems. We will return to Ostrom's views in chapter 4.

New Public Management sought (and seeks) to use market or private sector approaches in governmental administration. Encouraged by such decline as has occurred in belief in public interest, and encouraged by the political thinking represented in (say) Reaganism and Thatcherism, this shift occurred in Great Britain, New Zealand, and Australia as well as in the United States. It was also encouraged and shaped by Osborne and Gaebler (1992) in *Reinventing Government*. They advocated (see chapter 3) such features as competitive, results-oriented, mission-driven, customer-driven, decentralized, market-oriented government—a government that focuses on steering rather than rowing. In the U.S. government, there was the National Performance Review headed by Vice President Albert Gore—designed to establish a government that "works better [and] costs less." Among the results has been a vast increase in privatizing or outsourcing, the provision of "government" services through private mechanisms.

Grouping 7

Is there now emerging a pluralist or disconnect stage? That is, is there (or will there be) a different way of thinking? Will such a different way be encouraged not merely by disappointment with New Public Management but also by fundamental rifts (or disconnects) in society? Such rifts (or disconnects) might result from globalization, from multiculturalism, and from parallel changes. Such may encourage recognition of the potential of the epistemic pluralist model.

At the time of writing, contracting back-in of contracted services is evidenced and is being discussed in the public administration literature (e.g., Chen 2009, pp. 101–126). But the idea of a disconnect stage goes further.

Let's illustrate the disconnect characteristic. Orion and Cynthia McSwite (White and McSwain 1990, pp. 23–24), for example, offer what they call a rather "grim" picture. They speak of "fundamental historical disconnects of the sort we are currently experiencing (Foucault 1970). . . . [W]e see societies of the future afflicted with an extreme hyperpluralism—a hyperpluralism so deep and so widely spread as to deny the possibility for culture in the traditional sense of the term. . . ." In place of culture, which they define as the "indigenous, spontaneously arising symbols and rituals by which people are related to each other through their collective unconscious," Orion and Cynthia McSwite talk of technology installing control routines, amelioratives, and palliatives. (I will pass over their ideas about the public administrator providing a haven against such tendencies.) As they summarize their thought about the disconnect changes, "in short, we see a future where the foundations of meaning in life are idiosyncratically, rather than socially, based, and where in place of a regulating consensus there is outright behavior control of many varieties." Using the epistemic pluralist model as they continue with their reading, some readers may want (although I do not here) to fill out such a description of grouping 7.

What Is Traditional Public Administration? Does It Recognize Surface Challenges?

Yes, traditional Public Administration theory does recognize surface challenges. Examples of such surface challenges are paradoxes in the form of contraries, resulting from the profusion of paradigms (discussed above). The identity crisis is such a contrary.

The identity crisis of self-aware public administration thinking has been discussed almost ad nauseam. Waldo (1984) explains (as indicated above) that Wilson proposed a separation of politics and administration, making possible a generic science of PA that would aim at efficiency. Such a focus on efficiency is considered (e.g., by Riggs 1998 and others) to run up against the fact that the politics-administration dichotomy does not reflect the reality of political-administrative life. The politics-administration dichotomy of the orthodox period also ran counter to the paradigms proposed by Waldo and by Appleby. To give a different example, what Simon suggested ran counter to what Waldo suggested. Contraries are, as it were, all round.

Paradoxes in the form of contraries abound in traditional public administration. Contraries occur when two statements cannot both be true but may both be false; and, in Aristotelian terms, they are different from contradictories where two statements cannot both be true and also cannot both be false. Each of the underlying lines of development in traditional public administration yields results until it is clear that a contrary line of development should be pursued. This has been demonstrated in terms of what I have called the limits of particularism, of scientism, of technologism, of enterprise, and of hermeneutics (Farmer 1995, pp. 49–143). For example, there are advantages in traditional public administration as low tech and in public administration as sociotechnology. Yet as each reaches certain limits, needed are economic, political, and other types of inputs. There are advantages in traditional public administration as enterprise (as entrepreneurial); but again limits are encountered. (In fact, isn't there a political-business dichotomy—in the New Public Management grouping—that is parallel to the politics-administration dichotomy?) And so on.

There are ways out of such contraries (as well as of paradoxes) if certain implicit assumptions are relaxed or abandoned. (Contraries and paradoxes inevitably depend on assumptions.) However, relaxation or abandonment of particular assumptions often comes at a high price. As one way out for this field, it could be argued that traditional public administration is a developing subject, and the hope could be expressed that all would become clear with the onset of "maturity." As another possible way out for public administration, it could be asked "whether we can be content with the fact that public administration is essentially multidisciplinary, and maybe interdisciplinary, or should we continue to strive for a comprehensive theory?" (Raadschelders 1999, p. 281). Yet the reader may want to wonder whether it is part of the DNA of traditional public administration to strive for unidisciplinarity. The identity fire rages in traditional public administration (e.g., see Rabin and Bowman 1984).

What Is Traditional Public Administration? How Does It Echo Administrative Things?

Echoing and celebrating administrative practice is a feature of traditional public administration theorizing. But it echoes that part of administrative practice that is concerned with the shorter term.

"Echo" is a word taken from Richard Stillman, when he claims that "Overall, administrative theory served mainly to echo major lines of institutional development in America" (Stillman 1991, p. 105). He has just asserted that "Ideas about public administration that jelled into an identifiable field of study have, by and large, reflected the particular contours of state development in the United States." For a mixture of motives, there has been a tendency for traditional theory to justify itself through subordination to practice, especially subordination to administrative problems that administrators face in the here and now. Choosing to help the bureaucracy in coping with immediate circumstances (e.g., the arrival of e-government) seems like a no-brainer. Also, public administration's existence as an *independent* field seems *dependent* on the practitioner community, especially if the practitioners think (to the extent that they do—or don't) that the theorizing is really helpful for their varied and local needs. However, is focusing *exclusively* on immediate circumstances either necessary or desirable?

Echoing is also an oddity, furthermore, if Martin (1987) is right that "virtually every significant concept that existed in American public administration literature by 1937 (half the history of the field since Wilson's essay) had already been published in France by 1852. Most had been published by 1812" (p. 297). Speaking of public administration echoing what happened in the United States is odd if it had already echoed in France. Two echoes!

The existence of New Public Management, with its quantum jump in the volume of privatization, illustrates the subordination of theory to practice. Should traditional public administration theory focus on facilitating the new paradigm or on evaluating the new paradigm, or both? In the first option, thinkers must become involved in matters new to them. In the second option, thinkers must have some understanding of economics, which is also outside the traditional field, unless they want to do no more than repeat old slogans like "Don't forget the politics." Consider the first option—the practice of managing the contracting out of services, now required at the federal, state, and local levels. Managing of contracting out is said (e.g., by Barbara Romzek 2007, pp. 151–178) to require skills not possessed in abundance by civil servants. As the comedian George Carlin might have put it, the same civil servant group that was judged to be ineffective at producing services themselves are now asked to be effective at managing the production of goods by others. Romzek lists such challenges in managing contracting out as including specifying roles, defining performance, managing competition, maintaining relationships, sustaining staff capability, and managing accountability. She describes the complexities of indirect management that involves networks of contractees. Consider the second option—as she points out, "Evidence that privatization and contracting will save money is at least a questionable, and perhaps a faulty, expectation" (Romzek 2007, pp. 162–163). In either option, traditional public administration theorizing is being propelled to shift. It is following the leader. (The reader may also wish to reflect on whether public administration theory in support of New Public Management is attempting to row or to steer. To row, probably.)

See below for the claim that public administration's subordination to practice is subordinate only to a particular social construction of practice. It indicates that the subordination to practice is to what is in the short run and what is easier to implement. What counts as practice privileges what is considered to be practical—like reforms with payoffs in the short term and reforms that are easier to understand. In other words, traditional theorizing is not subordinate to the entire range of practice, but only to a part of that practice. Pushed to the margin are longer term needs and opportunities. When he said that the theory of administration is concerned with how an organization "should be constructed and operated in order to accomplish its work efficiently" (Simon 1976, p. 38), Herbert Simon neglected to add the words "in the short run."

What Is Traditional Public Administration? Is It the Whole or Part of the Story?

Truncated? Yes, traditional PA is truncated in terms of geography. Traditionally in the United States and in countries influenced by the United States, American public administration is regarded as the same as public administration. Basically, traditional public administration is limited to American administrative things.

There has been a subfield of comparative public administration (CPA), however. There has been a classical period of CPA, which included influences from the Alliance for Progress (1961–1972) and the New Directions (1973–1972), elements of American foreign aid, and an example of a prominent classical CPA thinker is

Fred Riggs. Influenced by globalization and New Public Management, there is interest more recently in what is called new CPA. Hasn't this had little impact on the heart of American public administration? So, we can read in a chapter entitled "Issues in Comparative and International Administration" that the "study of public administration has tended historically to concentrate on the administrative systems of individual nation-states. This is particularly characteristic of the discipline as it evolved and gained recognition in the United States. Such parochialism has often been deplored" (Heady et al. 2007, p. 605). Notice also an article by Fred Riggs (1998) entitled "Public Administration in America: Why Our Uniqueness Is Exceptional and Important."

Traditional public administration typically tends to operate as if there is little meaningful public administration outside the United States. There have been exceptions, such as the comparative public administration just noted, participation in international meetings, and some journal activity. Traditional American public administration is taught in odd contrast with, say, economics, where an introductory course on microeconomics would be the same (except for the language) whether it were given in the United States, Mongolia, or on the far side of the moon. Why should there be such a narrow public administration approach?

Traditional public administration has also been truncated in terms of time. This time truncation has been long recognized within the field. Traditional public administration is described as having started with Woodrow Wilson (1887) and his *Study of Administration*. Yet Edgar Gladden (1972) can point out the obvious, and that is that public administration goes back to ancient times. Dwight Waldo also writes that "American self-aware public administration needs to be viewed as part of the very long history that has been sketched. So viewed, it is not something altogether new and different, but another chapter in a millennia-length story" (Waldo 1980, p. 10). The whole story was what Waldo wanted recognized.

Implications

Haven't we experienced a lack of growing public confidence or public trust in government? To pick out one example, we can read Mitchell and Scott (1987, p. 455), writing that "we note a . . . waning in confidence of the public in its leadership that seems to cut across the major segments of the administrative state: government, business, unions, education." Look at most opinion polls.

Implication for Planning: Isn't There Help Enough from Traditional Public Administration?

Recall the description (in chapter 1) of the interrelationship of planning with the other public administration managing functions, such as planning of organizing, staffing, budgeting, and so on. Recall the description of policy studies and analysis straddling the circumference, at least partly outside the circumference. Planning is perhaps more associated with outlying disciplines (e.g., urban planning), and it long predated traditional public administration (ask any Roman emperor!). Outside and at least with some straddling of the circumference of public administration, there is the upsurge of projects like public policy and policy analysis. Public policy, it will be recalled, can be described as the "study of government decisions and actions designed to deal with a matter of public concern" (Cochrane and Malone 1999, p. 1), and policy analysis can be described as "an applied social science discipline which uses multiple methods of inquiry and argument to produce and transform policy-relevant information that may be utilized in political settings to resolve policy problems" (Weimer and Vining 1992, p. 2).

Turn to the macro. Distinctions between categories are often blurred toward the divide. Such blurring occurs in distinguishing macro and micro and higher and lower planning levels. Macro public administration concerns bureaucracy as a whole; this is distinguished from micro public administration, which is concerned only with an individual government. As indicated before, macro public administration resembles macroeconomics, which is concerned with the entire economy. But it is hard to allocate items like budgeting to the extent that they have one foot in the macro and the other in the micro, one being concerned with bureaucracy as a whole but the other functioning within an individual bureaucracy. "High-level" refers to officials and entities with authority to reshape a government; examples (noted above) would be Vice President Albert Gore and his National Performance Review Project, which accelerated New Public Management in the federal government. This higher level can be distinguished from middle management, which is the perspective of many master's of public administration students. Yet we would not wish to exclude from the higher level officials like the U.S. secretary of defense or even directors of major programs. But any blurring is neither an insuperable nor an unusual difficulty, except for dichotomous thinkers.

Let's start with one of the broadest categories—the macro and high-level planning of administrative activities as a whole. Early traditional public administration thinkers (i.e., in the orthodox period) planned four lines of administrative reform for achieving the happy uplands of public administration reformation. The first line of reform was in budgeting, and the aim was to develop a budgeting system that would move away from a green eyeshade or line-item way of conducting budgeting. The second line was in staffing, and that aimed to introduce personnel merit systems that would keep out the untalented but politically connected. In other words, it would defeat the spoils system and its remnants. The third line was in organization, and that would centralize organizations at all levels of government. It would unify hitherto independent units under the chief executive, like the president, the governor, or (a then-newish invention) the city or county manager. The fourth line of reform was in introducing the senior executive service, a class of senior generalist administrator who could move from one high-level management position in one department to that in another. The senior executive service in the federal government, imitating the British civil service administrative class (a category now abolished), would practice generalist public administration. So instead of a physician being the manager in a health department, for example, enter the administrator trained in traditional public administration.

At this broadest of macro administrative levels, there are writings on administrative histories and on administrative problems. Leonard White's administrative histories are examples of the former. For instance, in his book *The Jacksonians*, Leonard White shows how the "Jacksonians depended on experience, not on theory. . . . The administrative art was, in fact, obscured by the art of politics" (White 1954, p. 551). His previous books had been about the Federalists and the Jeffersonians; there would be others like that on the republican era. The narrower end of the macro included (and includes) some case study literature. Here, much is unconnected with academe. Some case studies explain or interpret specific administrative functions and macro problems, frequently using administrative judgments. Surely there is a useful literature, for example, Alice Rivlin (1971) on evaluation and Donald Kettl (2004), as mentioned before, on homeland security. I recall memoranda (Farmer 1968) I prepared for the National Advisory Commission on Civil Disorders (the Kerner Commission), as another example. They showed how the typical local government at that time could plan better. Commented the commission, "Without proper planning and objective evaluation of community resources available, mutual agreements [between jurisdictions] are largely worthless" (National Advisory Commission on Civil Disorders 1968, p. 284).

At the micro level, there is a long history of administrative and other commissions. For the federal government, the 1937 Brownlow Commission (the President's Commission on Administrative Management, headed by Louis Brownlow, Charles Merriam, and Luther Gulick) can speak of its focus on "administrative management—the organization for the performance of the duties imposed upon the president in exercising the executive power vested in him by the Constitution of the United States" (President's Committee on Administrative Management 1937, p. 1). The 1949 Hoover Commission (Commission on Organization of the Executive Branch of Government) can say that it "deals with the essentials of effective organization of the executive branch" (Hoover Commission 1949, p. 1). And so on. Then, every other major jurisdiction—and surely most minor governments—support and receive studies written about administrative topics. When with Public Administration Service and with the Jacobs Company (Planning Research Corporation), I conducted studies for some forty state and local governments. Reports were about public administration topics like management, organization, personnel, revenue administration, data processing, and performance measurement.

Return to budgeting, the first of the four lines of public administration's macro and high-level planning as a whole. Two reminders. To repeat, first, budgeting is itself a form of planning. Second, budgeting has contributed to both the macro and the micro.

Start with the positive side of the macro scoreboard. Wildavsky (1987) theorizes that budgets and budgeting are societal phenomena, and surely this is a valuable formulation. He described budgeting as a cultural phenomenon—or, as I (1995) have described public administration entities and facts, as socially engineered and socially constructed. As Wildavsky wrote, "Obviously, no society means no government and, hence, no budget. I reject this antisocial (worse still, this unbudgetary) view of the world" (Wildavsky 1987, p. 51). He adds that "[b]udgets and social life imply one another." The strength of this description is that it locates the subject matter of budgets and budgeting in society. It is not possible to understand budgets without exploring society. The nature of society conditions and shapes society's budgets and budgeting, and it is inadequate to think only of the way that budgets and budgeting shape society. A distinction is being drawn between budgets as the financial plan and budgeting as the structure for constructing budgets. The budgeting structure (the legal rules and the other prescriptions for budgeting) in American government differs from that in the Westminster governments, for example. The point is that both budgets and budgeting are, in Wildavsky's terms, cultural phenomena."Ask how budgets ought to be made and you will hear how social life ought to be lived," asserts Wildavsky (1987, p. 51). A strength of this view, I repeat, is that it invites the student of budgets to look first to the nature of society. What Wildavsky should emphasize is that budgeting is not merely a mechanical "thing." It is also a manifestation of societal consciousness and practice. Irene Rubin goes on to describe alternative theoretical ways in which this link between budgeting and societal phenomena has been theorized. These alternatives include neo-Marxist, Public Choice, incrementalist, and hierarchy theories.

There is a limit to the understanding of budgeting that is available from public administration theorizing by itself, however. Traditional public administration has not been—and cannot be—responsible for all the theoretical advances surrounding public budgeting. John Maynard Keynes changed understanding of budgeting, for example, describing how fiscal policy can have an ameliorative effect on business cycles. From his analysis come theoretical and practical consequences. The budget is now widely understood as an economic tool. An associated idea is that budgets should be balanced not annually but over the lives of business cycles. Some writers do not accept the monumental Keynesian analysis, but they have the hard task of rejecting the macroeconomics that Keynes created.

There is a view that budgeting does not have a theory. Rubin expresses a view of a theory, similar to what we have been calling a paradigm, explaining that its function "is to provide an orientation to a field, and to come up with some hypothesis about what causes what. In public administration, theory has the additional responsibility of culling practical problems and suggesting solutions. Budget theory in particular should be able to answer questions about why particular questions should be adopted, the importance of particular tasks, and the location of particular tasks in a larger process" (Rubin 1990, p. 3; 2006, p. 165). It is in this sense that Rubin can say that budgeting does not have a theory. She adds that writers "on budgeting do not agree on common assumptions or recommendations. While there are some common questions that have long stirred interest in budgeters, there is no widely accepted set of link hypotheses concerning cause and effect in budgeting" (Rubin 1990, p. 3). Regardless of the terminology about theory, it is hard not to sympathize with the idea that seems to lie within Rubin's comment. Rubin is not alone, of course. So V.O. Key (1940, p. 1), in his book *The Lack of a Budgetary Theory*, long ago could say that "American budgetary literature in singularly arid."

The claim that budgeting is theoryless can be contested, however. The concept of *theory* is elastic. On the description of a theory advanced by those like Andrew Sayer, certainly Wildavsky's and the other PA claims do constitute a set of theories. Sayer (a writer on the philosophy of social science) describes a theory as "a particular way of conceptualizing something" (1984, p. 50). Sayer identifies other senses of theory as "an ordering framework," or (as Milton Friedman puts it), as a "filing system" and as a term "often used interchangeably with "hypothesis" or "explanation." None of these views of a theory includes what appears to be Rubin's idea that X is a theory only if there are no competing theories, and none includes the idea that public administration theory should have the extra requirement of culling practical problems and suggesting solutions.

On the micro side of budgeting, the relationship between the use of better budgetary techniques and better governmental performance seems significant. The movement away from line-item budgeting to the various process improvements like performance budgeting, program budgeting, management by objectives, and zero-based budgeting seemed so promising. My very first job in government was as a budget analyst, and I recall the excitement in our Budget Bureau as we analyzed our assigned programs.

Return to the other three nonbudgeting lines of reform. Despite real benefits, didn't they fail to reach what we earlier called the happy uplands of administrative reform? On the personnel line, let us grant that the staffing or personnel line made significant strides in eliminating much of the spoils system through a succession of enactments that have extended the civil service system. Yet, despite talk about items like human capital, couldn't we well ask whether the staffing aim should not have been that of extending the pool of creative and imaginative personnel? On the organizational line, some progress has been made in centralizing bureaucracies. But should that have been the aim? On the generalist administrator line, a Senior Executive Service has been created in the federal government. Has it made the administrative reforming difference that was hoped for?

Implication for Management: Isn't There Help for Short-run Managing?

Recall (see chapter 1) that management is a broad term, no less than planning. In the orthodox period, it came to signify seven functions—POSDCORB. Later, it came to include others, for example, managing external relations, managing external coordination, managing public relations, and so on.

Haven't shorter-term improvements been made in directing, coordinating, and controlling in the public sector? Yet, surely, more profound upgrades could have been—and could be—made if management thinking could focus more on the longer run. It is in the longer run that what is socially constructed can be adjusted. Limiting management to the shorter-term constitutes overconcentration on the problems of practice as it is currently constructed. The issue is about overconcentration that limits theory from considering longer-term and more difficult problems—even identifying such problems.

Traditionally, there has been a limiting tendency to regard public administration practice as a given or a natural kind, rather than to recognize it as socially constructed. It is not only traditional public administration theory that is socially constructed, it is also practice. Jong Jun is referenced in later chapters as a writer who describes this tendency as *reifying* bureaucracy, where reifying means forgetting why and how concepts were originally constructed and "accepting them as real things that control bureaucratic life" (Jun 2006, p. 7) and that have lives of their own. He explains, as examples, that rules and roles and job descriptions are interpreted and constructed by people "as the necessary requirements for maintaining organizational order and operation" (Jun 2006, p. 7). Other examples of social constructions in traditional public administration practice, which I gave earlier (1995, pp. 21–22), include *government, employee, public sector, budget, paycheck,* and *supervisor.*

We should recognize that there is a back-and-forth movement between practice and theory, and that theory—if it has qualities like imaginative creativity—can shift understanding of what practice is. Theory can shift the social construction, rather than being a discipline that trails whatever is the latest style in practice. It can do this well only if it does not consider practice to be a given, to be nothing less than "as it really is." It can be said that the obvious involvement of public employees in the political perspective (obvious to those academics like Waldo who worked in government in World War II and to others who did so later) led to Waldo's paradigm that restructured public administration practice as including the political. Pre-Waldo, it may be said that the practical problems of public administration were not socially constructed as including public administration's legitimate involvement in the political. Seeing problems so defined as if they were natural kinds is inhibiting to theorizing. Similarly, the post-Waldo construction of problems is inhibiting if such constructions are regarded as natural kinds.

Implication for the Underlying: What Underlies Surface Systems and Problems?

Traditional public administration focuses so much on surface administrative problems. Yet couldn't more be achieved by turning more to the underlying? By *underlying,* the contrast is being made with the fact that many traditional thinkers tend to regard public administration theory and practice as dealing with administrative things independent of the societal and individual conscious, subconscious, and unconscious. Clearly this claim does not apply to all traditional thinkers; for example, there is Waldo. Some nontraditional thinkers, by contrast, regard the unconscious as primary.

Return to New Public Management and consider it as an example. Consider some (only some, and not even the deepest) of the layers that lie underneath "commitment" to this paradigm. Recall that the paradigm embraces market fundamentalism. With the adoption of this paradigm, public administration has drawn in its horns on its own macro administrative planning. Macro "administrative" plans (like New Public Management) come from *underneath* and outside public administration, for example, at least from the ideological and, to a lesser extent, probably through the upsurge of "outside" disciplinary projects like public policy and public analysis.

Rather than the result of theorizing or administrative practice, wasn't the New Public Management paradigm more likely the result of a spike in the popularity of what Waldo called this country's "business civilization"? Wasn't the shift to market fundamentalism, boosted by the political conservatism reflected in the election of presidents Ronald Reagan and George Bush, more important in deepening the belief that government is unacceptably inefficient? Wasn't the desire of business for the profits of privatization a co-driving force, bolstered by the idea that market economics sanctioned such a shift?

Yet market fundamentalism in the American culture, in the American psyche, goes much deeper than mere economic theory. Don't worry; it would be hard to eradicate such a psyche-set. A different matter is being self-conscious about, and tweaking, any details in the psyche-set that may or may not be less suitable for the current context. This is a topic that tugs at the heartstrings. But it is also a serious area of study; see, for example, Scott (1977), on American conceptions of property from the seventeenth to the twentieth century. Meanwhile, doesn't societal consciousness (and unconsciousness)—our culture's way of thinking—have more of a claim as "the" force that conditions economic attitudes like market fundamentalism, paradigms like new public administration, and public administration?

Using the perspectives discussed later, we can ponder the deeper levels! These deeper levels of societal unconsciousness impact public administration theory and practice, whether or not traditional theorists are conscious of the conditioning. At one level, it is the belief in the "mission of America" (Waldo 1984, pp. 15–21)—the spreading of democracy and the status of the Founding Fathers. Inspired unconsciously by American exceptionalism, it may appear natural to think that, say, traditional public administration is mainstream American public administration. So, constrained by its unawareness of societal unconsciousness, many in traditional theory can be prepared to commit self-hurting acts that American business management would not. For instance, many may be prepared to ignore benchmarking (e.g., steel companies watching to see how successful foreign companies produce steel) and thus ignoring any better approaches adopted in other cultures.

There are deeper levels. At another level, for instance, there is public administration's acceptance of the modernist view of the world as a machine (e.g., see Farmer 2005a). It appears unnatural not to center so emphatically on administrative things "out there," as if public administration problems were nothing more than an array of broken machine parts waiting to be fixed. And, when we come to the psychoanalytic perspective, we shall expect to encounter additional—and even deeper—levels.

Implication for the Public Administration Field: Isn't the Strategy for Coping All It Can Be?

Remember the public administration macro administrative plan (discussed above) used in the orthodox period. Does public administration currently have a compelling and fresh successor worthy of that forerunner? No. Should any such successor be designed with recognition of the changing context?

Complex changes in the context of administering include changes in technology, changes in knowledge content, and changes in the helping context, and coping with the changes requires reinvigorated theorizing. Compare and contrast managing that was limited by the quill pen and managing now limited by the computer.

Traditional public administration, to the extent that it is not on the upswing, can be expressed in terms of butts. On the academic side, traditional public administration is too often the butt of jokes from (say) political scientists—who in turn are too often the butt of jokes from (say) economists, who in turn are too often the butt of jokes from (say) physical scientists. On the practice side, public service practitioners are frequently the butt of jokes from private sector practitioners. In turn, practitioners are often dismissive of theory as *mere theory.*

Implication for Creativity: Aren't Public Administration Insights Imaginative Enough?

Three cheers for the 9/11 National Commission on Terrorist Attacks upon the United States (2004) for emphasizing the need for imagination in governmental bureaucracy. People don't take terrorism lightly, and here is a consensus commission—consisting only of political bluebloods—writing about the centrality of the imagination.

Two cheers for the 9/11 National Commission for claiming that there is a need to bureaucratize, to routinize, imagination in government! It's true that imagination occurs even in traditional agencies. But I think that to bureaucratize (in the manner of traditional bureaucracy) is to kill the imagination, like a python.

One cheer for the 9/11 Commission for failing to criticize traditional public administration theorizing for offering no help in saving the commission from making its central unimaginative recommendation. The recommendation was that, in addressing the problem of how to have an imaginative idea survive as it goes up the bureaucratic chain of command, the government should be content to appoint yet another bureaucratic layer to "force" such ideas up. Doesn't the traditional public administration mindset encourage such bureaucratic "one liners"? Clearly, there is more to be said about the imagination that public administration needs.

Epilogue

Please reflect on Feliz Nigro's definition of public administration, in view of your own experience and the comments in this chapter. How adequate is it as a definition of traditional public administration? Does it invite qualifications and exceptions?

Nigro (1970, p. 21) writes that public administration "is a cooperative group effort in a public setting; covers all three branches—executive, legislative, and judicial—and their interrelationships; has an important role in the formulation of public policy and is thus a part of the political process; is different in significant ways from private administration; [and] is closely associated with numerous private groups and individuals in providing services to the community."

Then, in the next chapter, let's turn to public administration from a business perspective, the first of the eleven perspectives discussed in chapters 3–12.

Suggested Readings

Harmon, Michael, and Richard T. Mayer. 1994. *Organization Theory for Public Administration*. Burke, VA: Chatelaine.

Simon, Herbert. 1976 (1945). *Administrative Behavior: A Study of Decision Making Processes in Administrative Organization*. 3rd ed. New York: Free Press.

Waldo, Dwight. 2007 (1948). *Administrative State: A Study of the Political Theory of American Public Administration*. New Brunswick, NJ: Transaction.

3

Public Administration from a Business Perspective

The business perspective has long been significant in the United States. Remember the words of Calvin Coolidge and of Dwight Waldo: "After all, the chief business of the American people is business," President Calvin Coolidge told the American Society of Newspaper Editors in Washington in January 1927. This is widely "misquoted" as "the business of America is business." It is true that Coolidge added toward the end that speech, "We make no concealment of the fact that we want wealth, but there are many other things that we want more . . . the chief ideal of the American people is idealism. . . . That is the only motive to which they give any strong and lasting reaction." Yet, it is close enough. In the same vein, Waldo would write that "Despite increasing pressure of population on resources and continuing prodigality in the use of resources, America remained a uniquely wealthy country, and ours became characteristically a Business Civilization" (Waldo 1984, p. 9). Business civilization—a term with a variety of meanings.

From this general standpoint, the aim is to begin by sketching the nature of a business perspective. The objective is to note what is critically important for public administration (PA) theory and practice about the general pattern. The following five questions are discussed.

1. What is a business perspective? What is an entrepreneur?
2. What is a business perspective? Are there alternatives to the entrepreneurial?
3. What is a business perspective? What, in a nutshell, is its past history with public administration?
4. What is a business perspective? Is it part of the underlying language of public administration?
5. What is a business perspective? What is business in today's terms?

The second part of the chapter discusses implications for public administration theory and practice of the business perspective. Reference is made to each of the five public administration elements noted in chapter 1—planning, management, underlying the administrative, the nature of the field, and imaginative creativity.

6. Implication for planning—What would Osborne and Gaebler do?
7. Implication for managing—Isn't supply chain management beneficial?
8. Implication for the underlying—Is there cultism in leadership?
9. Implication for public administration field—Shouldn't public administration seek the strategic?
10. Implication for public administration creativity—Does openness to business administration require imagination?

Recall Exercise 1 (see chapter 1). Readers should determine what insight or insights about public administration theory and practice interest them from a business perspective. The aim is to for the readers to generate PA-relevant insights.

Sketching the Business Perspective

Is the business perspective entrepreneurial? Like Osborne and Gaebler (1992), who speak of the entrepreneurial spirit, I agree with this characterization. Unlike them, I recognize that this characterization leaves us with difficulties in saying what entrepreneurial precisely means—and thus what the business perspective precisely means.

What Is a Business Perspective? What Is an Entrepreneur?

If the business perspective is to encourage the entrepreneurial even in government, what is an entrepreneur? Let's agree that an entrepreneur is one who undertakes and who is responsible for an enterprise. From the French *entreprendre* (meaning, to undertake). At least in this sense of economic theory, the entrepreneur is a leader of an enterprise. Beyond this, there are varieties in meaning. Consider one variety described by David Osborne and Ted Gaebler.

On the economic view, a core meaning of entrepreneur is to designate a person who is the owner of a business firm. That entrepreneur, whose actions in mainstream microeconomic theorizing are synonymous with the firm he heads, is an economic man in that his innovative actions are rational and entirely self-interested. That is, entrepreneurs seek to optimize their returns—to optimize their profits. The term "economic man" is used because that is the traditional term in economics, although we all know that many women are also in that position. Whether or not a type A personality, the entrepreneur has his eyes always set on the bottom line—on optimizing profits. In Public Choice theorizing, this concept of an entrepreneur is extended to public choice or nonmarket situations like the political. Thus we can have a political entrepreneur. Such Public Choice theorizing can seek to explain the actions of political entrepreneurs in providing public goods.

For a broader example, a core meaning of "entrepreneur" is "innovator." So say Osborne and Gaebler. They quote the French economist Jean-Baptiste Say, who says that the "entrepreneur shifts economic resources out of an area of lower and into an area of higher productivity and greater yield" (Osborne and Gaebler 1992, p. xix). They explain that this means that the entrepreneur "uses resources in new ways to maximize productivity and effectiveness" (p. xix). An entrepreneur could be the person capable of achieving entrepreneurial government, for example, where the desirable functioning (see below) is described as catalytic, community-owned, competitive, mission-driven, results-oriented, enterprising, anticipatory, decentralized, and market-oriented.

An entrepreneur has innovation as his or her specific tool, and must search "systematically for the sources of innovation, the changes and their symptoms that indicate opportunities for successful innovation" (Drucker 1993, p. 19). So explains Drucker, whom Osbrone and Gaebler quote and whom they call "the sage of management theory." For all of these writers, an entrepreneur is not a risk taker. On the contrary, he or she is a risk minimizer.

It is unsurprising when a word is taken and used in a new context, as word meanings are continually shifting over time. It is no surprise to see terms like public entrepreneur (to describe a Robert Moses, for instance, master builder in New York) and social entrepreneur (to describe a Baden-Powell, for example, founder of the Boy Scouts). But I am not sure why Osborne and Gaebler insist that the "true meaning" (as if words had "true" meanings) of *entrepreneur* cannot vary. They appeal to the long-ago economist Jean-Baptiste Say and his *Treatise on Political Economy* (1803). In a sense, this is a small point. The very words they quote from Say question their claim, and the translator (C.R. Princep of the 55th edition of Say's treatise in 1855) reports that he translates the economic "entrepreneur" as "adventurer." In another way, Osborne and Gaebler's point is not small if it leads us away from asking how the political or bureaucratic entrepreneur should be constrained (e.g., see McLean 1987, pp. 28–44). It is not trivial if it glosses over the source of the rhetorical power of the term *entrepreneur*.

Is the entrepreneurial what entrepreneurs actually do and actually think, or is it what they ought to do and think? Do small entrepreneurs have the same perspective as do big entrepreneurs, or should they? Or, is the entrepreneurial what mythology (e.g., entrepreneurs as risk takers versus as risk avoiders) or diverse ideologies picture entrepreneurs as doing and thinking?

What Is a Business Perspective? Are There Alternatives to the Entrepreneurial?

Rather than fostering the use of an apple pie concept like the entrepreneurial, an alternative is that a business perspective can be described as using wealth/power. This alternative perspective is to optimize profits through such means as securing legislation favorable to business, profitable government contracts, beneficial tax law changes, and interest group politics.

Business interest group politics can take such overlapping forms as business interest representation and payment. Interest group politics for business works in ways that are parallel to other groupings, except that the availability of larger funds adds clout. The National Association of Manufacturers is but one example; since 1895 it has had as its mission "to enhance the competitiveness of manufacturers by shaping a legislative and regulatory environment." Another example of an association is the U.S. Chamber of Commerce: it advocates for whatever governmental policy actions it is supporting, for example, protecting intellectual property and keeping business and other taxes low. There is a mass of national, regional, and local associations and others, representing economic activities and occupations and other features. Many are linked with lobbying firms and individuals. Individual corporations also have their own lobbyists and other representatives; lobbying is part of business practice. The volume of lobbying from business is large and growing (see chapter 1). Let the pharmaceutical industry, along with the makers of medical devices, serve as examples. They spent more than $189 million in 2007 lobbying the federal government (Center for Public Integrity 2005). The writing of legislation by lobbyists working for business interests is a commonplace. Lastly, there is influencing (indirect buying?) of awards of government outsourcing contracts.

There is a large literature on this subject. But the topic is not typically included in traditional public administration academic programs. Start with a book like *Is That a Politician in Your Pocket? Washington on Two Million a Day* (Sifrey and Watzman 2004), and check the Center for Public Integrity Web site (www. publicintegrity.org).

What Is a Business Perspective? What, in a Nutshell, Is Its Past History with Public Administration?

The entrepreneurial version of the business perspective has impacted public administration in two major waves. Being business-like, through system adjustment, has been a recurring aim in traditional public administration. The interest group version has grown dramatically as a factor since World War II and is now rapidly accelerating. Both versions have interconnections.

A first extensive use of the entrepreneurial version was at the outset of American public administration and through the orthodox period. A system change was to focus solely on the efficiency of the administrative, separating out the political. As Woodrow Wilson wrote, the "field of administration is the field of business" (Wilson 1887, p. 210). The paradigm was being efficient, like a business (see chapter 2).

The second extensive use of the entrepreneurial version has been in the more recent New Public Management period. The interest group version has also been in evidence. Certainly this includes an efficiency aim, but there is much else; there is a wish for more marketlike leadership and also significant outsourcing to the market. This paradigm in its earlier years of 1993–2001 had highest-level support in the United States in the form of the National Partnership for Reinventing Government (REGO), successor (as noted earlier) of the National Performance Review (NPR). Creating NPR in March 1993, President Bill Clinton explained the goal as making "the entire federal government less expensive and more efficient, and [changing] the culture of our national bureaucracy away from complacency and entitlement toward initiative and empowerment." Vice President Albert Gore described REGO (see chapter 2) as creating a government that "works better, costs less, and gets results Americans care about." The high level of support for this paradigm continued and intensified during the administration of President George W. Bush. Here the system change has been to focus on being more market oriented, even more like a business.

What Is a Business Perspective? Is It Part of the Underlying Language of Public Administration?

The business perspective is part of the language of thinking about PA. In the United States and in the world, the market currently is hegemonic, dominant, the master idea. As O.C. McSwite (2002, p. 86) explains, "The dominant fact of the world right now, it seems clear, is that free market capitalism has reached a position of hegemony. Many are raising and discussing the question of whether government is needed at all." The dominance is so entrenched in the United States and related societies that it is hard for public administration to have a way of thinking that is independent of the business perspective. For many people, the business perspective is part and parcel of the way of reflecting about public administration and government. O.C. McSwite (2002, p. xix) claims, "The United States has been overtaken by its shadow, its deeply embedded ideological side. Never before has it been so dominated by an ideological hegemony. The hegemony I mean, of course, is free market capitalism in its late capitalist incarnation, the leading edge of economic globalization."

There is much below this in terms of libidinal attachment, and we shall have to turn to other outlying disciplines for help—such as psychoanalysis. Clearly, the current form of Business Civilization has deepened popular and public administration attachment to what is business-like. Arguably, libidinal attachment to consumerism has intensified, as there are ever more goods and services, ever more advertising, and ever more rhetoric. Arguably strengthening the libidinal attachment, business has begun to play an even larger part in societal governance, for example, through massive involvement in lobbying, in think tanks and in corporate-owned news coverage. Arguably, the emotions of the long-gone cold war and the pressures and opportunities of globalization have added to the force of the libidinal attachment.

What Is a Business Perspective? What Is Business in Today's Terms?

For two nonmainstream views of the current form of our Business Civilization, see Robert Reich (2007) and Benjamin Barber (2007). Nowadays, business is *not* the same *in important respects* as it was in the 1950s. For a mainstream view, see Alan Greenspan (2007) and the *Wall Street Journal*.

Reich (2007) contrasts the economies of the mid-1950s with what he calls today's supercapitalism—capitalism that is global and Web-based. Since the 1970s, there have been pluses, for example, Reich's view is that large firms became more competitive, global, and innovative, and investors and consumers have better deals and better choices available. Yet logical outcomes of supercapitalism, in Reich's view, are such negatives as widening income disparity, increased job insecurity, and the spreading effects of global warming. The institutions shriveled that had served to "spread the wealth and protect what citizens valued in common . . . . Regulatory agencies faded. CEOs could no longer be corporate statesmen. Lobbyists swarmed over. . . . Thus did Supercapitalism replace democratic capitalism" (Reich 2007, p. 7). The extent to which this can, and will, be corrected in President Barack Obama's and later administrations remains to be seen.

Barber (2007) describes an economy where the primary goal of producers is no longer to produce goods and services, but to produce wants. This refers to the distinction widely learned in many kindergartens between needs and wants; Barber's suggestion is that producers are generating wants. There is what Barber calls market totalism, where the market is omnilegitimate (engaging in self-justification and self-rationalization), ubiquitous, and addictive. For more, see below. Barber explains that capitalism per se is not the issue he is raising. "The question is not whether there is an alternative to markets but whether markets can be made to meet the real needs capitalism is designed to serve, whether capitalism can adapt to the sovereignty of democratic authority that alone will allow it to survive" (Barber 2007, p. 4).

Greenspan (2007, pp. 268–269) repeats a mainstream and market fundamentalist view: "There is no denying capitalism's record. Market economies have succeeded over the centuries by thoroughly weeding out the inefficient and poorly equipped, and by granting rewards to those who anticipate consumer demand and meet it with the most efficient use of labor and capital resources. Newer technologies increasingly drive this unforgiving capitalist process on a global scale." Yet, "regrettably economic growth cannot produce lasting contentment or happiness." If that were the case, the tenfold increase in GNP in the past two hundred years "would have fostered a euphoric rise in human contentment."

Implications

Insights, both positive and negative, are available from the business perspective that can be used in public administration theorizing and practice. The benefits are optimal, it is suggested, when the insights are used as part of epistemic pluralism. They are not when the business perspective is applied on a "one perspective cures all" basis.

Implication for Planning—What Would Osborne and Gaebler Do?

The entrepreneurial business perspective suggests micro strategic planning and plans for leaders of public organizations. Micro, as will be recalled, refers to what applies to a single organization. Osborne and Gaebler (1992), in their *Reinventing Government: How the Entrepreneurial Spirit Is Transforming the Public Sector*, suggest a model for strategic planning for entrepreneurial government.

What is strategic planning? "Strategic planning is the major organizational intervention to develop a shared vision of your future and the values, culture, and business strategies needed to be implemented and managed to get you there," observes Stephen Haines (2000, p. 55), who describes himself as a CEO, strategist, entrepreneur, facilitator, systems thinker, and author. This entrepreneurial business perspective emphasizes the innovative role of the leader. Haines's account also emphasizes systems and sharing. Strategic planning could be less participative, of course. States Frederick Gluck (1986, p. 12), "Not long ago, I sat listening to a senior executive of a $10 billion corporation who described what he believed it took to bring about significant change in a rapidly evolving industry. . . . His objective for the business was clear: market leadership. His strategy was simple and direct: manage the business's products and markets in a focused, customer-oriented, profit-conscious way."

For a leader of a public organization, one option would be to select from among the aims listed by Osborne and Gaebler (1992). It is not at all essential for the strategic planner to regard this entrepreneurial model as a "take it or leave it" proposition. It can be used as an aid for creative thinking, stimulating the imagination and discussion. Some of the elements (e.g., anticipatory government) may have even more relevance in some organizational contexts than in others.

Osborne and Gaebler's model for entrepreneurial government consists of the following ten elements:

1. *Catalytic government*—steering, not rowing, serving as catalyst in generating alternate courses of action
2. *Community-owned government*—empowering communities and citizens

to be sources of their own solutions, rather than serving and producing dependence in clients

3. *Competitive government*—infusing competition into service delivery, fostering competition among public, private, and other service providers
4. *Mission-driven government*—transforming rule-driven organizations
5. *Results-oriented government*—funding outputs in the sense of achieving substantive public goals, rather than focusing so much on inputs like fiscal control
6. *Customer-driven government*—meeting needs of customers, rather than of bureaucracy
7. *Enterprising government*—earning through the profit motive by relying on charges and fees, rather than simply spending assigned monies
8. *Anticipatory government*—emphasizing the prevention of public problems rather than the cure
9. *Decentralized government*—from hierarchy to participation and team-based organization
10. *Market-oriented government*—achieving change through the market, such as by structuring the environment so that the market works optimally.

Recall that some Public Administration thinkers have criticized New Public Management and this entrepreneurial model. Janet and Robert Denhardt (2003) are among these, and they have suggested instead their *New Public Service: Serving, Not Steering.*

Alternatively, parts from the entrepreneurial business model could be used for management, to which we now turn.

Implication for Managing—Isn't Supply Chain Management Beneficial?

For management, the business perspective encourages mining the business management literature for useful techniques. Supply chain management (SCM) is an example of such a technique, clearly relevant to some public situations like (as suggested in chapter 1) homeland security. In fact, some SCM can already be found in parts of public administration.

Supply chain management (SCM) can be defined as "the design, maintenance, and operation of supply chain processes for satisfaction of end-users" (Ayers 2001, p. 35). Another, fuller, description is that it is "a set of approaches utilized to efficiently integrate suppliers, manufacturers, warehouses, and stores, so that merchandise is produced and distributed at the right quantities, to the right locations and at the right time, in order to minimize system-wide costs while satisfying service level requirements" (Simchi-Levi, Kaninsky, and Simchi-Levi 2000, p. 39). The literature of SCM is huge and growing. SCM has become an established feature of business management education, and it has professional associations (e.g., the Council of Supply Chain Management Professionals), as well as a flock of its own journals (e.g., *Journal of Supply Chain Management, Supply Chain Management Review*, and *Supply Chain Management: An International Journal*). Shouldn't supply chain management be capable of sparking insights about getting relief supplies to, say, post-Katrina New Orleans? Maybe it was used; it's so obvious. SCM has been described as a veritable tsunami that will sweep through business management.

Supply chain management has poked its head into parts of public administration. Dennis Wittmer and Robert McGowan report that adoption of SCM by government units has been problematic. The "shift to information-based supply chain systems in the public sector has met with more resistance and has moved far more slowly than in the private sector" (Wittmer and McGowan 2007, p. 324). They recommend extending use of SCM through educating employees and stakeholders, examining current processes and systems, instituting changes, and assessing and evaluating systems. As they add, the organization must be "willing to experiment with change and innovate" (p. 325). Steve New and Roy Westbrook (2004, p. v) note that "many writers observe that [SCM] is a field characterized by imprecise terminology, sloppily applied metaphors, and conflated or confused concepts." Yet Wittmer and McGowan (2007, p. 325) can reassure their readers that SCM is not a "fad."

Implication for the Underlying—Is There Cultism in Leadership?

Traditional public administration is wary of fads, as the existence of Wittmer and McGowan's reassuring comment hints. Yet it is not so alert to the underlying assumptions that are "bought" when a fresh approach or technique is imported.

Techniques like supply chain management have positive and nonfaddish implications for public administration. But such planning and management comes with underlying beliefs or attitudes. With the wheat can come either more wheat or chaff: it is important to identify which one you've got and to take any appropriate corrective action. Adaptation of any business perspective into the public administration context should be alert to underlying attitudes that are imported with the perspective, and to whether the underlying attitude is positive or negative. Identification of the underlying requires, among other things, awareness and sensitivity—attitudes surely fueled (see below) by imaginative creativity.

By definition (as it were), the entrepreneurial version of the business perspective celebrates the entrepreneur, the leader. The CEO is at the pinnacle of the business world, as evidenced (for instance) by the attitude toward any leader of a Fortune 500 company. "Leader" is a term intended here as a function over and above the function of a mere manager. A leader is someone over and above a person who directs, coordinates, and controls all the activities and personnel of the assigned unit—the latter being the words of the standard federal job description for a manager. The leader in this context is a heroic leader, the one who carries the venture and who carries the day.

Techniques like strategic planning and supply chain management do seem to be clearly positive borrowings, as mentioned. But let's repeat that any adaptation to public administration of a business implication should be alert to any unconscious or conscious baggage that underlies. Some will think that this emphasis on the supreme utility of leadership (as distinct from, say, effective management) is valuable in the public sector in the long run. Some will assert that nothing else but heroic leadership is needed in any and all situations. Some will assert that leadership is an idea that needs no discussion, thinking perhaps that all kinds of leadership are the same. But these and others are questions for inquiry independent of the benefit of (say) strategic planning or strategic management borrowings. There should be no free pass for what underlies.

It is true that the emphasis on the importance of the leader (the entrepreneur, the CEO) as the prime mover is mentioned so openly that it is only barely below the surface. But the leadership idea is emphasized and strengthened (some would say sustained) by its attachment to deeper underlying features. We will encounter them later.

Implication for Public Administration Field—Shouldn't Public Administration Seek the Strategic?

The business perspective suggests the advantages for public administration theorizing and practice of strategic planning and management. Some use has already been made in public administration, as may be expected; after all, "strategic" is an attractive word, a with-it term. All this was noted in the previous two implications, but it deserves reemphasis.

Strategic decisions are "those decisions that are concerned with the entire environment in which the firm operates, the whole of the resources and the people who constitute the company and the interface between the two," note Luffman and coauthors (1996, p. 6) in their textbook on *Strategic Management*. This is relevant to a major difficulty in government where departments often act in such a way as to optimize the interests of a given department but without doing so for the government as a whole. This often happens with units within a department: a unit's employees act for the benefit of that unit but without adequate consideration for the entire department. Isn't this a commonplace difficulty in large and small governments?

Strategic management in the business management area is well developed, and it makes use of multidisciplinary perspectives. Jenkins and Ambrosini (2007), for example, discuss advanced strategic management from institutionalist, economic, behavioralist, and emerging and integrating perspectives. The economic perspective, for instance, includes game theory, transaction cost, and agency perspectives.

Clearly, the idea of strategic management is not foreign to the public administration literature. But the business perspective is relevant if it reinforces and enhances it. As Rabin, Miller, and Hildreth (1989, p. iii) write, "Strategy is a concept born in politics but is employed most recently in business organizations. . . . Business schools and their M.B.A. curricula emphasize strategic management, both as a separate course and as a critical force in the teaching of finance, management, and marketing. Strategic management as a field of inquiry gains vitality from this attention."

Implication for Public Administration Creativity—Does Openness to Business Administration Require Imagination?

Public administration can learn from business administration. Yet belief in the un-qualified superiority of entrepreneurial private enterprise over public enterprise is so ingrained that it requires imaginative creativity in adjusting the field of PA in order to examine the meaning of what is imported from BA. Belief in the business perspective is part of the underlying language of PA, as discussed earlier. To express it in stark terms, the negative that is imported from the business perspective (accompanying the positive import) is a deep conviction that the private enterprise approach is *the* better approach than the public enterprise approach. To be even plainer, there is the belief that (with exceptions) government cannot run a two-car parade.

For the first of two examples, recall the alternative view of the business perspec-tive already emphasized. This is the interest group model. For a second example, consider the problem of benefiting from, say, the suggestions of Thomas Peters and Robert Waterman (2004) in their *In Search of Excellence*. They suggest eight characteristics of excellence. These are discussed under such headings of manag-ing as ambiguity and paradox; a bias for action; close to the customer; autonomy and entrepreneurship; productivity through people; hands-on value-driven; stick to the knitting; and simple, lean staff.

How can such insights be adapted while maintaining a realistic attitude to any underlying assumption about the priority of private enterprise? Surely, imagina-tive creativity is required in relating the claims of the business perspective with, say, the claims by Barber and Reich (noted above) about the changed nature of the contemporary economy. For instance, consider the former on market totalism and lovemarks. Barber claims that the private sector overproduces and targets children, as well as infantilizing adults. This results in kidults, rejuveniles, twixters, and adultescents. "In the first decade of the new millennium, consumers find themselves trapped in a cage of infantalization, reinforced by privatization and an identity poli-tics . . . of branding" (Barber 2007, p. 213). Corporations are concerned to brand themselves, and to imprint "lovemarks" on potential buyers—lovemarks being part of the "emotional propaganda that hijacks authentic emotions and sentiments and employs them in wholly instrumental ways to sell products for which there is little inherent demand" (p. 183). "It is not in the products, then," continues Barber, "but in the names and the brands they represent that the commercial value of consumer companies reside" (p. 186). Public administration thinking and creative imagina-tion should be adequate to assess such claims and features.

Epilogue

Should we change our ways? Peters and Waterman (2004, p. 1), for instance, write that, "At a gut level, all of us know that much more goes into the process of keeping a large organization vital and responsive than the policy statements, new strategies, plans, budgets, and organization charts can possibly depict. But all too often we behave as though we don't know it. If we want change, we fiddle with the strategy. Or we change the structure. Perhaps the time has come to change our ways."

Suggested Readings

Barber, Benjamin. 2007. *Consumed: How Markets Corrupt Children, Infantilize Adults, and Swallow Citizens Whole*. New York: W.W. Norton.

Drucker, Peter F. 1993. *Innovation and Entrepreneurship*. New York: HarperCollins.

Osborne, D., and T. Gaebler. 1992. *Reinventing Government: How the Entrepreneurial Spirit Is Transforming the Public Sector*. New York: Addison-Wesley.

Peters, Thomas, and Robert Waterman. 2004. *In Search of Excellence: Lessons from America's Best-Run Companies*. New York: Harper Business.

4

Public Administration from an Economic Perspective

The Nobel Prize in Economics was awarded in 1986 to James McGill Buchanan for his contribution in developing public choice economics. "Your Majesties, Your Royal Highnesses, Ladies, and Gentlemen . . . The first contribution from public choice theory, that is the most widely known outside the academic world, is the extension and use of traditional economic microtheory in the studies of the political system, the public administration, and interest organizations" (Stahl 1986). So proclaimed Ingemar Stahl in presenting Buchanan for the prize. Notice the words—for the extension and use of microeconomics to studies of areas including *the public administration!*

The economic perspective is important to public administration (PA) theory and practice, within and beyond public choice economics. First, economics possesses powerful analytical or theoretical tools and a distinctive way of looking at the world that can inform public administration understanding and functioning. It is a perspective not at all limited to the world of business. Sometimes called the Queen of the Social Sciences, economics has contributed in a distinctive manner to both some social and some natural sciences. Second, the economic is an important element in the context of administrative practice. To give but one example: following legislative enactments, the economic context co-shapes policy making and regulation formulating within public agencies by administrators and outside lobbying interests. Understanding of public-private relations, for instance, benefits from familiarity with both poles. Third, the economic forms a significant part of the dominant belief system that surrounds public administration. The free enterprise system, for instance, is widely considered to be the American way.

"The object of this Essay is to exhibit the nature and significance of Economic Science" (Robbins 1945, p. 1). Here, we can adapt this opening line of the economist Lionel Robbins's famous essay, a turning point in 1932 in the extension of the influence of economic theory. This chapter's object is to exhibit the nature of economic science and its significance for public administration theory and practice. The first set of questions asks about the nature of economic science.

1. What is an economic lens? What is economics?
2. What is an economic lens? What is public choice?
3. What is an economic lens? What are microeconomics and macro-economics?
4. What is an economic lens? What is market fundamentalism?
5. What is an economic lens? Does the "invisible hand" entail market fundamentalism?

Implications for public administration theory and practice are then discussed.

6. Implication for planning—What is Ostrom's paradigm?
7. Implication for managing—What is context, like budget maximizing?
8. Implication for the underlying—Is there any ideological indoctrination?
9. Implication for the field—How do macro public administration and macro-economics relate?
10. Implication for imaginative creativity—Does Arrow relate to citizen participation?

Recall Exercise 1 (see chapter 1, page 15). It asks readers to determine what insights about public administration theory and practice interest them from an economic perspective. The aim is for the reader to delve into the perspective in order to generate PA-relevant insights.

Sketching the Economic Perspective

The "first task therefore is to delimit the subject-matter of Economics—to provide a working definition of what Economics is about" (Robbins 1945, p. 1). In his *An Essay on the Nature and Significance of Economic Science*, Lord Robbins continued, "Unfortunately, this is by no means as simple as it sounds" (p. 1). About a decade after the second edition of Robbins's essay was published, when I heard my first freshman lecture in the Old Theater at the London School of Economics and Political Science (LSE), the lecturer was Lionel Robbins. With the innocence of any neophyte, I did not then know how his 1932 essay had redefined economics from a subject matter considered to be concerned with material wealth to a subject matter within the province of every other field (including public administration)— concerned with the allocation of scarce resources.

What Is an Economic Lens? What Is Economics?

What is economics? The now accepted description, as Robbins (1945, p. 24) wrote, is that the subject matter of economics "is concerned with that aspect of behavior which arises from the scarcity of means to achieve given ends." Or, as he also put it, economics is "the science which studies human behavior as a relationship between scarce means which have alternative uses." It is the study of the relationship between any scarce means and a set of alternate ends. If you won $10,000 in the lottery, you might decide whether to put that into your bank, or into the stock market, or into the space under your mattress. Economics concerns human behavior in deciding what to do with that scarce resource which can be used in different ways. It there were no scarcity, there would be no economics. If the resource had only one possible use, there would be no economics.

The materialistic understanding that Robbins's definition replaced can be seen in the famous definition advanced in 1890 by Alfred Marshall (1920, p. 1): "Economics is a study of mankind in the ordinary business of life; it studies that part of individual and social action which is most closely connected with the attainment and with the use of the material requisites of well-being." After Robbins, economics is not limited to lucre, to business, and to the material requisites. Robbins's means and ends—or the scarcity—go beyond these items. On means, for instance, think about scarce time. Imagine a public manager who is limited to eight hours in a working day. She could invest the eight hours (or whatever portion you care to consider) in writing a certain report, in meeting with superiors, in meeting with subordinates, or in preparing for. . . . As another example, isn't span of control mainly about limited time? On ends, the economist in this definition is not interested in the nature of the ends or "ends as such." Adds Robbins (1945, p. 24), "[T]o speak of any end as being itself 'economic' is entirely misleading."

Mainstream economics has gone through changes since the publication in 1776 of Adam Smith's *Inquiry into the Nature and Causes of the Wealth of Nations* and has experienced many varieties like Austrian economics and behavioral economics. The classical period gave way to Alfred Marshall's *Principles of Economics* (1890) and to the neoclassical period, which later was transformed by John Maynard Keynes's *General Theory of Employment, Interest and Money* (1936), which gave way to. . . . This history also includes the mainstream economists of the Chicago School, which was founded by Frank Knight (1885–1972), who taught Nobel prize–winning economists like Milton Friedman (1976), George Stigler (1982), and James Buchanan.

From among the mass and variety, two features should be emphasized here. Mainstream economic theory is deductive, and it uses the concept of economic man in rational analysis of scarce means with alternative ends. By deductive, I mean that the development of economic models proceeds from general propositions to particular propositions. In this way, economic theory is like geometry, a subject undeniably useful in designing constructions of all kinds. In this respect, it is unlike traditional public administration, which is basically inductive—proceeding from particular observations to, hopefully, general propositions.

By *economic man* (or economic woman, to modernize the traditional term), I mean that in *mainstream* economic modeling the assumption is complete self-interested rationality among the actors. Economic man *always* seeks to optimize his own utility, and his rational choices are internally coherent. Readers may wonder about this, if they recognize that they themselves are not always self-interested (that sometimes we commit acts that are altruistic) or rational (that sometimes we are guided by the emotional and nonrational). But two points on the "that's OK" side. First, recall from chapter 1 the comment by Milton Friedman (1953, p. 15) that the truth or falsity of premises does not count: the "only relevant test of the validity of a hypothesis is comparisons of its predictions with experience." Second, it can be said that economic man does live; he lives entirely in the world of the model. That is, if there were no right-angled triangles outside Pythagoras's model, Pythagoras's theorem would still be true in his model. It's the same for the economic man.

What Is an Economic Lens? What Is Public Choice?

Public choice applies microeconomics to political science and incidentally to public administration. "Public choice can be defined as the economic study of nonmarket decision making, or simply the application of economics to political science," writes Dennis Mueller (1989, p. 1). Or, as Jac Heckelman (2004, p. 1) puts it, "The field of public choice applies neoclassical economic analysis to areas of political interest." Mueller adds that the subject matter of public choice is the same as that of political science; the methodology is that of economics.

The methodology of public choice embraces the decision making of economic man, complete rationality and self-interestedness. It is the decision making of an "egoistic, rational, utility maximizer" (Mueller 1989, p. 2)—all decisions are made to optimize personal satisfaction. Between them, Mueller and Ostrom describe this as within a tradition of political thinking that includes Thomas Hobbes, Benedict Spinoza, James Madison, Alexander Hamilton, and Alexis de Tocqueville. Note the inclusion of founding fathers. But contemporary public choice uses the tools of economic theory, and so Mueller points out that public choice "developed as a separate field largely since 1948." Public choice came to public administration *primarily* through Vincent Ostrom, as we will see, in 1973.

What Is an Economic Lens? What Are Microeconomics and Macroeconomics?

Microeconomics looks at the smaller picture, macroeconomics at the larger. These are the two major divisions of economics.

Microeconomics analyzes how individuals and firms allocate scarce resources, that is, how a person or a business makes economic decisions. The basic model of microeconomics is how price relates to the supply and demand for the selected good or service. Microeconomic supply and demand models have the two features already discussed. That is, the star of microeconomic modeling is economic man, utterly egoistic and utterly rational. The modeling is deductive, deducing from universal generalizations (like economic man and the so-called law of diminishing marginal utility, that is, the more you have of x, the less marginal utility will you obtain from another unit of that x).

Macroeconomics analyzes an economy—a national, regional, or even the world economy, for example. It deals with an economy as a whole (as it were), rather than with units like the individual, the family, or the firm. It deals with entities like gross national product, inflation and price indices, and unemployment levels. For an example of macroeconomics, think of John Maynard Keynes's 1936 general theory analyzing the nature of the business cycle and ways of mitigating the cyclical swings. Keynes analyzed decisions of firms to produce (affecting income and employment levels) in terms of the interaction of aggregate demand and aggregate supply. For instance, he analyzed aggregate demand in terms of the determinants of consumption and of investment and their effects (like the accelerator). And more. Of course, macroeconomics has proceeded since Keynes's death, for example, to post Keynesianism. Other examples of macroeconomics could have been given, such as monetarism.

What Is an Economic Lens? What Is Market Fundamentalism?

Market fundamentalism holds that market exchange is the best guide for all human actions; it maintains that the free market is the only true ethical, or prudential, guide to life. Market fundamentalism is also known as neoliberalism—or as the 1980s Washington economic consensus.

The icon of market fundamentalism is Friedrich von Hayek (1899–1992). He had strong associations with Ludwig von Mises and the Austrian school of economics, which shared a neoclassical view of economics. After leaving Vienna, Hayek taught at the London School of Economics and then (among other places) at the University of Chicago. He received the Nobel Prize in Economics in 1974. Most are familiar with his celebrated *Road to Serfdom* and *The Constitution of Liberty*. The former made him famous, and Milton Friedman (1994, p. ix) described Hayek's ideas in that book as "timeless." The book also made Hayek the golden boy of certain conservative money (his Chicago professorship was financed by the Volker Foundation) and led to "his" creation of the Mont Pelerin Society—which inspired the establishment of "free market" societies in Washington and in London.

Hayek is a market fundamentalist in the sense that he regards the market as a self-organizing system, a spontaneous order or catallaxy. It is the result of human action but not design: we create the conditions in which the system arranges itself. The market self-generates by cultural evolution. Because of our epistemological condition, the market is our best device for allocating resources. By this epistemological condition, I mean that Hayek is a skeptic about the limits of human knowledge. For him, the market compensates for our ignorance. For instance, he thinks that prices (discovered as a result of market interactions) give us information in coded form, and do this without participants agreeing to common ends. For Hayek, the real importance of the market is to transmit knowledge, not to achieve equilibrium. Also, Hayek thinks that the market is the best survival arrangement. For example, he claims that the market has won the evolutionary battle against closed and tribal arrangements—ancestors of contemporary collectivism. Our ideas have also evolved, and so our present moral views "undoubtedly contain layers or strata deriving from earlier phases of the evolution of human societies" (Hayek 1982, p. 142). Again, these layers are unhelpful moral impulses from the hunter-gatherer stage. And Hayek thinks survival dictates that we should reject these in favor of open market values. The neoliberalism associated with Hayek recommends individual entrepreneurial freedoms within a framework emphasizing strong private property rights, free markets, and free trade. The role of government, in this view, is to create and preserve this framework, including the creation of markets where they do not exist and including the use of supporting force. This is consistent, as we know, with privatization, deregulation, and "withdrawal" of social provision of services.

On the plus side for Hayek's neoliberalism, market decision making does have certain advantages over nonmarket decision making, in terms of market signals, for example. The market has given us lots of "stuff" (witness the consumer society), and anyone who visited a Moscow grocery store in the old Soviet days knows that that is not to be sneezed at. I doubt whether we have the capability of running all aspects of an entire economy on a collectivist basis; that seems almost as hard as consciously running all the functions of a brain with 100 billion neurons. A counter-argument, however, is to deny that totally collectivist versus totally market are the only two options—and Hayek himself talked about the need to make exceptions. I should explain this counterargument about collectivist versus market options in terms of car versus bicycle. Undeniably, a car has certain advantages over a bicycle, for example, in terms of speed. Does that mean that I must always ride in a car? What about the middle way? Take your own self-test. Which is more efficient— the market or the government? The answer is to decline to answer as is. A test is whether you believe the phony dichotomy that it's only either/or. It is whether you believe that, in all circumstances, it comes down to one or the other—either all-market or all-government.

Neoliberalism also has minuses. Alan Haworth, for example, sees arbitrariness in Hayek's theory of spontaneous order. He describes this as "little more than a gesture of faith in the free market"—"as a grandiose rhetorical trope for this attempt" (Haworth 1994, p. 129). He describes it as "just a story."

What Is an Economic Lens? Does the Invisible Hand Entail Market Fundamentalism?

No, the invisible hand does not entail market fundamentalism. Consider what Paul Samuelson said about the failures of the invisible hand. Samuelson won the Nobel Prize for Economics in 1970 and wrote (among other things) a famous textbook entitled *Economics* (1948; Samuelson and Nordhaus 2004).

What is the invisible hand doctrine? It says that the pursuit of individual self-interest inevitably leads to an optimal social result. In other words, if each and every person strives selfishly only for his or her own individual satisfaction, it is as if an "invisible hand" arranges that society is thereby better off than if people tried to act for the public interest. In developing the doctrine of the invisible hand in 1776, Adam Smith famously wrote, "It is not from the benevolence of the butcher, the brewer, or the baker, that we expect our dinner, but from their regard to their own interest. We address ourselves not to their humanity but to their self-love, and never talk to them of our own necessities but of their advantage" (Campbell and Skinner 1976, pp. 26–27).

Paul Samuelson explains how and when the invisible hand fails—how its benefits are accompanied by harmful side effects. The invisible hand, according to Samuelson, fails on occasions of inefficiency, inequality, and instability. It fails when inefficiencies occur in the form of monopolies and oligopolies, externalities, and public goods. It fails when there are unacceptable inequalities of income and wealth. It fails in terms of instability. It cannot prevent the economic cycles that produce unemployment and inflation, and it does not yield economic growth. Others would dismiss all this, of course.

Implications

Throughout its history, American public administration has typically existed in the shadow of the economic—like Hamlet in the shadow of his ghostly father. With American public administration's creation in the orthodox period, celebration of the economic supported the regulative ideal that the bureaucracy should be run like a business. In its new public management period, public administration is even more in the shadow of the economic—deregulation, privatization. Said Hamlet to his ghost of a father, "Whither wilt thou lead me? Speak!" (I.5.734).

Implication for Planning—What Is Ostrom's Paradigm?

For planning, change the dominant public administration paradigm. Adopt the Paradigm of Democratic Administration. Abandon the likes of Wilson's paradigm. This was the prescription recommended in 1973 by Vincent Ostrom in his *Intellectual Crisis in American Public Administration*. Ostrom's Paradigm of Democratic Administration is a fruit of public choice economics; it results in looking at public administration from such an economic perspective. Ostrom explains his paradigm as relating to "a science of democratic administration inherent in a paradigm that grows out of the work of modern political economists and that of early democratic theorists" (2008, p. 98).

Recall that the Paradigm of Democratic Administration stands against "perfection of hierarchical ordering" relating to "a single center of power." Ostrom summarizes his paradigm in terms of eight propositions; two of the eight mention opposition to such hierarchical ordering. One opposes such hierarchical ordering of "a professionally trained public service," as that will reduce the capability to respond to different citizen preferences and environmental conditions. The other opposes accountability to such a single center, as that will not maximize efficiency. Ostrom (2008, p. 25) contrasts these claims in the Paradigm of Democratic Administration with the perfection of hierarchical organization in the Wilsonian paradigm.

Instead of any such perfection of hierarchical ordering, Ostrom's Paradigm of Democratic Administration seeks fragmentation "of authority among diverse decision centers with multiple veto capabilities within any one jurisdiction and the development of multiple, overlapping jurisdictions of widely different scales. . ." (Ostrom 2008, p. 99). Instead of perfection of hierarchical ordering, his paradigm seeks a "variety of different organizational arrangements" for different goods and services, "coordinated through various multiorganizational arrangements including trading and contracting to mutual advantage, competitive rivalry, adjudication of conflicts, and the power of command in limited hierarchies" (Ostrom 2008, p. 98). There are four other propositions that add to this picture.

Don't worry about items like traditional balance and orderliness in organization charts. "Attention will shift from a preoccupation with the organization to concerns with the opportunities individuals can pursue in multiorganizational environments." The proposed paradigm will turn from such features as simplicity and neatness and symmetry to "diversity, variety, and responsiveness to the preferences of constituents" (Ostrom 2008, p. 115). Ostrom urges that a task should be to develop "a theory of association" (p. 115) that will help communities to fashion organizational arrangements that will make optimal use of individual self-interest.

Implication for Managing—What Is Context, Like Budget Maximizing?

Managing in public administration is facilitated by understandings and insights available from public choice economics. Consider the understanding provided by the analysis of the budget-maximizing bureaucrat—inside the bureau. Notice insights available about bureaucratic efficiency (outside the bureau, e.g., in outsourcing) and interest groups (both inside and outside the bureau, e.g., in impacting budgets and in resolving hollow legislation). To be helpful, shouldn't public administration's strategic management engage such ideas?

Turn to the inside of bureaus. Proposing his model of the budget-maximizing bureaucrat, William Niskanen (1971) argues that bureaus will tend to overproduce. He indicates that the budget-maximizing bureaucrat and her context will produce twice the optimal level of output. First, the rational and self-interested bureaucrat wishes to maximize her budget because she wants to maximize her utility. Her utility function is made up of salary, perquisites, reputation, power, patronage, output, ease of making changes, and ease of managing the bureau. Except for the last two, each of these functions is a positive monotonic function of the budget. That is, the greater her budget, the greater her reputation, her power—and so on. In addition, she wants to survive. The greater her budget, the greater the cooperation and efficiency of her subordinates. The reason is that, the greater the budget, the greater opportunities employees have for promotions and for their own security. Second, in budget discussions the bureaucrat has greater information about unit costs than the entity overseeing the budget request. For example, a bureau chief in the federal government has a staff who can provide her with extensive information about plans, such as the proposed production of *x* number of new units of, say, airplanes. The congressional budgeting committee, on the other hand, cannot be expected to match this intimate level of understanding of the projected costs.

Whether this is the complete story is a different question. Objections have been raised against the validity of Niskanen's model. For instance, one has been to deny that bureaucrats are budget maximizers, and another has been to deny the positive relationship between budget and personal interests. Reviewing these objections, Andre Blais and Stephane Dion (2007, p. 142) conclude that the evidence supports "a budget-boosting strategy but not a budget-maximizing strategy, and that it refutes the assumption of a passive sponsor." It is possible to specify such alternatives. For one, Jean-Luc Migue and Gerard Belanger (1974) model bureau managers pursuing nonoutput goals other than mere budget maximization. Niskanen (1974, p. 43) himself suggested that this latter model and his own should be regarded as special theories of bureaucratic behavior.

There is much else that could be said about the inside of bureaus. One example is the use of competitive arrangements rather than the traditional public administration default position of eliminating duplication. The market embraces competition, as long as the competition is real; could not public administration aim for such arrangements within its own strategic management? Martin Landau was a writer who indicated the benefits that redundancy could have in public administration, that is, in suppressing error: "[a] commercial airliner is a very redundant system, a fact which accounts for its reliability of performance; a fact which also accounts for its adaptability" (Landau 1969, p. 338).

Turn to the outside of bureaus. Performance is a critical issue in planning outsourcing. How can performance goals be achieved unless the outsourcing is to a competitive context? Recall that economic theory recognizes that demand for a service (like an outsource contract) can be from a monopsonist (a single buyer), from an oligopsonist (one of a few buyers), or from a buyer in a perfectly competitive context. (Perfect competition, to speak only of the supply side, occurs when neither the buyer—nor the seller—can set the price. There is the demand side, however, where the additional conditions for perfect competition make up a situation that is much less likely to be achieved.) Oligopsonies are the general rule in the market to buy such outsourcing contracts. Microeconomic theory critiques oligopsony because—like monopsony—oligopsony yields price distortion. It is not the price that would obtain in perfect competition. The critique is not that oligopsony can lead to such distortion. Rather, it is that such a distortion, given that market structure, is rational. The oligopsonist is being irrational if she does not distort the price in order to optimize her profits.

Turn to the inside and the outside of bureaucracy, especially to the economics of lobbying, for example, in relation to budgeting and hollow legislation. The economics of lobbying relates to budgeting on both the expenditures and taxation sides. For instance, how do lobbying-related benefits fit into the budget-maximizer's utility function (see above)? As another instance, the condition of the U.S. tax code (which is replete with special interest provisions) has significance for policy making and administration, especially when entitlements and other trends are discussed. Shouldn't strategic policy making include understanding of the impact of various interest groups? Recall the economics of lobbying in relation to hollow legislation. The latter is legislation where the act's provisions require the bureaucracy to make regulations that will resolve holes left in the legislation—holes typically left deliberately. Involved in the resolution process are officials within the bureaus and lawyers representing lobbyists. Shouldn't strategic planning include an attempt to protect the public interest in this regulation-resolution process, where the public is not typically represented? The economics of lobbying is outside the scope of traditional public administration, unfortunately.

Implication for the Underlying—Is There Any Ideological Indoctrination?

Commonplace throughout the world is the translation of economic ideas into ideology and then indoctrination through such economic ideologies, which (in part) link with the unconscious. This has been the case, as Hoover (2003) points out, in the growth to ideologies of the competing ideas of Harold Laski, Keynes, and Hayek, respectively—a market governed by socialism, a market requiring macro management, and market fundamentalism. In the United States, the dominant ideology has been and is the latter, the unfettered free market. Such ideology has many aspects, such as its connection with the American dream, the celebration of rugged individualism, and so on. Let's consider only one aspect of this entrenchment of market ideology.

Indoctrination as a concept is usually viewed as a negative, understandably. Consider two preliminary difficulties. First, it is easier to notice how other cultures indoctrinate their youth, for example, that the Communist Soviet Union indoctrinated its children. It is harder to recognize that, even if with the best of good intentions, our own culture indoctrinates. Second, so repulsive is the term "indoctrination" that it is hard to see that education and indoctrination can overlap, and that that indoctrination sometimes can be better than nonindoctrination, like when we use it to induce children to brush their teeth, or to use their seat belts, or to avoid street drugs, or to do their homework.

Indoctrination into market fundamentalist ideology is encouraged in kindergarten, as the standards of learning (SOLs) of elementary and high schools in the

United States reveal. The indoctrination is supplemented and bolstered by the media, myths, legends, and what is considered common sense. From the SOLs, it can be seen that many kids are being prompted, unconsciously and often enough consciously, to privilege the market and market values. The unfettered market is privileged as being as natural as apple pie, and self-interest is celebrated. Individual success is equated with financial success. This brand of economic ideology rules as part of the social construction of individuals and society. All this limits and channels dreams—and constrains the public administration context.

Under the heading of promoting economic literacy, teaching economics that favors market fundamentalism in elementary schools has been growing over the past half century. The kind of economics promoted by the SOLs presents a happy, happy version of economics—which is striking for a subject that, since 1800 and the Reverend Robert Malthus, has traditionally been described as the "dismal science." Adverse economic features are not emphasized in the SOLs, such as, the business cycle, the traditional problems of monopolies and oligopolies, and other difficulties for the market fundamentalist ideology. Here are the standards of learning for kindergarteners and early graders in a suburban and prosperous school district in Virginia: For kindergarten graduates, the relevant SOL provides that they will know two economics things. The first is to identify the difference between basic needs (food, clothing, and shelter) and wants (things people would like to have). The second is to "recognize that people use money to purchase goods." Grade 1 wants the graduate to know the difference between goods and services, that people are both buyers and sellers, that people make choices because they cannot have everything they want, and that people save money for the future to purchase goods and services. Grade 2's SOL wants the graduate to know the distinction between natural and human and capital resources. It is true that economic literacy bears on life. But how does what is learned in this way in kindergarten and the early grades bear on economic literacy?

Focus on the triviality of these standards—for example, the kindergarten standard that money purchases goods. Such disjointed bits are hardly "essential" for any later study of economics: it looks like a time waster. An ideological feature of this standard is that a particular version of economics, named as economics, is being taught in kindergarten at all. This is being taught at a most impressionable level. The start is being made in kindergarten perhaps with latent reference to ideas that evoke appetitive pleasure to little kids, such as money for toys, for chocolates. The message is that money is what it is all about. Yes, people do make money to purchase goods, and knowing that makes us feel warm and happy. But isn't it ideological to gloss over the detail that some people have much more money than others? Isn't it implicitly ideological to gloss over the detail that some people obtained their money other than from the metaphorical sweat of their brows? Against the objection that these negative aspects cannot be treated in kindergarten, it may be asked "Why bring it up at all?"

Trivia in kindergarten—as a servant of indoctrinating ideology—is not at all limited to economics. A major SOL in civics, for instance, includes the student being able to recognize—among other things (like the flag)—the fact that "the President is the leader of the United States." Recognition of the flag also occurs each morning at the reciting of the Pledge of Allegiance. Yes, there is value in taking such a pledge; but the value doesn't mean that it is not ideological.

Implication for the Field—How Do Macro Public Administration and Macroeconomics Relate?

Two contrasts between macroeconomics and traditional public administration should be pursued. First, there is no doubt that macroeconomics exists. If traditional macro public administration exists, it does so by exception. Exceptions have been noted in this book (e.g., Dwight Waldo) and in this chapter (e.g., Vincent Ostrom). For instance, Ostrom's recommendation for a paradigm change is macro, and the paradigm change deals with the longer run. But it is one of the exceptions.

Second, macroeconomics is a sophisticated set of theory, as in, whether true or false, Keynesianism, post Keynesianism, and monetarism. Do you know of a traditional public administration "exception" that reaches that level of sophistication?

What kinds of issues "require" macro public administration? There are at least two kinds of topics, which (I agree) do overlap significantly. A first is macro problem–focused. For example, how should government and bureaucracy cope with escalating corporate lobbying that distorts public policy and administration? As another example, how should government and bureaucracy administer the work of private contractors in, say, war zones? A second is lens-focused. For instance, how should public administration respond to Ostrom's lens? To a feminist lens? To a post-structural lens? To a critical theory lens? Or, to all four lenses together? And so on. On a "day-to-day" basis, "practical" public administration macro issues currently are shortchanged.

Implication for Imaginative Creativity—Does Arrow Relate to Citizen Participation?

The utility of making imaginative connections is underscored in applying economic theory to public administration. The play of creative imagination in public administration is not limited to fantasizing. Consider the relevance of Arrow's possibility theorem to any citizen participation in administrative policy setting, speaking to the matter of mere voting.

Kenneth Arrow received the Nobel Prize for Economics in 1972. His possibility theorem (Arrow 1963) shows that it is impossible to guarantee any system for aggregating individual wishes that will not violate the most trivial set of assumptions. These assumptions are not difficult aims. Instead, they are run-of-the-mill rationality requirements like transitivity, that is, if x is preferred to y and if y is preferred to z, then y is preferred to z. Putting it one way, "no voting scheme has ever been devised—and Arrow proved it impossible to find one—that can guarantee majority voting will be consistent and will move the society to its most desirable point" (Samuelson and Nordhaus 2004, p. 765). Putting it another way (in the words of the speech given when Arrow was presented for the Nobel Prize), "Let us assume that in a society one has a number of alternative conditions to choose between and that each individual in the society can rank all these alternatives in order of desirability. Is it possible, in this case, to find ethically acceptable, democratic rules, for making a collective (or social) ranking of the different alternatives in order of desirability? Arrow showed that the question must be answered in the negative. It is impossible in principle to find such rules" (Bentzel 1972). How does this relate to planning and management for citizen participation? Imagine.

Epilogue

The economic perspective is so powerful in contemporary society that the ideas of economists should be approached by public administration seriously and directly. As John Maynard Keynes (1936, pp. 383–384) wrote, "the ideas of economists and political philosophers, both when they are right and when they are wrong, are more powerful than is commonly understood. Indeed the world is ruled by little else. Practical men, who believe themselves to be quite exempt from an intellectual influence, are usually the slaves of some defunct economist. Madmen in authority, who hear voices in the air, are distilling their frenzy from some academic scribbler of a few years back. . . ."

Suggested Readings

Harvey, David. 2005. *A Brief History of Neoliberalism*. New York: Oxford University Press.

Heilbroner, Robert L. 1999. *The Worldly Philosophers: The Lives, Times, and Ideas of the Great Economic Thinkers*. 7th ed. New York: Simon & Schuster.

Mueller, Dennis C. 1989. *Public Choice II: A Revised Edition of Public Choice*. New York: Cambridge University Press.

Ostrom, Vincent. 2008 (1973). *The Intellectual Crisis in American Public Administration*. Tuscaloosa: University of Alabama Press.

5

Public Administration from a
Political Perspective

There is close kinship between political science (PS) and public administration (PA). For practice, there is a close and intimate working relationship in coping with, and in exercising, political and administrative power and service. Even though the relationship is unequal and often shifting, ranking public administration managers and ranking political officials cohabit government—and relate, at the federal level, to congressional and other politicians and their staffs. It is increasingly easy to see daylight between politics and administration as the watcher descends the governmental ladder.

For theorizing, there is also a close but unequal relationship. There has been ongoing involvement of public administration theory with the political, as discussed in chapter 2. Recall Dwight Waldo and the reaction to the politics-administration dichotomy, a dichotomy "established" by a practicing politician—President Woodrow Wilson. The relationship has been unequal to the extent that the study of politics has involved larger theoretical and more consequential concerns. This inequality has been encouraged to the extent that public administration has focused on technical and short-term concerns. Both in practice and in theory, the mainstream political and the traditional administrative have tended to share and support, adamantly and with few questions, the traditional narrative about the American political experience—the meaning of the founding fathers, the Constitution, and so on.

Recognizing this close kinship, this chapter explores the political perspective and selected implications for PA. The first set of questions sketches selected features of a political perspective.

1. What is a political lens? What is political science?
2. What is a political lens? What is political theory?
3. What is a political lens? Are political science and public administration cousins?

4. What is a political lens? What are political ideologies?
5. What is a political lens? Are bureaucracy and democracy compatible?

The second set of questions examines implications for public administration theory and practice.

6. Implication for planning—Shouldn't it be more philosophical?
7. Implication for managing—Shouldn't more democracy be an aim?
8. Implication for the underlying—Is what counts as common sense reliable?
9. Implication for public administration field—Shouldn't political science be an example?
10. Implication for public administrative creativity—Wasn't Harold Lasswell right?

Recall Reflection Exercise 1, discussed in chapter 1. In reading this chapter, readers are asked to determine what insight or insights about PA theory and practice interest them from a political perspective.

Sketching a Political Perspective

The American Political Science Association (APSA) held its first annual meeting in 1903, thirty-six years before the creation of the organizational home of traditional public administration—the American Society for Public Administration (ASPA). APSA's first meeting postdated the discussion of government and public administration in Plato's *Republic* by some 2,370-plus years. It postdated the discussion of government and public administration in the *Analects of Confucius* by some 2,480-plus years.

What Is a Political Lens? What Is Political Science?

The first APSA president, Frank J. Goodnow, warned in 1903 of the danger of defining political science. "It is tempting to answer the question: What is political science? To this temptation, I have determined not to yield. For it seems to me that such an attempt at definition is dangerous, particularly if it shall result in the endeavor to formulate a definition of political science which is at the same time inclusive and exclusive" (Goodnow 1903). PS resists one-liner definitions no less than PA, even (after Lasswell 1963) politics as who gets what, when, and how. Referring to Goodnow, Theda Skocpol (2003, p. 1) in her centenary presidential address reaffirmed that ASPA "aspires to be inclusive."

Political science is "the study of governments, public policies and political processes, systems and political behavior" (APSA 2008). This "answer" presently appears on the APSA website. Frank Goodnow in 1903 had described political science as "that science which treats of the organization known as the State. . . . It has to do with the State at rest and with the State in action" (Goodnow

1903). Goodnow explained that the "State, as an object of scientific study, will be considered from the point of view of the various operations necessary to the realization of the State's will" (Goodnow 1903). He identified three parts. The first was "the expression of the State's will," and the second was "the content of the State's will as expressed." The third was "the execution of the State's will." Seventeen years earlier, when the first issue of the *Political Science Quarterly* appeared, Munroe Smith had stated that the domain of political science was the comparative and historical study of the state. Since Goodnow and Smith, there have been shifts in political science not only in subject matter but also in method.

Political science "subfields include political theory, political philosophy, political ideology, political economy, policy studies and analysis, comparative politics, international relations, and a host of related fields" (APSA 2008). The APSA website entry, "What is political science?" goes on to list 38 subfields. Public administration is one of the organized sections of APSA. The broad and somewhat diffuse subject matter (echoes of Goodnow's boundary danger) of PS is reflected in that list of organized sections. The list shows the difficulty of specifying the nature of "the" political lens. In a sense, there is no "the" political perspective. In another sense, however, there has been enough congruence to represent a mainstream American view of the political. The APSA sections include:

federalism and intergovernmental relations
legislative studies
political organizations and parties
conflict processes
representation and electoral systems
religion and politics
science, technology, and environmental
    politics
comparative politics
information technology and politics
international security and arms control
European politics and society
political communication
foundations of political theory
political science education
politics, literature, and film
elections, public opinion, and voting behavior
race, ethnicity, and politics
international history and politics
Canadian politics

qualitative and multi-method
    research
law and the courts
public policy
public administration
presidency research
political methodology
urban politics
new political science
human rights
state politics and policy
politics and history
women and politics research
political economy
political psychology
sexuality and politics
foreign policy
health politics and policy
comparative democratization
political networks

Not all of these organized sections are equally important for describing the political science lens. Yet the length of the list does promise that attending a political science conference, like the annual meeting of APSA, typically provides confirmation of happy—if limited—doses of deviance and interesting ideas.

Public policy, defined in one textbook as "what government ought or ought not do, and does or does not do" (Simon 2007, p. 1), should be highlighted. There has been since 1970 an APSA section on public policy, and APSA cosponsors (along with the Policy Studies Organization) The Policy Studies Journal. Of course, there are other programs and journals concerned with public policy. Late in the 1970s, the Association for Public Policy Analysis and Management (APPAM) was established, for instance. The MPP degree (master of public policy) is now widespread, and so on.

Let's reemphasize the shifts in content and character of the American study of political science. As Theda Skocpol put it in her 2003 ASPA presidential address, "An association once founded on the formal arrangements of law and government now encompasses a much broader understanding of politics; and presidential addresses over the decades document the emergence of behavioralism, systems theories, and rational choice to coexist with new variants of institutional analysis" (Skocpol 2003, p. 1). Twists and turns in PS are indeed reflected in the presidential addresses. Robert Axelrod in his 2007 address, commenting on how well ideas had been imported from other subjects (like psychology, sociology, and economics), advocated an emphasis on exporting ideas from political science to other disciplines, for example, exporting cooperation theory to cancer research (Axelrod 2007, p. 5). Ira Katznelson in 2006 talked about PS emphasizing the study of power in circumstances of fear (Katznelson 2006, pp. 3–15). Margaret Levi in 2005 asked for a new and more "dynamic" theory of government (Levi 2005, pp. 5–19). Suzanne Rudolph urged situated knowledge, warning against the imperialism of categories (Rudolph 2004, pp. 5–14).

What Is a Political Lens? What Is Political Theory?

Turn to political theory (PT), which the American Association of the Humanities described as a discipline that had "died and been reborn several times" (Herbert 1981, p. 35).

On the upside, plurality of subject matter and method is now emphasized in political theory; so urge David Leopold and Marc Stears (2008). Political theory "is an exceptionally wide-ranging and open-ended branch of scholarly enquiry, within which there is very little in the way of settled agreement with regard to questions of method and scope" (Leopold and Stears 2008, p. 9). On the downside, John Gunnell (1983, p. 38) judged that the history "of the subfield of Political Theory does not demonstrate any great ability to transcend American political culture."

On the upside, Steven Jay Gold in 1993 was optimistic about the prospects of political philosophy. He described the four main paradigms as liberalism, Marxism, feminism, and postmodernism. For most of the twentieth century political philosophy has played "a relatively minor role in Anglophone philosophical debates" as metaphysics, epistemology, ethics, and philosophy of language have dominated. Gold claims that things have changed. "Not only has political philosophy become a central, even dominant part of the philosophical dialogue; the diversity and richness of the emerging traditions has become staggering" (Gold 1993, p. vii). On the downside, Leo Strauss in 1959 had said that "We hardly exaggerate when we say that today political philosophy does not exist any more, except as matter for burial . . . " (Gildin 1989, p. 12).

A distinction is drawn between PT and pt. PT is a subfield of political science, and pt is a more general interdisciplinary body of literature, activity, and intellectual community. John Gunnell reports that there is a burden on pt to contribute to the practice of the "discipline" of political science. And pt could extend beyond political theory to philosophy, anthropology, law, economics, history, sociology, psychology, and so on.

History of political theory can be stimulating. Ancient and medieval, modern, and contemporary—from Socrates to Rawls; I have taught these for some fifteen years in the pt tradition. Aims have included stimulating student reflection, especially on what is outside one's routine political exposure.

What Is a Political Lens? Are Political Science and Public Administration Cousins?

There is a close, but strained, relationship between political science and public administration. The relationship is exemplified in methods and in constricting assumptions. It is also reflected in the facts that the American Political Science Association does house a section on public administration, and it is doubtful that many ranking public managers are unaware that they administer in "political" organizations. Should the close relationship be categorized as between cousins or in a more distant way?

On methods, behavioralism and rational choice theory have had somewhat parallel trajectories in both PS and PA. The word "somewhat" reflects that there are differences, for example, typically public administration's responses have been of relatively lower voltage and more readily diluted and easily abandoned. Consider the behavioral revolution in PS of 1950–1959, the embrace of "rigorous" science. Compare that upsurge with Herbert Simon and his advocacy for a science of administration in his *Administrative Behavior*, still the most cited book in PA. Gunnell explains that behavioralism in PS introduced a "meta-theoretical consciousness" about scientific explanations. It involved an emphasis on pure science rather than on such aims as liberal reform. It involved political theorists (including David Easton, Robert Dahl, Heinz Eulau, and Herbert McClosky) "of the historical or normative kind: they were what they sought to replace" (Gunnell 1983, p. 15). As for Herbert Simon, behavioralism in PS resulted in large part from the inspiration of logical positivism. On the subsequent disappointment with behavioralism, see writers like John Nelson. Behavioralism in PS became "the theoretical, quantitative, and empirical study of the directly observable behavior of persons in political science" (Nelson 1998, p. 103). He notes "how the purportedly behavioral political science, which was to become more scientific by restricting itself to the external movements of bodies, instead comes to be dominated by attitudinal and mentalist concepts" (Nelson 1998, p. 14). Did relying exclusively on observable variables really cut it in terms of yielding interesting theory, either in public administration or political science?

On constricting assumptions, a striking and debilitating feature in political science (and in public administration) is the difficulty of modifying or escaping *American exceptionalism*. It is not merely that APSA is the *American* Political Science Association, just as ASPA is the *American* Society for Public Administration. The fact that the APSA Web site can claim correctly that it has 15,000 members in 80 countries does not deny exceptionalism in American PS. Exceptionalism is the belief that a country, or a group, is different from all others in critical respects. Such exceptionalism can be based on various grounds such as the religious (God is on our side), or the genetic (our race is the purest), or the environmental (we are separate geographically from the rest of the nasty world), or the political (our freedom is unique). In this context, a first difficulty is that "is different from" tends to slip into "is superior to." The second difficulty is that tweaking (adjusting) of the content of exceptionalism (the grounds for the exception) tends to become disallowed, to the extent that exceptionalism tends to be regarded as beyond discussion by, say, "patriots." American exceptionalism was a term used in 1831 by Alexis de Tocqueville. In practical politics, it can lead to such political consequences as claims of Manifest Destiny. In disciplinary or theoretic terms, exceptionalism can severely limit conclusions. The idea of American exceptionalism certainly has been discussed in PS and other literatures (e.g., in Seymour Martin Lipset's *American Exceptionalism: A Double-Edged Sword*, 1996).

What Is a Political Lens? What Are Political Ideologies?

Political and other ideologies are entrenched belief systems, and they limit PS as well as PA. That is, ideologies like conservatism, liberalism, and exceptionalism are entrenched lenses. An ideology (distinguished from a philosophy) is a set of beliefs that tends to trump understanding of what is and what should be done, where such beliefs are grounded in features of the unconscious. Another description, offered in a textbook by Terence Ball and Richard Dagger (2002, p. 5), is that an ideology "is a fairly coherent and comprehensive set of ideas that explains and evaluates social conditions, helps people understand their places in society, and provides a program for social and political action." That is, an ideology has explanatory, evaluative, orientative, and programmatic functions. This description is deficient to the extent that it overstresses the place of rationality rather than the appearance of rationality, and that it does not connect ideology with the unconscious. Since the concept of ideology was proposed for the "science of ideas" in 1798 by Destutt de Tracy, it has been variously used and interpreted. So we can read Emmet Kennedy writing that "Consequently, it has not yet been fully explained how 'ideology' the synonym Destutt de Tracy proposed in 1798 . . . could come to mean false consciousness . . ." (Kennedy 1979, p. 353).

Ideologies typically are not the products of the philosophical spirit, the open kind of philosophy that Socrates and others lived. Rather than remaining open, the ideologue typically has settled beliefs that tend to be proof against argument and reflection. This is what is intended in making a distinction between ideology and philosophy. Yet the word "typically" is used to respect that gray area that exists between any such distinctions. To put it another way, Mark Tiller speaks of political socialization, which determines "which ideologies attract our attention. It begins during childhood, as parents and schoolteachers teach reverence for patriotic historic events, myths and symbols and tell idealistic stories of heroic leaders and role models. It continues via friends and peer groups such as interest groups, political parties, and churches. In the current information age, the media plays an increasingly large role in socialization" (Tiller 1997, p. 4). It is socialization that can lead to what is meant by "false" consciousness.

There is a multitude of political ideologies, and each ideology contains a multitude of variations. There is liberalism, conservatism, socialism, communism, fascism, environmentalism, for example. Within liberalism, there is classical liberalism and neoclassicial liberalism. Within environmentalism, there is deep ecologism and. . . . Within conservatism, there is. . . . Within each and every ideology, there are variations. There are also overlappings, such as anarcho-socialism, eco-feminism, and so on.

All descriptions of ideologies are themselves a tad ideological, even mine and even yours. The description from Ball and Dagger, for example, separates political ideology from religion, which in the dominant ideology of the United States is reserved. All schemes or mappings that display the relationship of one ideology to another are themselves ideological. For instance, ideological is a one-dimensional depiction of ideologies as sitting on a line, ranging from left to right—or right to left.

What Is a Political Lens? Are Bureaucracy and Democracy Compatible?

Is bureaucracy incompatible with democracy, and in what ways? Can they be made more compatible? The relationship between bureaucracy and democracy has long been a concern for some public administration and political science thinkers. Subsidiary questions relate to whether democracy in this context is limited to an idealized version of what Abraham Lincoln called democracy in a republic. Some would want to emphasize the existence and place in the United States of the U.S. Constitution, which contemplates both bureaucracy and democracy.

Prominently, Dwight Waldo was a PA and a PS theorist who objected that incompatible with democracy was PA's emphases on efficiency and hierarchical thought patterns. Concerns about incompatibility, in various forms, have been expressed by other thinkers like Marshall Dimock (1936), Robert Dahl (1947), and Emmette Redford (1969). More recently, they have been voiced by such public administration writers as O.C. McSwite (2002) and Robert Denhardt (2004). The incompatibility, in one way of talking, is described variously and in such terms as encouraging calculative inhumanity, technological efficiency, subordination of the individual to the agency, and nonparticipation. Needless to say, many public administration thinkers have taken a different point of view, beginning with Woodrow Wilson, who advocated the politics-administration dichotomy. Many more have ignored the question.

The subsidiary question, typically passed over, is whether democracy is limited to whatever we think that we have in the United States. Robert Dahl identified five criteria of the democratic process, and he thought that they were necessary "if the members (however limited their numbers may be) are to be politically equal in determining the policies of the association" (Dahl 1998, p. 38). The five criteria were effective participation, voting equality, enlightened understanding, control of the agenda, and inclusion of adults. He gives fairly short shrift to direct democracy (what he calls assembly democracy), compared with our representative democracy. He criticizes Greek democracy in comparison with our form on the basis of noninclusion, for instance, as if the United States always gave the vote to women and slaves. Yet he acknowledges that other advocates of democracy favor direct democracy—down to American antifederalism, the Swiss cantons, and towns in Vermont.

Implications

Cousins should learn from the good habits of their close relatives. Public administration has inherited good habits from political science, and probably it could inherit more. Like a good cousin, though, it must also be wary of the counterproductive.

Implication for Planning—Shouldn't It Be More Philosophical?

Implications point the way to the more philosophical. They include those relating to policy analysis, to political philosophy, and to the Constitution. Each of these is likely to provoke controversy.

A first implication for strategic planning for public administration is to embrace policy studies and policy analysis more thoroughly. The place of policy studies and analysis in political science underscores the extent to which public policy making and analysis are practiced in governmental administration—especially at higher levels. It occurs under various names in various sites in the federal government, ranging from the White House and the Office of Management and Budget to locations throughout agencies. Yet this embrace of policy studies and policy analysis need not be limited to the existing patterns dominant in the policy disciplines. For instance, it could (in my view, should) extend to the philosophical. Some such philosophizing is currently conducted in the Public Administration Theory Network (www.patheory.org) and by others, and in journals like *Administrative Theory and Praxis* and *Administration and Society*.

A second implication for strategic planning for PA is to embrace political philosophy in a genuine philosophical sense exemplified by political philosophers like (say) Leo Strauss, applied to public policy issues of relevance to bureaucracy. Such increased emphasis on political philosophizing implies, in turn, a greater emphasis on public administration theory. It also implies encouraging such philosophizing in public administration education and research and practice, with a de-emphasis in public administration education and research on technical and short-term microproblems. The aim of such philosophizing is *reflection*.

For the nature of the philosophical, turn to Leo Strauss. Strauss explains that the aim of political philosophy is to seek truth, not to possess it. Strauss explains that philosophy "is essentially not possession of the truth, but quest for the truth. The distinctive trait of the philosopher is that 'he knows that he knows nothing' and that his insight into our ignorance concerning the most important things induces him to strive with all his power for knowledge. . . . This would not make philosophy futile. For the clear grasp of the fundamental question requires understanding of the subject matter with which the question is concerned . . ." (Strauss 1989, p. 5). Political philosophy is a branch of philosophy thus understood. For more on this, see Strauss's essays in *An Introduction to Political Philosophy: Ten Essays by Leo Strauss* (Strauss 1989.) In his introduction to the collection, Hilail Gilden claims Strauss (1899–1973) was seeking "to revive political philosophy as it was practiced by thinkers like Plato, Machiavelli, Hobbes and Montesquieu" (Gilden 1989, p. vii). He is being chosen here in spite of (or perhaps because of) the fact that he wrote the quote attributed to him earlier: "Today, political philosophy is in a state of decay and perhaps of putrefaction, if it has not vanished altogether" (Strauss 1989, p. 12).

Yet there would be resistance to such changes from some in traditional public administration. The president of ASPA in October 2007 pointed to disturbing developments "pushing public administration towards academic obfuscation" (White 2007). Following this, an ASPA task force, chaired by Nicholas Henry, issued what became known as the Larry Lynn Report (Henry et al. 2008). It commented on White's claim that there is "an increasing propensity to subvert the master of public administration (MPA) degree programs to prepare students for almost everything except careers in public administration" (White 2007, p. 16). The task force itself asserted that the MPA degree "is, and ought to be, distinctly different from those in the realms of policy, management and public affairs." What the task force had in mind is what it saw as the second goal of the MPA (see below for the first aim): the "transmittal of the essential professional, or 'craft' knowledge of the field, along with experiential exposure of students to the world of practice by means of nonclassroom projects, internships, case studies, practitioner involvement in teaching, etc." (Henry et al. 2008, p. 7).

A third implication for strategic planning for public administration is to emphasize the sovereign and guiding character of the U.S. Constitution. Adopted in 1787 and subjected to amendments, the Constitution provides the framework for government in the United States. "We the People of the United States, in order to form a more perfect Union, establish Justice, ensure domestic Tranquility, provide for the common defense, promote the general Welfare, and secure the Blessings of Liberty to ourselves and to our Posterity, do ordain and establish this Constitution for the United States of America." So begins the Preamble to the Constitution, which has a treasured place in the nation's life.

Those urging such an emphasis on the Constitution in public administration would not be expected to attach weight to the idea that the focus on the Constitution should underscore a division between American and non-American public administration (the latter consisting of public administration practiced in countries that do not enjoy an American constitution). They would have little interest in the fact that other countries have different traditions. But most might be sympathetic or open to the importance of that part of political philosophy, at least, that illuminates the Constitution and the ongoing work of forming a more perfect union.

Implication for Managing—Shouldn't More Democracy Be an Aim?

Bureaucracy should be managed consistent with democracy, and not just like a business. More visionary and reflective management analysis is needed that focuses on the longer run. Public administration theorizing should contribute to refining understanding of the basis of such democratic-bureaucratic policy (e.g., as in political philosophy) and to shaping specific policies for such a democratic purpose. This should speak, for example, to appropriate citizen participation. It should speak to obstacles (again) like lobbying.

Why is more theorizing needed in this respect? Rather than mere assertive claiming, required are reflective analysis and deliberation. (For a view of this, see O.C. McSwite, 2009.) To what extent is it true that bureaucracy should be unbusinesslike? To what extent and how should citizens participate in bureaucratic management? To what extent should answers to such questions recognize the different levels and programmatic characteristics of bureaucracy? How can we evaluate alternative theories of how to make bureaucracy consistent with democracy? What is democracy? And so on. The theorists should not feel constrained to "come up with" something that is technocratic and system-bound and that is limited to the short run.

There is—naturally—a significant literature in public administration on the question of how government should be run, and the political perspective would suggest that this should be intensified and broadened. Let's offer one example.

"Government shouldn't be run like a business; it should be run like a democracy" (Denhardt and Denhardt 2003, p. 3). With these words, Janet and Robert Denhardt open their book. They go on to specify seven elements of what they call the "New Public Service." They indicate that "theorists of citizenship, community and civil society, organizational humanism and the new public administration, and postmodernism have helped to establish a climate in which it makes sense today to talk about a New Public Service" (p. 42). They speak of the following seven lessons for strategic management in public administration. These are:

1. Serve citizens, not customers,
2. See the public interest,
3. Value citizenship over entrepreneurship,
4. Think strategically, act democratically,
5. Recognize that accountability is not simple,
6. Serve rather than steer,
7. Value people, not just productivity.

These lessons should not be read on a "take it, or leave it" basis. I think that the authors would welcome questioning, for example, asking more (or not asking), as to question 4, why it should not be worded: "Think democratically, act strategically." The lessons should be pursued by the public administration reader in the light of political philosophy.

Suggested by the political science lens is an emphasis on citizen participation, speaking of democracy. There is a literature, and public administration has had its own experience with citizen participation. On literature, for example, James Creighton (2005) gives good advice on what he calls the three stages in designing a public participation program—decision analysis, process planning, and implementation planning. And he does make clear that one-size-does-not-fit-all. The higher priority for the public administration discipline, the political perspective would suggest, is reflection and re-reflection on the broadest and most unrestricted basis. What is needed here is theorizing that links with political philosophy.

On public administration experience, citizen participation was an aim in the U.S. government's Model Cities Program (1966–1974), for instance, and that was where I first encountered it—in directing a major consulting project that was funded by the U.S. Department of Housing and Urban Development (HUD) on the management of model cities programs. The Model Cities Program was part of President Lyndon B. Johnson's Great Society and War on Poverty, and it was a program that called for comprehensive planning, rehabilitation of social service delivery, and creation of citizen participation for selected urban neighborhoods. I carry two lasting memories from that experience. The first is the great benefit of citizen participation. The second is the ease with which the illusion of participation can be substituted for, and mistaken for, meaningful participation.

Implication for the Underlying—Is What Counts as Common Sense Reliable?

An important implication is to improve on what is socially constructed in public administration talk as common sense, and we will return to this in chapters 13–18. This need is illustrated by the existence of the same problem in political science talk. Such improvements in public administration talk should recognize the relevant underlying societal unconscious where such social constructions are typically grounded.

John Nelson (1998, p. 81) points out that "political science often yokes itself to dubious assumptions implicit in the ordinary language of talk about politics." So does public administration. Nelson goes on to give the example of growth in government; when reading this, it is suggested that the public administration reader should think about growth in governmental bureaucracy. He writes that "if politicians start talking globally about 'growth in government,' many political scientists clamor to investigate it as a single coherent phenomenon—because that is how politicians discuss it. Too few political scientists ask whether there is a single such thing as 'growth in government,' let alone what its components and dynamics must be. Instead empiricists (especially) rush in to say where it is present and what causes it. Hence they sacrifice the chance to improve on the conventional wisdom" (Nelson 1998, p. 81). When it comes to "growth in bureaucracy" and "big government" talk, don't public administration writers sacrifice the chance to improve on the conventional wisdom? And this is but one example.

Return to American exceptionalism. American exceptionalism is linked to the idea of the American dream, and the contents of the American dream were developed in a historical period when conditions were different from those obtaining today. Jeremy Rifkin writes that the "American Dream is far too centered on personal material advancement and too little concerned with the broader human welfare to be relevant in a world of increasing human risk, diversity and interdependence. It is an old dream, immersed in a frontier mentality, that has long since become passé" (Rifkin 2004, p. 3). Unlike Rifkin, many will not want to replace that dream with others available—and he spoke of a new and different European dream being born. Most of us will want to keep the American dream. But, retaining the American dream (or any other dream) does not rule out tweaking. As asked in chapter 2, can we not tweak the dubious equation of individual success with material success? Also, isn't it practical—and not un-American—to be open to each individual dreaming her own dream(s)?

Implication for Public Administration Field—Shouldn't Political Science Be an Example?

In the style of PS, traditional PA should embrace the political. For this, studying and practicing public policy is a good tonic.

On not taking the political for granted, the same ASPA or Lynn report (noted in the Implication for Planning discussion) seems supportive. That report recommended MPA coursework stressing "the constitutional and legal foundations of public administration" (Henry et al. 2008, p. 18). The first aim of an MPA degree, in its view, is "transmittal of a full awareness of the broad issues of constitutionalism, politics and democratic theory that are innately embedded in the practice of public administration in a republic such as ours" (p. 7).

Public policy studies and analysis can serve as a tonic for public administration. *Modernizing Government* (Cabinet Office 1999) was an approach for upgrading policy formulation in the British government. It stressed core competencies, labeled as forward looking, outward looking, innovative and creative, using evidence, inclusive, and joined up. Hugh Bochal and Sue Duncan (2007, p. 67) describe and evaluate these features, and they describe the entire process as "hierarchical." Right or wrong, how can such studies not be a tonic for the public administration theorist and practitioner?

Implication for Public Administration Creativity—Wasn't Harold Lasswell Right?

Harold D. Lasswell emphasized for the study and teaching of political science the importance of the cultivation of creativity. The cultivation of imaginative creativity should be no less a priority in public administration. In his *The Future of Political Science*, Lasswell (1902–1978) devoted two chapters to the cultivation of creativity in PS. "No static certainty is to be found in politics or political science, hence the importance of cultivating an affirmative, inventive, flexible mind" (Lasswell 1963, p. 147). Later he added that, "Whether a conventionally named body of scholars called 'political scientists' will continue to play a prominent part in the study and appraisal of politics depends chiefly on its vigor and imagination" (Lasswell 1963, p. 241). Public administration and political science: two cousins in search of the imaginative?

Epilogue

Shouldn't public administration deepen its knowledge of the democracy our systems seek to serve? "Like many beautiful ideas, however, democracy travels through our minds shadowed by its doubles—bad ideas that are close enough to be easily mistaken for the real thing. Democracy has many doubles, but the most seductive is majority rule, and this is not democracy. It is merely government by and for the majority. The ancient Athenians who invented democracy learned this lesson the hard way. . . . They tinkered with the system for nearly 200 years, and it was working smoothly when the overwhelming power of the Macedon brought it down . . ." (Woodruff 2005, p. 1).

Suggested Readings

Denhardt, Janet V., and Robert B. Denhardt. 2003. *The New Public Service: Serving, Not Steering*. Armonk, NY: M.E. Sharpe.

Kramnick, Isaac, and Theodore J. Lowi. 2009. *American Political Thought: A Norton Anthology*. New York: W.W. Norton.

Lasswell, Harold D. 1963. *The Future of Political Science*. New York: Prentice-Hall.

Woodruff, Paul. 2005. *First Democracy: Challenge of an Ancient Idea*. New York: Oxford University Press.

6

Public Administration from a
Critical Theory Perspective

The Frankfurt School of Critical Theory is about emancipation. The school began in 1923, with the creation of the University of Frankfurt's Institute for Social Research. Max Horkheimer became its director in 1930. With the rise of Nazism, the Frankfurt School relocated in 1933 from Germany to Switzerland—and then to the United States. From 1934 to 1943, the institute was affiliated with Columbia University. There was emigration to New York in 1935 and to California in 1941. The school returned to Germany several years after World War II, the institute being reestablished in 1953. The school was enriched by fresh writings from Jürgen Habermas and others—including those like Herbert Marcuse, who remained in the United States. The term *critical theory* is interpreted here as referring to the mainstream tradition of the Frankfurt School.

The Frankfurt School is neo-Marxist. Two preliminary points. First, the Cold War is over. It should now be possible to evaluate Karl Marx without ideological bias. Yet recall that no significant thinker batted (a baseball analogy) either 1,000 or 0. Second, to focus on the Frankfurt School as neo-Marxist, while true, is somewhat misguided. The more important point is that the Frankfurt critical theorists take a quantum leap forward in their PA-relevant analyses of society and of emancipation.

The first part of this chapter sketches the nature of critical theory. The objective is to note what is significant for public administration practice and theory.

1. What is critical theory? What, in a nutshell, is a description?
2. What is critical theory? What are the three generations of critical theory?
3. What is critical theory? Who were Herbert Marcuse and Theodor Adorno?
4. What is critical theory? Who is Jürgen Habermas?
5. What is critical theory? What is critical theory outside the Frankfurt School?

The second part of this chapter discusses implications for public administration of a critical theory perspective. The following questions are discussed:

6. Implication for planning—Shouldn't public administration seek emancipation toward the lifeworld?
7. Implication for managing—Is anti-administration emancipative?
8. Implication for the underlying—Does public administration suffer from one-dimensional thinking?
9. Implication for the field—What does "public" mean in public administration?
10. Implication for creativity—What does emancipation ask from public administration?

In reading this chapter, the readers are asked (per Reflection Exercise 1) to determine what insights about public administration theory and practice interest them.

Sketching Critical Theory

Critical theory aims to complete the emancipatory project of modernity, the intensions of the Project of Enlightenment. As Jürgen Habermas explains, "The project of modernity formulated in the 18th century by the philosophers of the Enlightenment consisted in their efforts to develop objective science, universal morality and law, and autonomous art according to their inner logic. . . . The Enlightenment philosophers wanted to utilize this . . . accumulation . . . for the enrichment of everyday life—that is to say, for the rational organization of everyday social life" (Habermas 1983, p. 9). Public administration is one form of this "rational organization of everyday social life."

What Is Critical Theory? What, in a Nutshell, Is a Description?

Critical theory aims to emancipate, to free. It analyzes constraining power (or bondage or exploitation or domination), with the aim of guiding human action toward emancipation. As an example, critical theory has included critiques of constraining ideology or false consciousness. It has sought to explain how and why people accept worldviews and forms of thought and belief systems that sustain the existing power structure rather than their own realistic self-interest. It has studied the pathologies of reason itself. It has stood opposed to instrumental reasoning and to the administered industrialized society where ideological control is exercised over people considered to have no consciousness of their exploitation. It wants to show that a freer and happier society is possible, offering understandings that can aid self-consciousness among social agents and that can promote emancipation. Its method is reason, but it aims for consciousness that is self-critical and self-conscious.

Critical theory is interdisciplinary and varied. It is interdisciplinary in that it interweaves variously such disciplinary traditions as, for example, the sociological, the psychoanalytic, and the philosophical. It is varied in both views and methods; it is not monolithic.

"The work of the critical theorists provides criticisms and alternatives to traditional, or mainstream, social theory, philosophy, and science, together with a critique of the full range of ideologies from mass culture to religion. At least some versions of critical theory are related to politics and an interest in the emancipation of those who are oppressed and dominated." That is how Douglas Kellner (1989, p. 1) puts it. He adds that "Critical theory has become a major force in the debates about the nature, trajectory and impact of what has become known as modernity" (p. 3).

What Is Critical Theory? What Are the Three Generations of Critical Theory?

First Generation

Extending beyond the return to Germany after World War II, the first of the three generations of critical theorists included at its core Max Horkheimer, Theodor Adorno, Herbert Marcuse, Leo Lowenthal, and Friedrich Pollock. Others were associated with the institute, like Erich Fromm, Franz Neuman, Otto Kirchheimer, Henryk Grossman, and Arkadij Gurland. In varying ways, they emphasized philosophy of consciousness. They wanted to transform society, the meaning of culture, and the relation between individual, society, and culture (Held 1980). Much of the work was directed toward the forces that would impel society toward rational institutions, completing the work of modernity and aiming for free, true, and just lives.

Second Generation

The dominant figure of the second generation was Jürgen Habermas. A primary focus was to turn from a philosophy of consciousness to a philosophy of language, with the overall purpose remaining self-emancipation of people from domination. It was a communicative turn. Habermas's view was that communicative forms of language are primary, and that communicative discourse is emancipatory. Some see the second generation as the culmination of critical theory; others do not. For more about Habermas, see the questions below.

Third Generation

The emerging third generation currently centers on Axel Honneth. Others associated with this generation include Seyla Benhabib. Honneth (2004, pp. 336–337) tells us that "Critical Theory, whose intellectual horizon was decisively formed in the appropriation of European intellectual history from Hegel to Freud, still relies on the possibility of viewing history with reason as its Leitfaden. But there may be no other aspect of Critical Theory more foreign to today's generation, which has grown up conscious of cultural plurality and of the end of 'Grand Narratives,' than social criticisms founded upon this sort of philosophy of history." He goes on to say that "historically effective reason" is incomprehensible "if one can no longer recognize the unity of a single rationality in the diversity of established convictions" (Honneth 2004, p. 337). The reasoning and emancipatory pursuit remains; but times and context, at least, have changed.

What Is Critical Theory? Who Were Herbert Marcuse and Theodor Adorno?

These are prime representatives of critical theory's first generation. Herbert Marcuse (1898–1979) was a philosopher and a sociologist. Theodor Adorno (1903–1967) was a philosopher, a sociologist, and a musicologist. Two of the many books written by Marcuse were *Eros and Civilization* (1955) and *One-Dimensional Man* (1964). Two of the many books written by Adorno were *Dialect of Enlightenment* (1944 in German; an English edition was published in 1973 and co-authored with Max Horkheimer) and *The Authoritarian Personality* (1950).

All these publications analyze contemporary civilization, with (as suggested) the aim of facilitating emancipation. Here are illustrative snippets. Take Marcuse, for example. *Eros and Civilization* begins by stating that "Sigmund Freud's proposition that civilization is based on the permanent subjugation of the human instincts has been taken for granted. His question whether the suffering thereby inflicted on individuals has been worth the benefits of culture has not been taken too seriously— the less so since Freud himself considered the process to be inevitable and irreversible" (Marcuse 1955, p. 1). Its concern was with "philosophical and sociological implications." So, the book critiques contemporary civilization as being based on features like production and repression. Instead, it advocates an alternative model of aesthetics, sensuality, and play. It is not a matter of eliminating (say) labor; rather it is a question of eliminating labor as an organizing principle of society.

One-Dimensional Man begins by stating that "A comfortable, smooth, reasonable, democratic unfreedom prevails in advanced industrial civilization, a token of technical progress. Indeed, what could be more rational than the suppression of individuality in the mechanization of socially necessary but painful performances . . ." (Marcuse 1991, 1964, p. 1). The book describes the one-dimensionality of thinking that is limited to the uncritical and conformist acceptance of existing structures, norms, and behaviors. As an alternative, Marcuse argues for a Great Refusal as a means toward emancipation. For more, see below.

What Is Critical Theory? Who Is Jürgen Habermas?

In an important sense, Jürgen Habermas (born 1929) is the second generation. Habermas is a philosopher and a sociologist, and he is a prolific writer. He shifted the second generation, as noted above, to philosophy of language, with the same critical and emancipatory aim. Most usually, he is associated with such ideas as communicative action, communicative rationality, discourse ethics, and (see below) deliberative democracy. Communicative action, for instance, refers to agency in the form of deliberative communication. Discourse ethics is argumentation ethics.

Among Habermas's publications, the most celebrated is his *Theory of Communicative Action* (1987). It is written in two volumes. Volume I is called *Reason and the Rationalization of Society.* Volume II is *Lifeworld and System: A Critique of Functionalist Reason.* Habermas gives an account of communicative reason and communicative action, based on inter-subjective searching for understandings. Communicative reason is contrasted with instrumental rationality that serves functional purposes—and that facilitates oppressive choices. See below for comments on lifework and systems, and the rationalization and colonization of the lifeworld.

Deliberative democracy is emphasized, as Habermas continued his thinking in *Between Facts and Norms* (1996). He rejected what he called "liberal" (grounded in Hobbes) and "civic republican" (grounded in Aristotle and Rousseau) democracies. He favored *deliberative democracy*, with an emphasis on mutual consultative discourse and shared meanings rather than implementing summed preferences.

What Is Critical Theory? What Is Critical Theory Outside the Frankfurt School?

Critical theory can be interpreted in a wider way to include more than the Frankfurt School. Such a category of those with emancipatory intent would include, for example, postcolonialism, queer theory, and Marxism. Each could have had a chapter in a larger version of this book. I've mentioned that I find postcolonialism very valuable, and I have written about Homi Bhabha's *Location of Culture* on three or four occasions (e.g., in Farmer 2005a, pp. 40–41). The concept of the "in-between" applies importantly to public administration, such that "in-between spaces provide the terrain of elaborating strategies of selfhood—singular or communal—that initiate new signs of identity, and innovative sites of collaboration and contestation, in the act of defining the idea of society itself" (Bhabha 1994, p. 4). For a description of each of these perspectives, see Malpas and Wake (2006, pp. 127–140; 102–114; and 28–42). Included in separate chapters of this book are still other emancipatory perspectives, post-structuralism, and feminism.

Implications

"In such a field [as PA], one would think a body of theory that offers critique of public institutions plus a vision of a better future would appeal to writers. Critical theory does these things, but it appears infrequently in the literature of public administration," writes Richard Box (2005, p. 14).

*Implication for Planning—Shouldn't Public Administration Seek
Emancipation Toward the Lifeworld?*

Shouldn't emancipation be a principal aim of strategic planning for the future of
public administration theory and practice? This is implied by critical theory.

For public administration theory, shouldn't a principal aim be to constrain the
world of bureaucratic and other systems and to privilege the lifeworld? This aim,
as indicated above, is described by Jürgen Habermas. First, in this paragraph let's
sketch some of what Habermas intended. The background in Habermas's account
is that there is a tendency toward rationalization and colonization of the lifeworld.
Shouldn't Public Administration discourse operate against this tendency, and promote means to pursue and sustain the lifeworld? The lifeworld is the open-ended
world of living a life that is conducive to communicative action. It is the informal,
lived world of culturally grounded discourse. It is the world of everyday sociabil-
ity. The systems world consists of systems governed by nonlinguistic institutions
like power, money, and the media. The systems world includes government and
the economy and traditional bureaucracies. Communicative action in the lifeworld
results from shared understandings shaped by shared circumstances. This stands
against instrumental rationality that attempts to promote functions in the systems
world, for example, to advance the interests of a bureaucracy, to make money, to
dominate. The problem is that the systems world and its instrumental rationality
tend to destroy the capacity of the lifeworld to achieve this communicative action. Consider how rationalization, as a single example, can act in constraining
communicative action. Lifeworld discourse (and deliberative democracy) can be
contaminated by rationalization that includes the conscious (e.g., to defend against
ridicule) and the subconscious (e.g., to block guilt feelings) concoction of stories
to justify this or that action. In terms of bureaucratic agencies, there are stories of
success (e.g., we are kicking their derrieres in this war), stories of the practitioners
as heroes (e.g., we support our troops), and stories of dangers faced (e.g., the enemy
hates us, and they are sneaky). Communicative reason is induced to accept oppression when discourse is reduced by such instrumental rationality.

Second, let's turn to discourse within public administration. Richard Box
observes that discourse theory "is emerging in public administration as a way to
recapture a sense of public administration outside the narrow confines of management technique and efficiency. It seeks to free citizens and administrators from
reified, theoretical preconceptions and institutional constraints, allowing them to
recreate themselves and their institutional arrangements in current discourse settings" (Box 2005, p. 91). He goes on to refer to the work of O.C. McSwite (1997b)
and Charles Fox and Hugh Miller (1997) "on the discourse process," and he refers
to me (Farmer 1995) as working "from multiple perspectives to offer a broad view
of interrelationships in governance systems" (p. 91). Recognizing the differences,
he describes the themes among discourse theorists as including "antifoundational
resistance to metanarratives (disbelief in the primacy and objectivity of any single

theory or description of phenomena), a constructivist view of knowledge, . . . and the search for free and uncoerced communication in open discourse settings" (Box 2005, p. 91). He notes McSwite (2000, p. 55) describing people as creating "themselves in the interactive process of working together on problems," rather than as individuals coming to the process as "predetermined packages of interests . . ." (Box 2005, p. 92). He describes Fox and Miller (1995) as framing the current social situation in terms of a "postmodern 'thinning' of reality in which terms and images are increasingly separated from 'authentic' discourse, and a genuine sense of community can only be found in small, localized enclaves. . . . [And] we find ourselves in a situation in which some people (but not others) participate, and it is a matter of creating them from something like Jürgen Habermas's 'ideal speech' situation" (Box 2005, p. 92). Box references me (Farmer 2000, p. 81) as opposing discourse that leaves out "important elements of what it is to be human."

Box (2005, pp. 126–145) analyzes citizen participation, designed to upgrade discourse in the bureaucracy. Aptly reflected in the chapter title "Critical Practice and the Problem of Finding a Public," he offers a framework for understanding and for responding to the fact that "most people are not interested in traditional forms of participation in public decision making." His framework is "based on critical social theory," and elements include "contradiction and dialectical change, critical imagination, and self-determination" (p. 126).

Emancipation by privileging self over system is an aim. Systems have clear functional advantages; but prioritizing systemization comes at the expense of selves. Early post-traditional thinkers, like Max Weber and Hebert Marcuse, wrote about the inhumanity of privileging systems. That is, they wrote about "the anti-human effects of modern economic and bureaucratic systems" (see Farmer 2005a, 33–34). Weber described our entrapment in the economic-bureaucratic "iron cage" (1958, p. 181). He wrote of the Faustian bargain we make with the economic-bureaucratic system. We trade our "full and beautiful humanity" in return for a narrow vocation where we are "specialists without spirit, sensualists without heart" in a rationalized and disenchanted world (Weber 1958, p. 182). Other thinkers have said similar things in different ways. Importantly, there is Habermas, discussing his distinction between the lifeworld and the world of systems.

Implication for Managing—Is Anti-Administration Emancipative?

Critical theory aims toward emancipation. Managing anti-administratively seeks to emancipate clients, subordinates, and ideas.

Anti-administrative discourse (mentioned in chapter 1) exhibits radical openness in public administration thinking and action. It seeks to include not only mainstream ideas and people, but also ideas and people that are *other*—excluded or marginalized. It seeks to include people and ideas that are subordinate. For people, examples are financially poor clients and citizens, minorities and women, and employees dealing with their bosses. For ideas, the example I (2005a) have given is greater inclusion of nonmechanical understandings. For a management bumper sticker, there is "Think and act anti-administratively; not ant-administratively!"

What is a practical example of anti-administration? Robert Cunningham and Robert Schneider give examples of the gifting aspect of anti-administration. "Examples are the social service worker who at the end of the day drives the client home so the client will not have to spend 90 minutes waiting for the infrequent buses, the public housing manager who leads the boy scout troop made up of boys from public housing on camping trips, the building inspector who on Saturdays participates with other volunteers in the framing of Habitat for Humanity houses. Each of these acts is a freely given gift. . . . They cannot be programmed or predicted" (Cunningham and Schneider 2001, p. 581). As they say, "Modern administration has become a unidimensional concept, concretized into Weberian legal-rational governance. The administrative model no longer has legitimacy in the eyes of many U.S. citizens" (p. 584).

Why? There are utilitarian and altruistic reasons for public administration to take care of marginalized or vulnerable groups. On the utilitarian side, one reason is the benefit not only to the excluded group but also to the mainstream or dominant group. Consider the claim that public administration theory is essentially top-down, thinking of administration from the perspective of the manager—as explained in discussing public administration thinking and practice in terms of the cult of the leader (see Farmer 2005a, pp. 141–153). As such, it tends to marginalize or dominate clients or subordinates. In such a case, public administration thinking inspired by critical theory can be useful in adding insights that can strengthen "mainstream" or dominant thinking.

I first started writing about anti-administration in *The Language of Public Administration* (1995), describing it as a main point of postmodernism. Such anti-administration included what I called imaginization, deconstruction, deterritorialization, and alterity. I continued thinking about this through my edited book *Papers on the Art of Anti-Administration* (1998a). Later I attempted to separate anti-administration from postmodernism by speaking about it in terms of a medieval (and then a modernist) framework (e.g., see Farmer 2002, pp. 271–287).

That thinking was also carried forward in a 2001 symposium. In that symposium, McSwite (2001, pp. 493–506) provided a Lacanian rationale for anti-administration. Michael Spicer (2001, pp. 507–528) argued for value pluralism, suggesting that the monist ethical view is dangerous. Patricia Patterson (2001, pp. 529–540) used the trickster figure to illustrate the anti-administrative contention that prevailing questions need reframing. Richard Box (2001, pp. 559–572) focused on public administrators exercising their imaginative faculties to protect private lives. Robert Cunningham and Robert Schneider (2001, pp. 573–588) discussed witnessing and gifting as anti-administrative strategies for reclaiming what they describe as a trust relationship between civil servants and citizens. Janet Hutchinson (2001, pp. 589–604) maintained that anti-administration is anti-melancholy, and she suggested that multigendering is one remedy for what she described as the pervasive melancholy that afflicts men, women, and children. Debra Jacobs (2001, pp. 605–620) offered an ecological argument for anti-administration: "Life within the machine is ordered being. . . . The chaos of nature is the other. . . . Imagine for an instance a cow standing in the middle of the highway as you drive to work. The chaos destabilizes your world" (pp. 618–619). As she adds, the "cow simply does not belong on the road."

Implication for the Underlying—Does Public Administration Suffer from One-Dimensional Thinking?

Emancipate us, critical theory implies, from the one-dimensionality of public administration theorizing and practice. Frequently such one-dimensionality is unconscious. Consider Marcuse and then public administration.

One-dimensional thinking is described by Herbert Marcuse in his *One-Dimensional Man* (1991 [1964]). Recall Question 3 above and its description of one-dimensionality as thinking that is limited to the uncritical and conformist acceptance of existing structures, norms, and behaviors. Marcuse is opposed to the oppression and domination (imposed on self and others) associated with the "new conformism which is a facet of technological rationality translated into social behavior" (Marcuse 1991 [1964], p. 84). Instead of submission to one-dimensionality, Marcuse argues for emancipation through a Great Refusal (discussed earlier).

One-dimensionality is exemplified in the top-down character of traditional public administration practice. As James Scott observes, "With rare, but significant, exceptions the public performance of the subordinate will, out of prudence, fear and the desire to curry favor, be shaped to appeal to the expectations of the powerful" (Scott 1990, p. 2). Speaking in a non–public administration context, Scott later adds that on "a daily basis, the impact of power is more readily observed in acts of deference, subordination and ingratiation" (Scott 1990, p. 28).

Power has been extensively and intensively studied outside the public administration field, for example, by Marcuse, Foucault (see chapter 7), and by Scott (just mentioned). Such study is rare within a number of the social sciences, like economics. It is rare in public administration. An exception was a 2003 symposium on the Great Refusal—including thinkers who wrote in the symposium just discussed. O.C. McSwite (2003, pp. 183–204) offered a theory of social change through personal, deconstructive refusal. I (Farmer 2003, pp. 205–232) discussed how to correct the imbalance in PA thinking between speaking-from-power and speaking-to-power. Patterson (2003, pp. 233–242) discussed one-dimensionality in terms of William Butler Yeats's lines that include "The best lack all conviction, while the worst/Are full of passionate intensity." Box (2003, pp. 243–260) wrote of the relevance of refusal in the areas of democracy, the "Warfare" state, research, and gender. Lisa Zanetti (2003, pp. 261–276) considered the implications of refusal in the context of dialectic and depth psychology. Louis Howe (2003, pp. 277–298) dramatized possibilities for an ethos of refusal in public administration by drawing upon what he called subaltern ethics.

Implication for the Field—What Does "Public" Mean in Public Administration?

Human emancipation is *the* aim that critical theory would urge for the public administration discipline. See Questions 6 and 7 above, for example. Clearly the choice of optimal boundary limitations for public administration would be impacted, if not determined, by choice of such an aim. Beyond this, critical theory does imply questions about the adjective "public" in public administration.

Public administration draws a boundary line between the public and the non-public; otherwise, the field would not be called public administration. Jürgen Habermas's work implies that PA's boundary is artificially or socially constructed, and it should raise the question for the discipline whether the boundary line could be drawn more helpfully.

"The usage of the words 'public' and 'public sphere' betrays a multiplicity of concurrent meanings," begins Habermas (1989, p. 1) in *The Structural Transformation of the Public Sphere*. Here Habermas includes a description of the rise of the "bourgeois public sphere" in the early years of modernity. The sphere was the scene of rational debate, mediating between the public and the private. It included the political club, the newspaper, and the journal. Habermas then describes the decline of this sphere, increasingly taken over by private corporations and the state. Recall the rise of public relations and advertising, and corporations becoming dominant over culture. Rational individuals become culture consumers. The "criteria of rationality are completely lacking in a consensus created by sophisticated opinion-molding services under the aegis of a sham public interest" (Habermas 1989, p. 195). As I (1995, p. 61) noted earlier, Habermas's description is much different from the socially constructed view of the public and private spheres "implied in, say, Samuelson and Nordhaus's *Economics*."

Implication for Creativity—What Does Emancipation Ask from Public Administration?

Embracing the goal for public administration of emancipation, in imitation of the aim of critical theory, would require creative imagination in at least two respects. First, it would require imagination to see through what we currently count as common sense truths. Second, it requires imagination to help public administration make a virtual 180-degree turn from what I will explain as *inward* discourse and action to *outward* discourse and action.

As to the first respect (what counts as common sense truths), check the imaginative connections that you can make from the following four claims in Marcuse's *One-Dimensional Man* to the situations in your work or your life.

Claim 1: "Today this private space has been invaded and whittled down by technological reality. Mass production and mass distribution claim the entire individual, and industrial psychology has long ceased to be confined to the factory" (1991 [1964], p. 10).

Claim 2: "Domination is transfigured into administration. . . . The slaves of developed industrial civilization are sublimated slaves but they are slaves, for slavery is determined . . . by the status of being a mere instrument and the reduction of man to the state of a thing" (pp. 32–33).

Claim 3: "The prescriptions for inhumanity and injustice are being administered by a rationally organized bureaucracy, which is, however, invisible at its vital center" (p. 71).

Claim 4: "We are again confronted with one of the most vexing aspects of advanced industrial civilization: the rational character of its irrationality" (p. 9).

Regarding the second respect, consider the imaginative creativity needed to help PA theorizing and practice change, for instance, from *inward* discourse and action to *outward* discourse and action. By inward discourse and action, I mean discourse and action that relate primarily to the *internal benefit* of the bureaucracy or the program. While the stated goals and rhetoric may be outward, for instance, don't bureaucratic goals typically and in reality point inward? This inward direction is contrasted with *outward benefit* in discourse and action to what is *beyond* the bureaucracy and *beyond* its program. From public administration thinkers and practitioners, it requires imagination to shift from primary concern with the bureaucratic machine (inward, as we are using the term) toward primary concern with the human-in-society (outward). It does require imaginative creativity to seduce and encourage public administration into switching its comfortable privileging of the *systems world* to an uncomfortable privileging of the *lifeworld*.

Epilogue

Isn't the lifeworld worth privileging? Horkheimer and Adorno write (2002, pp. 124–125), "Existence in late capitalism is a permanent rite of initiation. . . . Individuals are tolerated only as far as their wholehearted identity with the universal is beyond question. From the standardized improvisation in jazz to the original film personality who must have a lock of hair straying over her eyes so that she can be recognized as such, pseudo-individuality reigns."

Suggested Readings

Box, Richard C. 2005. *Critical Social Theory in Public Administration*. Armonk, NY: M.E. Sharpe.

Habermas, Jürgen. 1987. *Theory of Communicative Action*. Vol. 1. Boston, MA: Beacon Press.

Horkheimer, Max, and Theodor W. Adorno. 2002. *Dialectic of Enlightenment*. Stanford, CA: Stanford University Press.

Marcuse, Herbert. 1991 (1964). *One-Dimensional Man: Studies in the Ideology of Advanced Industrial Society*. Boston: Beacon Press.

7

Public Administration from a Post-Structural Perspective

Post-structuralism stands against structuralism. It contests a basic structuralist idea that underlying all phenomena are deep structures that shape them. It opposes the views that each of these structures functions according to its own grammar and that the structures are interrelated. Post-structuralism objects to the structuralist idea that, at least in principle, the world is completely comprehensible through analysis of these systems and structures. For the post-structuralist, excluded from this structuralist view are emphases on unknowability, luck, and even human agency. For the post-structuralist, this focus on solid foundation has no solid foundation. For the post-structuralist, the surface swamp (as it were) should not be misleadingly discounted.

All this is uncomfortable to the habit of mind of traditional public administration, to the extent that this habit of mind privileges the systemic. This traditional habit of mind is uncomfortable when encountering a definition that is not definite and systematic—and preferably, short and easy to understand. It is uncomfortable with descriptions that do not fit in with the hearer's existing conceptual framework, with the familiar system. Post-structuralism invites an uncomfortable shift away from this traditional habit of mind.

This chapter sketches the nature and implications of a post-structural perspective in terms of the points where post-structuralism and postmodernism overlap. A reason for this choice is that both post-structuralism and postmodernism share the view that thinking realistically about the world lies in giving adequate recognition to the nonstructural, the nonsystematic. Five questions discuss the nature of this perspective, with the objective of noting what is significant for public administration practice and theory.

1. What is a post-structural lens? What is structuralism, in straightforward public administration terms?

2. What is a post-structural lens? What do structuralism and post-structuralism share?
3. What is a post-structural lens? What is postmodernism?
4. What is a post-structural lens? What is modernity?
5. What is a post-structural lens? Who are the "big" names?

The second part of the chapter examines the significance for public administration theory and practice of a post-structuralist perspective.

6. Implication for planning—What is deconstruction?
7. Implication for managing—What is anti-administration?
8. Implication for the underlying—What are normalization and hyperreality?
9. Implication for the public administration field—What is deterritorialization?
10. Implication for imaginative creativity—What is imaginization?

In reading this chapter, readers (per Reflection Exercise 1) may wish to reflect on ideas about administrative theory and practice suggested by a post-structural perspective.

Sketching the Post-Structural

Jacques Derrida issues the post-structural invitation to interpret texts better. Interpreting "interpret" as "understand the meaning" and interpreting "texts" as "situations," he invites us to understand situations better. By implication, public administration is invited to understand situations better.

Post-structural interpretations are not easy, however, nor is any serious philosophy. Here is Derrida (1978, p. 17) asking how interpretation should be interpreted: "There are . . . two interpretations of interpretation, of structure, of sign, of play. The one seeks to decipher, dreams of deciphering a truth or an origin that escapes play and the order of the sign, and which lives the necessity of interpretation as an exile." He continues, "The other, which is no longer turned toward the origin, affirms play and tries to pass beyond man and humanism, the name of man being the name of that being who, . . . throughout his entire history . . . has dreamed of full presence, the reassuring foundation, the origin and the end of play." For Derrida, the first interpretation is a delusion.

What Is a Post-Structural Lens? What Is Structuralism, in Straightforward Public Administration Terms?

If the standard description (in the opening paragraph) of structuralism sounds too general and too abstract, try this preliminary procedure of using the following two steps in applying that standard description to public administration and to what is familiar to you. Then, the reader may feel emboldened to turn to language (to signifiers and signified) and to writers like Ferdinand de Saussure.

First, recall the description of why post-structuralism stands against structuralism. It was noted (in the first paragraph) that post-structuralism objects to the structuralist idea that, at least in principle, the world is completely comprehensible through analysis of systems and structures. Post-structuralism contests a basic structuralist idea that underlying all phenomena are deep structures that shape phenomena. The post-structuralist invites us to focus on the surface swamp of phenomena.

Second, imagine phenomena to be all the public administration, economic, political and social, and other activities in the world—such phenomena are stuff that happens, in all its variety and confusion. Imagine structuralism to be saying that underlying each of these categories (public administration, economics, politics, etc.) is a structure with its own grammar (or logic) that can be studied. So public administration phenomena can be understood as having a distinct underlying structure—and the grammar (or logic) of that structure can be best studied in the way that, say, traditional public administration studies such phenomena. Similarly, economic phenomena have a distinct underlying structure that can best be studied by means of the grammar (or logic) of deductive microeconomic and macroeconomic modeling. Such deductive modeling is a grammar that is foreign to the inductive grammar of public administration. However, these grammars may well have similarities and parallels with the grammars of other structures or disciplines. For instance, public administration may have a grammar that is quite similar to the grammar of, say, business administration. But the differences in grammar are sufficiently marked that public administration and business administration "deserve" to be analyzed in different disciplines, by specialists with different experience and educational backgrounds. It is easy to see that, in principle, it would be possible eventually to know everything about the entire world by completely analyzing all of the interlocking structures that underlie the world. Post-structuralism stands against this.

What Is a Post-Structural Lens? What Do Structuralism and Post-Structuralism Share?

At least three features are shared by structuralism and post-structuralism. These are critiques of the human subject, of historicism, and of meaning. Structuralists like Claude Lévi-Strauss and post-structuralists like Derrida can be found on the same sides of such critiques. Madan Sarap (1993, pp. 1–5), who explains these differences in more detail, also adds a fourth—critique of philosophy.

The human subject is the free, intellectual, fully conscious, self-knowing agent. Such a conception was formulated most famously by Descartes, who wrote, "I think, therefore I am." Some philosophers have taken Descartes's implied argument apart; but its influence has been central in thinking about the human "sciences."

For me, this view of the human subject reaches its zenith in economic man, the perfectly rational construct who dominates mainstream economic theory. No, say both structuralists and post-structuralists.

Historicism takes it that history has an overall pattern. No, there is no onward-and-upward, no general (repeat, general) progress, no end point—say both camps.

Meaning embraces the talk about signifier and signified. *Cat* is the signifier in English for a variety of animals, including the animal that purrs and has pointed ears and whiskers: in French, it is *chat*. The signified in this case is the set of animals themselves. Both structuralists and post-structuralists point to the precarious balance between signifier and signified. Sarap describes Saussure himself as stressing that "each signifier acquired its semantic value only by virtue of its differential position within the structure of language" (Sarap 1993, p. 3). Derrida goes much further, writing of floating signifiers. For social science examples, consider the floating signifiers "depression" and "recession" and "rolling readjustment." Arguably, these signifiers have the same referent.

What Is a Post-Structural Lens? What Is Postmodernism?

Post-structuralism offers with postmodernism the invitation that people should interpret texts better. As Stuart Sim puts it, postmodernism is taken "to encompass figures and debates within poststructuralism. . . . Postmodernism, we might say, subsumes postructuralism . . ." (Sim 1999, p. ix). Post-structuralism also is described as including streams of thought that lie outside postmodernism, such as (some say) Lacanian psychoanalysis.

Let's describe postmodernism.

Postmodernism, like post-structuralism, wants to understand the world as it is, warts and all. It wants us to interpret in what it considers to be the most "realistic" way. The word "realistic" is put in scare quotes because realism is often used in a different way; here it refers to "as it is." The world is "as it is" in all its uncomfortable complexity.

Ideas prominent in the postmodern, as in post-structuralism, are unknowingness, luck, human agency, and anti-foundationalism. Unknowingness can be understood as skepticism about human capability to have absolutely certain knowledge about the ultimate reality of the world. We cannot have what elsewhere I (Farmer 2005a, pp. 62–72) have called Big T Truth, full-throated and confident assertions of "The Truth, the whole Truth and nothing but the Truth" about ultimate reality. This does not mean that there is no truth in the world. There is truth: to give an example, it is true that I have just written that "there is truth"—and isn't that obviously true? Doesn't such little-t truth abound? But that is different from the whole Truth and nothing but the Truth. The question of the existence of "The Truth, the whole Truth, and nothing but the Truth," is also quite different from whether I can know that Big T truth. Skepticism is not concerned with being optimistic or pessimistic; it intends to be realistic about the human condition.

Luck can be part of the skeptical condition, to the extent that it is not predictable. If luck operates in the working of phenomena, doesn't this exercise some limit on my capability of explaining such phenomena? As one example, Karl Marx advanced his historical materialist explanation of the dialectical development of society, noting how opposing forces (thesis and antithesis) give rise to new conditions (synthesis). In this way, Marx can give an account of how human history is led to develop through the ancient, feudal, capitalist, socialist, and communist stages: we are bound within the structures of historical development. Marx did not emphasize the luck of the draw.

Human liberty is a way of speaking about an aspect of human agency. Earlier I (1995) described postmodernism as aiming for radical human liberation. It has been described as not merely liberty in a familiar liberal sense, for example, of freedom within certain constraints. Such radical liberty can be recognized as liberty from the shaping of deep systemic structures.

Foundationalism is the "reassuring foundation" of which Derrida wrote (in the quote in the second paragraph of this section). Anti-foundationalism challenges the availability of any beyond-all-doubt, self-evident basis on which thinking and belief can be based, pointing out that any such foundation inevitably presupposes a prior assumption. Derrida has challenged the validity of the law of identity ($x = x$), for example. One motivation for such a challenge is the view that foundationalism is authoritarian in intent, keeping people in their places.

What Is a Post-Structural Lens? What Is Modernity?

Postmodernism is not a matter of historical eras, as Lyotard (1984) has explained. Premodern Socrates (in the early dialogues of Plato) was a sort of postmodernist, for example. In the famous story when he wondered why the Delphic Oracle had designated him as the wisest person, suddenly he recognized that (unlike so many of those he questioned) not only did he not know but also he knew that he did not know. Despite the fact that it is not a matter of historical eras, postmodernism can be introduced by contrasting it with what it opposes—in the same way that post-structuralism can be made clearer by considering structuralism. So we will speak of modernity—as a lens to the postmodern.

The project of Enlightenment is the project of modernity. In the words of Jürgen Habermas (discussed in chapter 6), "The project of modernity formulated in the 18th century by the philosophers of the Enlightenment consisted of the efforts to develop objective science, universal morality and law, and autonomous art according to their inner logic. . . . The Enlightenment philosophers wanted to utilize this accumulation of specialized culture for the enrichment of everyday life—that is to say, for the rational organization of everyday social life" (Habermas 1983, p. 9). The project of modernity was evidenced beginning in Europe in at least the sixteenth century. It was encouraged by revolutionary scientific discoveries, such as those of Isaac Newton. It can be described in terms of the *philosophes*, reaching a culmination in France in the Enlightenment. Elsewhere, I have followed the historian Thomas Carlyle and described the Festival of Reason, held in the Cathedral of Notre Dame and elsewhere in France on November 10, 1793. The congregations worshipped the goddess Reason (in Notre Dame in the form of Madame Momoro, who was borne into the cathedral). The project of modernity, the project of the Enlightenment, maintained that *more and more reason* means *more and more morality* and *more and more human happiness.*

Two traumatic practical and two theoretical blows are often described as undermining this confidence in the project of modernity. For practical blows, there was the slaughter of World Wars I and II: no rational person, it is supposed, would have decided to initiate war that could result in 50 million deaths. There were the genocides of the concentration camps, when one of the most advanced countries committed acts beyond the most uncivilized. For theoretical blows, there was Karl Marx's recognition that our reason is shaped by economic unthoughts—as history proceeds on its course. There was Sigmund Freud's emphasis on how our rational thoughts are dominated by unconscious forces.

About the project of Enlightenment, critical theorists like Habermas (1983) assure us that modernity is an incomplete project. The postmodernists argue against the validity of such a project.

What Is a Post-Structural Lens? Who Are the "Big" Names?

Among the "big" names of postmodernism are Jacques Derrida, Michel Foucault, Jean Baudrillard, Gilles Deleuze, and Jean-Francois Lyotard. Both Derrida and Foucault denied that they were postmodernists. Among the "big" names of post-structuralism are Jacques Derrida, Michel Foucault, Roland Barthes, and others. All these thinkers are French. But, as we will see, their thinking extended significantly to the United States.

It is hard to say whether a thinker is an X (e.g., a postmodernist). If you believe that the Law of Gravity is true, are you a Newtonist? If you believe that all or some postmodern (and critical theory, and economic) ideas are true, does this mean that you must declare that you are a postmodernist (plus a critical theorist, plus an economist)? If I wrote a book on public administration and postmodernism (1995) and if I believe—as I do—that many ideas and implications are true and valuable, should I declare that I am a postmodernist (as well as a critical theorist and all the other chapter topics in this book)? It is an implication of epistemic pluralism that this would be a counterproductive requirement. Being put in conceptual "boxes" is a modernist or structuralist fate not only of thinkers but also of groups, and it can be not only a mechanism of understanding but also a weapon of defense and control. It is in this light that we can understand that Derrida, the inventor of deconstruction, also denied that he was a deconstructionist. Putting thinkers in deconstructible "boxes" runs counter to the spirit of post-structuralism, let alone to good sense!

Implications

Postmodernism entered public administration theorizing in the mid-1990s (Fox and Miller 1994; Farmer 1995), late even among the social sciences. Unlike philosophy at its best (which, for example, can study seriously even the hylomorphism of the pre-Socratics), traditional public administration is a fashion-conscious discipline—in spite of the discipline's own self-image and its often-expressed fear of fads. Its interests tend to wax and wane. Such public administration interest in the word "postmodernism" has subsequently waned, albeit traces remain. Interest in post-structuralism has been even slighter.

Postmodernism is described by various writers as having made a significant impact on non–public administration areas. These areas include philosophy, critical and cultural theory, politics, feminism, lifestyles, science and technology, architecture, art, cinema, television, literature, music, popular culture, and the tradition of dissent (Sim 1999).

Implication for Planning—What Is Deconstruction?

Deconstruction is a significant resource for strategic and other kinds of planning. Developed by Jacques Derrida, it was introduced into the United States in a seminal 1966 seminar at Johns Hopkins University. It took until 1995 to reach public administration theorists. Opportunities abound for applications of deconstruction in PA planning. Readers are encouraged to develop their own examples. For instance, a start could be made by considering the relevance of liberating public administration from entrapment in the efficiency metaphor, with the binary opposition of efficient-inefficient. Another possibility is to start by analyzing the relevance of freeing PA from entrapment in various capitalist metaphors, with such binary oppositions as private-public and productive-unproductive.

Deconstruction is essentially good reading of a text. Text, as hinted earlier, is used in its widest sense to include narratives and meanings not only in documents but also implicit in situations, events, and even lives; thus, it includes administrative situations, events, and other phenomena. Deconstruction has been compared to x-raying a painting to reveal underlying pictures. As Culler (1983, p. 109) puts it, "Deconstruction does not elucidate texts in the traditional sense of attempting to grasp a unifying content or theme; it investigates the work of metaphysical oppositions in their arguments and the ways in which textual figures and relations . . . produce a double, aporetic logic."

For a reminder that this is not at all far-out talk, recall New Rhetoric and symbolic interactionism (see chapters 6 and 12). It suggests the primacy of the symbolic. Think of the importance of symbols in PA, such as big government, leader, balanced budget, American dream, and the rest. Think of how hard it is, as it were, to penetrate through symbolism to what otherwise could be considered real issues.

Deconstruction pays attention to two features prevalent throughout any text.

The first is binary opposition, and the second is metaphor: both have a distorting effect. Derrida wants to break down binary opposites like inside-outside, true-false, private-public, masculine-feminine, politician–civil servant, subject-object, health-disease, and good-evil. He wants to reverse the polarity; he wants to show that the superior term—as rational is to irrational and as good is to evil—is in fact subordinate. He wants to blunt, but not deny, this opposition; he would put the words under "erasure." His reason is his view that the privileged terms cannot serve as a ground or first principle for our beliefs.

The distorting effect of metaphor is that it not only disguises and shifts a text's meanings but also yields multiple meanings. He points out that even the most apparently literal text contains metaphors, for example, Newtonian physics resting on the metaphor of the mechanical universe. Sarap mentioned that we think of theories as buildings, "with foundations and superstructures, and we think of organizations spatially, in terms of up and down" (Sarap 1993, p. 47). Morgan (1980) writes of metaphors in organizational analysis, mentioning metaphors like *machine, organism, loosely coupled system, theater, culture, text, language game, instrument of domination,* and *catastrophe.*

Earlier, I (Farmer 1997, p. 15) mentioned that Derrida opposes logocentrism, the attitude that rational language can represent the essence of things—that signifiers "capture" the signified. For him, signs can also refer to what is absent or to relations between signs; for example, he asks whether it is possible to know the meaning of "I" without knowing its relationship with other signs like "you, she, he, it, we, and they." For him, meaning emerges at the end of sentences and passages, and it is not invariant between contexts. For him, reason tyrannizes by excluding the uncertain and the marginal.

Implication for Managing—What Is Anti-Administration?

Different perspectives often can yield the same, or similar, implications. Anti-administration is implied by critical theory (see chapter 6). It is also implied by post-structuralism. In such circumstances, is repetition really undesirable?

Anti-administration is a slogan for management that is simultaneously directed at negating administrative-bureaucratic power and that negates the rational-hierarchical outlook that Weber described. It was developed with the inspiration provided by Michel Foucault, who spoke of "the fascism in us all"—including in all managers, good people though they might be. In his introduction to Deleuze and Guattari's *Anti-Oedipus,* Foucault explained with prescriptions that included the following:

- "Free political action from all unitary and totalizing paranoia.
- Develop action, thought, desires by proliferation, juxtaposition, and disjunction, and not by subdivision and pyramidal hierarchization.
- Withdraw allegiance from the old categories of the Negative (law, limit, castra-

tion, lack, lacuna), which Western thought has so long held sacred as a form of power and access to reality. Prefer what is positive and multiple, difference over uniformity, flows over unities, mobile arrangements over systems.
- Do not use thought to ground a political practice in Truth, nor political action to discredit, as mere application, a line of thought." (Foucault 1977b, pp. xiii–xiv)

The style of anti-administration is implied not only by these comments from Foucault but also in the style of rewriting discussed by Jean-Francois Lyotard. Lyotard indicates that such *rewriting* is not an attempt to grasp the past correctly. Rewriting is similar to free association. Attitudes include a kind of thinking as play that includes suspending judgment, being patient, and giving attention to everything that happens.

Anti-administration is presented as such a model for management thinking and action. It wants to include not only mainstream ideas but also ideas that are *other*. "Other," here, are the ideas of people who are excluded and marginalized, for example employees in dealing with their bosses, minorities and women, and financially poor clients and citizens. "Other" also refers to ideas from discourses that are not dominant, for example, nonmainstream economics, queer theory, ecological views. In analyzing bureaucratic questions, anti-administration includes more focus on the nonbureaucratic, the nonsystematic, and the nonmechanical. For more about this, see chapter 6.

Anti-administrative thinking is similar to epistemic pluralism described in this book. It is designed, as noted, to include a style of management and contemplation that includes voices excluded from, or marginalized, in traditional discussions of governance.

I did first describe anti-administration in terms of postmodernism (Farmer 1995, pp. 227–243). But later I also discussed that the same implication is available from both the medieval and the modernist standpoints (e.g., see Farmer 2002). The point here is to emphasize that, while the approach is implied by the postmodern, anti-administration is not at all limited to the postmodern perspective. For instance, nonhierarchical management and nonhierarchical bureaucracy are implied by, say, anarchism.

Implication for the Underlying—What Are Normalization and Hyperreality?

Aren't normalization and hyperreality facts of public administration life? These two features underlie and condition what theorists and practitioners think and do. Conscious of such features, I can hope to try to struggle free of the constraints.

On normalizing, turn to Michel Foucault and his account of how power socially constructs what-counts-as-true. Foucault describes the normalizing role of the prison, and this normalization proceeds beyond the prison. "Is it surprising that prisons resemble factories, schools, barracks, hospitals, which all resemble prisons?" (Foucault 1977a, p. 228). What counts as true is what produces the right kind of person and the right kind of behavior—or, more precisely, what is socially constructed as the right kind of person and the right kind of behavior. This truth is not discovered; it is *invented* in order to produce a normalized person who *fits in*. The end products of such normalization are particular ways of thinking and of acting—or, as is often said, particular discourses.

The hardest discourse (a product of normalization, among other things) to identify is one's own, because our own seems exceptionally *natural*. (It's similar to accents. The Long Islander can say that the Virginian has an accent, but suppose that a Long Islander does not; and vice versa.) For examples of discourse variations that result from normalization among public administration practitioners, chapter 12 mentions differences between (say) some police officers and some social workers. In terms of the discourse context, one world tends to consist of good guys and bad guys; the other world tends to consist of needy clients and others. In terms of discourse constraints that marginalize, one view is that the true cop is a crime fighter, and the other is that the true social worker is a helping professional. In terms of discourse situated in a practice of a particular time and place, one world may value macho and paramilitary values now privileged in some agencies; the other will not. For examples of discourse that results from larger-scale normalization, recall the discussion of the indoctrination of schoolchildren with a particular view of economics. Remember the third implication in chapter 4. There it was suggested that indoctrination—the normalization—into market fundamentalist ideology is encouraged in kindergarten, as the standards of learning (SOLs) of elementary and high schools in the United States reveal. It was suggested that this brand of economic ideology shapes individuals and society—and thus public administration's context.

On hyperreality, turn to Jean Baudrillard. Baudrillard describes people in postmodernity as living with hyperreality (more real than real), which blurs distinctions between real and unreal. Mass media, information systems, and technology, for him, are new forms of control that change government and life. Baudrillard claims that boundaries are imploding between information and entertainment, between images and politics. He argues that society and meaning themselves are imploding. For him, postmodernity is the destruction of meaning. "All that remains is to play with the pieces. Playing with the pieces—that is postmodernism" (Baudrillard 1984, p. 84).

"We live in a world where there is more and more information, and less and less meaning," Baudrillard later writes (1994, p. 79). When he wrote this in his *Simulacra and Simulation*, he was referring to (as that chapter was titled) "the implosion of meaning in the media." (Oddly, traditional public administration does not consider the ramifications for PA of such a media implosion, in a context where governing appears so constrained by the perceived need to placate the media.) Yet Baudrillard did not intend to confine the implosion to the media. The implosion extends to governance and to all else.

This is difficult "information" for public administration specialists. To those unversed in any philosophical quest for the *real* and the *ultimately real*, some might find the terms themselves unreal. Such a philosophical quest was started by (again) the pre-Socratics, who suggested various alternatives—like air, water, the unlimited, and so forth. It continued through Plato (with his Forms) and Aristotle and beyond. It is a quest pursued now also by other academics like physicists, who talk of (say) quarks. Despite the difficulties, public administration should be alert to such considerations underlying its discipline. To the extent that Baudrillard is right (if he is), public administration's total frame of reference may be shifting.

Implication for the Public Administration Field—What Is Deterritorialization?

Deterritorialization means removal of the disciplinary boundary limits that are currently imposed on professional public administration thinking. A post-structural alternative could be to encourage, for example, the study of governance. It is worth repeating that *governance* includes all that makes up the fractured subject of what Michel Foucault calls *governmentality*—a term he used to replace what he earlier called *power-knowledge*. It is limiting to seek insights from too narrow a public administration turf fragment (e.g., military out, intelligence out, nonpublic out, society out, and so on). For more on deterritorialization, see chapter 16.

Implication for Imaginative Creativity—What Is Imaginization?

Modernity aimed to extend rationalization more and more through society, aiming for more and more moral behavior and human happiness. Postmodernity will act, as it were, like a mirror image—but with imaginization. The imagination will break out, as it were, from its virtual confinement to the arts. More and more imaginization will yield more and more moral behavior and human happiness. In public administration, managers should be held accountable for their imaginative creativity, and they will expect in turn others in their agencies to privilege the imagination. For more, see chapter 17. So much is implied by the post-structural.

Epilogue

Shouldn't we be careful about claiming with certainty to know Big T Truth about Public Administration—the Truth, the whole Truth and nothing but the Truth? Writes Michel Foucault (1972, p. 131), "truth isn't outside power, or lacking in power: contrary to a myth whose history and functions would repay further study, truth isn't the reward of free spirits, the child of protracted solitude, nor the privilege of those who have succeeded in liberating themselves. Truth is a thing of this world: it is produced only by virtue of multiple forms of constraint. And it induces regular effects of power. Each society has its regime of truth, its 'general politics' of truth: that is, the types of discourse which it accepts and makes function as true; the mechanisms and instances which enable one to distinguish true and false statements, the names by which each is sanctioned; the techniques and procedures accorded value in the acquisition of truth; the status of those who are charged with saying what counts as true."

Suggested Readings

Baudrillard, Jean. 1994. *Simulacra and Simulation*. Trans. Sheila Glaser. Ann Arbor: University of Michigan Press.

Deleuze, Gilles, and Félix Guattari. 1977. *Anti-Oedipus: Capitalism and Schizophrenia*. Trans. Robert Hurley, Mark Seem, and Helen R. Lane. New York: Viking Press.

Farmer, David John. 1995. *The Language of Public Administration: Bureaucracy, Modernity, and Postmodernity*. Tuscaloosa: University of Alabama Press.

Lyotard, Jean-Francois. 1984. *The Postmodern Condition: A Report on Knowledge*. Trans. G. Bennington and B. Massumi. Minneapolis: University of Minnesota Press.

8

Public Administration from a Psychoanalytic Perspective

Consciousness of the unconscious deepened. Sigmund Freud (1856–1939) published *The Interpretation of Dreams* in 1899. In 1895 (a rival for the birth date of psychoanalysis), Freud had published *Studies on Hysteria*. In such writings and in his associated work, Freud made possible the potential of psychoanalysis and psychoanalytic insights to revolutionize public administration (and much else). He made possible not only better understanding of human individuals, institutions, and society, but also their better functioning. While not the first to discuss the unconscious, he illuminated the nature and workings of the unconscious for the individual, for the group, and for civilization. Such understandings of the unconscious were further deepened—changed and supplemented—by others, including Carl Jung (1875–1961) and Jacques Lacan (1901–1981).

Human understanding of what it is to be human began to overturn when Freud studied the case of a person who came to be named Anna O. In 1882, Josef Breuer had consulted with Freud about her, and Freud began to treat her case (see, e.g., Freeman 1972). As a result of the case, Freud conceptualized free association. It was Anna O who called it the "talking cure," the free association being like a "chimney sweeping" of the mind. From this case, Freud also developed concepts like transference, countertransference, resistance, repression, and symptoms as disguised wishes. Over his lifetime, Freud's ideas evolved. The Freud of *The Ego and the Id* (1923) and later, for example, differed in important respects from the Freud of 1882 and 1899. That dynamism is typical of a creative genius who lives long enough.

The first part of this chapter sketches the nature of a psychoanalytic perspective. Five questions are discussed:

1. What is the psychoanalytic? What, in a nutshell, is psychoanalysis?
2. What is the psychoanalytic? What is the Freudian unconscious?

3. What is the psychoanalytic? What is the Jungian unconscious?
4. What is the psychoanalytic? What is the Lacanian unconscious?
5. What is the psychoanalytic? Are there parallel psycho-perspectives?

The second part of the chapter examines the significance for public administration theory and practice of the psychoanalytic perspective.

6. Implication for planning—Shouldn't public administration planning recognize the unconscious?
7. Implication for managing—What is psychoanalytic organization theory?
8. Implication for the underlying—Is there an unconscious workplace?
9. Implication for the field—Shouldn't public administration expand interpretation of its narrative?
10. Implication for imaginative creativity—Where does free association point?

Reflection Exercise 1 (see chapter 1) asks readers to reflect on insights available about public administration theory and practice from a psychoanalytic perspective.

Sketching the Psychoanalytic

Psychoanalysis came to the United States in a major wave after Freud's 1909 visit to Clark University in Massachusetts. A second wave arrived with European émigrés in the 1940s. In 1911, the American Psychoanalytic Association (APA) and the New York Psychoanalytic Society (NYPS) were founded. As Robert Coles (1998, p. 142) indicates, "The Freud who visited America very early in [the 20th] century, but who had no great love for it, would one day exert an enormous influence on that nation's cultural and intellectual life. Since, in many ways, [the 20th] has been an American century, it has also been a psychoanalytic one." And the rest is history? Not quite.

What Is the Psychoanalytic? What, in a Nutshell, Is Psychoanalysis?

The *unconscious* is the dynamic root in psychoanalysis. As Richard Chessick (1993, p. 306) puts it, "all psychoanalytic models have the same conceptual base, the dynamic unconscious, although they may differ in fundamental ways." He adds that all the models use free association; all use transference and countertransference; all view childhood and infant experiences as critical. "All in various ways and to varying degrees emphasize repetition, the role of the analyst, and the importance of interpretation."

By contrast, psychodynamic has been described (see Berzoff, Flanagan, and Hertz 2008, p. 5) as a broader term than psychoanalytic. The former includes conscious, as well as unconscious, forces that shape the human, that is, mental and emotional development.

Psychoanalysis ranges from the purely *mechanical* to the *nonmechanical*, from the purely *medical* to the *philosophical-also*. By mechanical, I mean rote or routine or uncreative—applying the ideas of others, off the shelf. By nonmechanical, I mean what the psychoanalyst Sandor Ferenzci exemplified in his mutual analysis. Ferenczi was a close associate of Freud, accompanying Freud and Jung on the 1909 trip to Clark University. Ferenczi's mutual analysis involved alternating sessions in which the analyst and the analysand rotated functions. It involved the analyst sharing with patients insights about his own blind spots. Later, mutual analysis evolved to a dialogue of unconsciouses, where both analyst and analysand would fall "into a trance simultaneously . . . free associating and also giving vent to their feelings in gestures and expressive movements" (Dupont 1988, p. 84). By purely medical, I mean what you expect when you visit your therapist to get rid of an annoying neurosis (or worse). By philosophical-also, I mean what is exemplified in the piles upon piles of books like, say, Freud's *Civilization and Its Discontents* (1930). It is what is exemplified by what you could expect when psychoanalysis is studied as part of philosophy.

What Is the Psychoanalytic? What Is the Freudian Unconscious?

Sigmund Freud's major contribution was changing our understanding of the human with his account of the dynamic unconscious. What this implies is suggested in Walter Kaufman's list of Freud's achievements. Kaufman (1980, pp. 108–172) explains that Freud created a poetic science of the mind and a new therapy. Freud also made contributions to understanding the importance of childhood experiences (for character development) and of sex. He contributed to our understanding of dreams and their interpretation, of the psychopathology of everyday life, and of literature, art, and religion.

For Freud, a primary fact is that each person has an unconscious, a psychic structure. The unconscious shapes and co-shapes a person's thinking and feeling and acting; and psychoanalysis is radically helpful because it permits coping with the functioning of the dynamic unconscious. Let's recall some well-known features of the unconscious. Freud discussed in earlier years the pattern of the individual mind (e.g., in *The Interpretation of Dreams*) in terms of the unconscious (Ucs), the preconscious (Pcs), and conscious (Cs). For him, what is in the preconscious is forgotten but accessible. What is in the unconscious is repressed and inaccessible, and it can enter conscious awareness only in disguise. To greater or lesser degrees, such unconscious desires and drives and memories shape what the person does and feels and thinks. Sometimes what action appears on the surface and beyond conscious control is dramatic, as when Anna O experienced a hysterical pregnancy or when she became mute. At other times, what appears on the surface may seem more pedestrian. A person might instantly dislike a newcomer, for instance, and she might be able to give a rational account. But her account is wrong; unconsciously, her mind may associate a feature of that newcomer with someone entirely different (but with a similar psychological or other feature) that she knew previously. Beginning in *The Ego and the Id* (1923), Freud added another pattern. This was his structural theory of the psyche. The pattern of unconscious elements in the psyche is threefold. First there is the "id" or the "it." Second, there is the "ego" or the "I." Third, there is the "superego" or the "over-I." Those of us who admire Plato like to remember that Freud was influenced by Plato's threefold division of the psyche.

This description requires a warning label. Warning: the unconscious is a repressed voice; it is widely mischaracterized, and it is uncanny. First, it is typically trivialized for defense mechanism reasons like repression and resistance (see the first implication, below). Second, misrepresentations abound about the unconscious and about psychoanalysis. In a later edition, Freud complained that "the assertion that all dreams require a sexual interpretation, against which critics rage so incessantly, occurs nowhere in my *Interpretation of Dreams*. It is not to be found in any of the numerous editions of this book and is in obvious contradiction to other views expressed in it" (Freud 1932, p. 397). Third, the unconscious is not easily understood in conscious terms. It is not a mere add-on to consciousness. The unconscious does not distinguish between fantasy and reality, for instance. Again, in *The Interpretation of Dreams*, Freud can be found explaining that—despite any and all analysis—we are always left with a core of mystery at "the dream's navel, the spot where it reaches down into the unknown" (p. 397). Indeed, the unconscious is, as is reiterated in the Epilogue, uncanny. *Unheimlich* was the German word used by Freud and translated as uncanny.

What Is the Psychoanalytic? What Is the Jungian Unconscious?

Focus on the *collective unconscious*, only one but probably the most dramatic of Carl Jung's contributions. Jung explains that the collective unconscious is "not individual but universal . . . it has contents and modes of behavior that are more or less the same everywhere and in all individuals. It is, in other words, identical in all men and thus constitutes a common psychic substrate of a supra-personal nature which is present in every one of us" (Jung 1980, p. 4). Jung contrasts this with what he describes as Freud's view that the unconscious is of an "exclusively personal nature." What Jung calls the personal unconscious is "a superficial layer of the unconscious." It rests upon a deeper layer, which does not derive from personal experience and is not a personal acquisition "but is inborn." (Jung 1980, p. 3). That deeper layer is the collective unconscious.

"The form of the world into which [a person] is born is already inborn in him as a virtual image" (Jung 1953, p. 188). My experience of the world is significantly (though not completely) shaped by the collective unconscious, which I inherit. The collective unconscious is a "storehouse of latent memory traces inherited from man's ancestral past, a past that includes not only the racial history of man as a separate species but his pre-human or animal ancestry as well. It contains the psychic residue of man's evolutionary development . . ." (Hall and Lindzey 1957, p. 80).

The contents of the collective unconscious are archetypes. Simply expressed, archetypes are universal thoughts, charged with emotion—representational images with universal symbolic meanings. Examples are mother, father, hero, wise old man, child, and God. Important in Jung's theory are the persona (i.e., the public personality), the anima (the feminine side of a man), the animus (the masculine side of a woman), the shadow (animal instincts inherited in evolving from lower forms of life), and the self ("life's goal," explain Hall and Lindzsey 1957, p. 86). The point is that a complex (say, a mother complex) is determined not merely by mother-child interaction but also by the relationship between the archetypal mother expectation and the experience with the actual mother. And so on. As anyone knows who has experienced a Jungian program (like Centerpoint) for several years, there is more. The aim of Jungian analysis for a person is what is understood as individuation.

What Is the Psychoanalytic? What Is the Lacanian Unconscious?

For Jacques Lacan, the unconscious is like a language, a discourse. Famously, Lacan (1993, p. 167) said that the unconscious is "structured like a language." As such, it is transpersonal and in the order of symbols. He discusses the unconscious in terms of speech, discourse, and signifiers. It is also the discourse of what Lacan meant by the Other. Hill (1997) and Evans (1996) are among the helpful introductions to Lacanian theory.

As Evans (1996, pp. 217–219) explains, Lacan thought that it is false to suppose that the unconscious is primarily primordial or instinctual. Instead, it is (again) like a language. For one reason, the unconscious is only understood in that part which "is articulated by passing into words" (Lacan 1992, p. 32). Just noted was Lacan's view that the unconscious is transpersonal, rather than "inside." For him, this "exteriority of the symbolic in relation to man is the very nature of the unconscious" (Lacan 1966, p. 163). Lacan uses linguistic metaphors to conceptualize the unconscious. He also speaks of the unconscious as a kind of memory and an unknown knowledge. As Hill (1997, p. 294) states, Lacan's unconscious is "a topological space where hidden desires live," and desires "only have expression as symptoms, signifiers or words."

The "unconscious is the discourse of the Other" (Lacan 1966, p. 16). In discussing the Other, Lacan distinguishes between *little a* and *big A* (*a* and *A* being the first letter in *autre*, French for *other*). This translates into English as little o and Big O. The *little a* is a reflection of the ego and is in the realm of the imaginary. The *big A* is radical alterity and it is unassimilable. As Evans (1996, p. 133) explains, "Lacan is stressing that speech and language are beyond one's conscious control; they come from another place, outside consciousness." As Hill (1997, p. 160) puts it, "The *other* is another word for *object*. An object is any item that creates or supports subjectivity. These include the little object, which is the cause of desire and the object of desire, the big other, that is, the other of language, the Names-of-the-Father, signifiers or words, and the phallus."

The role of the therapist is "to interpret the semiotic text of the personality structure," as Sadock and Sadock (2003, p. 223) note. This is because primary process thoughts are in fact "uncontrolled free-flowing sequences of meaning" and symptoms are signs "of underlying meaning." Lacanian therapy is engaged in "the need to become less alienated from the self and more involved with others."

Capturing Lacan in a few paragraphs is impossible to do—impossible to say. Evans (1996) covers more than 200 Lacanian terms, for instance. O.C. McSwite (1997a, pp. 43–63) complains that within the limits of a full article "it really is not possible to convey anything like the full meaning of even the key concepts of [Lacan's] thought." Nevertheless, McSwite notes that Lacanianism has been important not only in such areas as film and literary theory and in feminism but also in the study of society and culture. Thus the Association for the Psychoanalysis of Society and Culture was created.

What Is the Psychoanalytic? Are There Parallel Psycho-Perspectives?

There are many other psychoanalytic and related models or systems. It is a long laundry list. Sadock and Sadock (2003, pp. 217–228) list other schools derived from psychoanalysis and psychology: Karl Abraham (1877–1925), Alfred Adler (1870–1937), Michael Balint (1896–1970), Wilfred Bion (1897–1979), John Bowlby (1907–1990), Melanie Klein (1882–1960), Kurt Lewin (1890–1947), Otto Rank (1884–1939), William Reich (1897–1957), B.F. Skinner (1904–1990), Donald Winnicott (1896–1971), and others. Take clinical social work interventions, for another example; a standard work by Francis Turner (1986) discusses twenty-two chapters of "interlocking theoretical approaches." Yes, Freud, Jung, and Lacan are discussed here. But some may prefer others.

Implications

Public administration was once defined as getting things done through people. Psychoanalysis is also about people, including people getting things done (or not)—and even including people getting things done through administration (or not). Looks promising for public administration?

Implication for Planning—Shouldn't Public Administration Planning Recognize the Unconscious?

Macro and micro strategic planning should recognize the fundamental importance of the unconscious in shaping—again what will be discussed in chapter 18—what counts as public administration common sense. Common sense in public administration planning—for the discipline, for theorizing, and for practice—is socially constructed and limited by unconscious factors; the point is that unanalyzed common sense may or may not be harmful to such planning. Unexamined, what counts as common sense for planning may (or may not) be harmless: without analysis, we will never know.

Public administration should search among the Freudian, the Jungian, *and* the Lacanian. Work on the unconscious is already available; see below. We should have more.

Recognize Sigmund Freud's description of the unconscious (see Question 2). Consider how Freud describes the defense mechanisms that distort recognition of what is the case, possibly harmful for public administration planning (or any kind of decision making). Freud describes how drive components evoke what he considers to be ego defenses. This is complex. Sadock and Sadock (2003, p. 207) explain that in Freudian theory there are twenty-eight different defense mechanisms. Three of these are categorized as narcissistic, eight as immature, eleven as neurotic, and (on a relatively happier note) six as mature. The narcissistic defenses are denial, distortion, and projection. Sadock and Sadock (p. 207) describe denial in part as "avoiding the awareness of some painful aspect of reality by negating sensory data." Distortion (in part) is "grossly distorting external reality to suit inner needs"; projection (in part) is "perceiving and reacting to unacceptable inner impulses and their derivatives as though they were outside the self" (p. 207). The following are the eight kinds of immature defenses: acting out, blocking, hypochondriasis, introjection, passive-aggressive behavior, regression, schizoid fantasy, and somatization. And so on. These twenty-eight defenses are associated with different levels of libidinal development. "The anal phase, for example, is associated with reaction formation, as manifested by the development of shame and disgust in relation to anal impulses and pleasures . . . and neurotic 'defenses' are encountered in obsessive-compulsive and hysterical patients as well as in adults under stress" (Sadock and Sadock 2003, pp. 205–206). As an experienced public employee, cannot you remember a manager (or an agency) who was awful because s/he was anal, or obsessive-compulsive, or hysterical, or under stress? What could be said about a manager under the stress of fear for his or her job or a stressed agency fearful of reductions in force, or an agency like Homeland Security established after 9/11?

Recognize Carl Jung's description of the collective unconscious (see Question 3). Such recognition sheds helpful light on public administration's acceptance of the "inevitable" and "common sense" character of, say, hierarchy and the cult of leadership. Jung describes the collective unconscious as coming to each of us (including the strategic planner) not only from our human but also from our prehuman past. He speaks of archetypes that the public administration planner should not ignore. Surely, public administration plans that rely upon such "common sense" ideas as *PA hierarchy and PA leadership are essential* must also take into account that what counts as common sense is shaped under influences that include archetypes in the collective unconscious. The planner should recognize that these archetypes include, for instance, the hero and the wise old man. At least two questions require reflection.

First, how "real" are the planner's unanalyzed assumptions about common sense relating to bosses and bossism? How realistic are such unconscious dispositions from an earlier era that might be different from our own, for example, in such terms as proximity to starvation and to carnivores? In other words, is what was good for the Neanderthals close enough for contemporary planning, if unanalyzed?

Recognize Jacques Lacan's description of the transpersonal unconscious (see Question 4). O.C. McSwite (1997a, pp. 43–63) employs the Lacanian theory of the human subject to deny the utility of what counts as common sense in PA. Recall that the Lacanian view is that the human subject is the subject of the unconscious, rather than the subject of the conscious. (Well, it was arbitrary for Descartes to imply that I am my consciousness, and my consciousness is me.) The Lacanian ego is an object, rather than being the center of the self. It is a social construction whereby the subject becomes alienated from the self; it is an imaginary formation. Lacan has more to say. For him, the ego is structured exactly like a symptom. "At the heart of the subject, it is only a privileged symptom, the human system par excellence, the mental illness of man" (Lacan 1988, p. 16). The ego is structured similarly to paranoia.

McSwite suggests that four implications undermine public administration views of what counts as common sense. The first is that truth is available only by "admitting the unconscious into the realm of consciousness" (McSwite 1997a, p. 57). The second is to deny economic epistemology for public administration; administrative man is not economic man. Third, "the idea of administration as the rational attainment of goals [should] be abandoned." Fourth, public administration has unwittingly tied itself to the assumptions of modernism. This precludes Lacanian understandings. It discourages the anti-administrative idea that administrators should seek to administer without, for instance, giving primacy to the administrative. "Lacan's psychoanalysis cannot only help us understand such prescriptions but, indeed, can indicate that such approaches are essential to the condition of the human subject" (p. 61).

Public administration should reflect on these four claims. Take the claim, for instance, that administrative man is not economic man. Is public administration planning basically trapped in a common-sense and limited view of the human subject as fully rational economic man—more precisely as a man without the complexities of an unconscious? Economic man's preferences, when revealed, involve none of the complexity of, say, the Alcoholics Anonymous member who wants to stay on the wagon but who puts his money down and "demands" a drink. Interest in the mainstream economic model ends, as it were, at the water's edge of where preferences are revealed; there is no further concern with motivation.

Recall the views of Cornelius Castoriadis (1922–1997), a thinker (first mentioned in chapter 1) always difficult to pigeonhole but certainly writing also from a psychoanalytic viewpoint. His interest goes deeper than the water's edge of revealed preference. Note the relevance for planning (and much else) of Castoriadis's idea of magma, used as one element (but only one element) in macro study. Castoriadis

explains magma as referring to society's creative framework or world of signification. He depicts each society as instituting itself in terms of an "originary" creation,
describing the institution of society's magma of "social imaginary signification" as
shaping what can be constituted in that society. It is worth repeating his explanation
that "Each society, like each living being or species, establishes, creates its own
world, within which, of course, it includes itself" (Castoriadis 1997, p. 7). Castoriadis continues, "In brief, it is the institution of society that determines which is
'real' and what is not, what is 'meaningful' and what is meaningless. Sorcery was
real in Salem three centuries ago, but it is not now. . . . Each society is a construction, a constitution, a creation of a world, of its own world."

Implication for Managing—What Is Psychoanalytic Organization Theory?

Traditional public administration has long included important psycho-elements.
Psychoanalytic organization theory is available, arguably again toward the circumference. More psycho-storying and re-storying are needed to facilitate more
effective managing.

Indeed, important psycho-elements, designated as human relations theory, have
long been a part of traditional public administration. Michael Harmon and Richard
Mayer describe what they call the later human relations tradition. "In a nutshell,
these (later human relations) theorists argued that the rationalistic, organization-
dominant view of organizational behavior, by effectively ignoring the rights, values,
and personal development of individuals in organizations, causes serious damage
both to the individuals involved and to the larger society" (Harmon and Mayer 1986,
p. 198). Adopted into this later human relations category was Abraham Maslow
and his hierarchy of psychological needs—where the self-actualizer can experience what he called a peak experience, a transcendental state of consciousness.
Included was Douglas McGregor and his Theory X (the conventional theory of
management) and the alternative, Theory Y. Included was Chris Argyris, seeking
the integration of individual and organization. In his *Organization Man: Rational
and Self-Actualizing*, written in debate with Herbert Simon, Argyris (1973, p.
356) declared that "It is the design and administration of organizations that do not
encourage the discussion of emotions and emotionally loaded substantive issues
(when they are relevant) that is the shackle." There were others, like Warren Ben-
nis. There was organizational development, which was sometimes called a sort of
applied sensitivity training (according to Harmon and Mayer 1986, p. 215).

Michael Diamond writes about psychoanalytic organization theory. For him,
psychoanalytic organization theorists believe that "the mysteries of organizational
life reside in the intersubjective world of organizational members' experience—
what [he calls] their organizational identity" (Diamond 1993, p. 37). These theorists
discuss, for example, how "people, particularly those in power, use their experiences with and fantasies about organizational membership [and how that] affects

their relationships . . ." (1993, p. 37). The emphasis is on interpreting "the patterns of human interactions and perceptions of members in their respective roles and groups." For him (is he right?), an organization is "not analyzable as a single entity, an organization with its own psyche" (Diamond, 1993, p. 37). The rationale of Diamond's 1993 book is "to encourage organizational members to confront institutional forms of oppression. This is not possible, [he] believes, without a willingness to confront ourselves as producers of and collaborators in our own oppression." The book includes discussion of the psychodynamics of ritualistic organizational defenses, of organizational culture, of organizational identity, of individual and group regression in the workplace, and of organizational change.

Important results have been obtained. Diamond himself gives public administration case examples. He also reviews the literature. From the works available, he selects Levinson's *Executive* (1981), Kets de Vries and Miller's *The Neurotic Organization* (1984), Baum's *The Invisible Bureaucracy* (1987), and Hirschorn's *The Workplace Within* (1988). Clearly, even these writers have written more. Isn't it useful to recognize, after Hirschorn, how rules and procedures can be used in management as a defense against anxiety? Doesn't it fit with our own bureaucratic experience to read how managers can prefer holding subordinates responsible for rules rather than producing results? Isn't it helpful, after Kets de Vries and Miller, to read about neurotic styles? The literature has continued since that time.

Managing should seek to utilize Freudian, Jungian, and Lacanian insights in re-storying traditional accounts that do not use psychoanalytic insights. The re-storying can aim to change the way of thinking about, say, managing.

Reader, can you offer a Freudian example? Maybe it could address a question like how those in hierarchical organization are discouraged from taking public-spirited actions because they will displease the father figure. In Oedipal terms, Rosemary Farmer (1998) has described the boss as symbolizing the father, while the organization is symbolic for the mother. In this triangle, the public servant "may react as Hamlet did when he encountered Claudius, i.e., feeling guilty as he too secretly wants to kill the father in order to possess the mother. So he hesitates, and his hesitation is in the form of seeking approval from the boss" (p. 81).

Can you offer a Jungian example? Maybe it could be a story that utilizes Jung's introvert-extrovert distinction. Introverts, as we know, relate primarily to the inner world, while extroverts relate primarily to the outer world. Each person has a mixture of both elements. Reader, what stories come to mind? There must be one from public administration relating to human resources management.

Can you offer a Lacanian example? Maybe it could take up the huge significance of Lacan's idea that a signifier represents the subject for another signifier. At first, this sounds too odd; but it is not. Hill (1997, p. 31) illustrates by saying that the "lawyer represents the client for another lawyer. . . . [Your] lawyer will communicate with my lawyer." The lawyers are separated from their clients by their lawyerly language and bound to their clients by the language of money. "We are all alienated by language" that we must use (p. 32). Dear reader, what stories come to mind? There must be one, like the manager who represents his subordinate for another manager—or like the public agency that represents its customer(s) for another agency.

Implication for the Underlying—Is There an Unconscious Workplace?

There are unconscious dynamics that underlie public administration and surely psychoanalysis itself. The unconscious workplace for all these functions should not be suppressed or repressed. In addressing the unconscious workplace, the importance of free association in psychoanalysis supports the suggestion that there is value for public administration in thinking as play.

For an example in public administration practice, see O.C. McSwite's (2006) appeal to the Lacanian unconscious and especially to public administration impelled by underlying pressure to be the carrier of what they call "the new social bond." In particular, McSwite's appeal is to the Sinthome, which they describe as the general neurotic symptom that is the "foundation stone" of the personality. As they summarize it, the failed bond of modernism is replaced by what they call the "unstable and necessarily temporary" bond of market fundamentalism. An impulse to develop a new bond must underlie public administration practice "in the process of carrying out the work of public agencies. In order to accomplish this, public administrators must develop a different, psychoanalytically informed relationship to themselves" (McSwite 2006, p. 176). " For another and less complex example, recall Question 6 above and check which defense mechanism is relevant to the following police administration story. Given the finger by a fleeing felon on a motorcycle, a group of police officers (on catching the felon) may act out by beating him and then by charging him with a long list of extra crimes—and the administration may, or may not, support the police officers.

There is a tendency to soft-pedal examples of public administration and the dynamic unconscious; hard-pedaling carries the risk of alienating the reader. Dear reader, can a connection be drawn between a taboo public administration subject like (say) managerial sadomasochism and (say) the taboo Freudian idea of the death instinct? This is the Freud of *Beyond the Pleasure Principle* (1922), with its implications for the autonomy and rationality of the subject. As Jean Laplanche and Jean-Baptiste Pontalis (1973) explain, the Freudian death instinct is opposed to the life instinct. Directed inward, it strives to reduce tensions toward zero, while turning toward the external world (e.g., toward academic complexities and to other perspectives in public administration's case) in an aggressive and destructive way. It struggles to bring the living back to an inorganic state. Paul Ricoeur (1970) explains that "the extreme is this: living things are not put to death by external forces which suppress them, as in Spinoza; they die, they go to death by an internal movement." If this sounds macabre in terms of what counts as common sense, is macabre the right litmus test?

For two examples of what underlies psychoanalysis, consider the dynamics that underlay the reception of psychoanalysis in the United States and then the bureaucratic horror that greeted Lacan's flexible adjustments in the length of the analytic session. The first example concerns what Robert Coles (1998, p. 143) describes as the post-1909 "deliberate, sought-after absorption [of psychoanalysis] into the conservative medical profession." Underlying and shaping the interpretation and expression of psychoanalysis in the United States was the medical model. The second example is described as relating to what was among Lacan's "most controversial beliefs" and this was that "psychoanalytical sessions should be standardized not to time, but rather, to content and process" (Sadock and Sadock 2003, p. 223). There was intense resistance among the relevant French hierarchy to changing the bureaucratic rule about the 50-minute session. In both cases, what psychodynamics underlay the shaping of psychoanalysis itself?

Implication for the Field—Shouldn't Public Administration Expand Interpretation of Its Narrative?

The public administration field should give higher priority to psychologically informed self-examination. The field should shift farther toward inclusion of the unconscious. Consider, as an example, visioning as a form of dreaming.

Cannot public administration deepen understanding of its own narratives? Consider, for instance, applying Freud's interpretation of dreams to self-visions and to other-visions of public administration theorizing and practice. By self-vision, I mean the matter of the public administration discipline's or an agency's or a manager's self-conception. Examples of such self-visions might be: public administration is eminently practical. Or New York's finest! Or I am a strong manager, a great leader! Examples of self-vision proclamations can be found in titles like Department of Homeland Security or in statement of goals like "To protect and serve." Examples can be found in the multiplicity of statements that are commonly said or chanted about our discipline, agency, or activity, like, we are a family. Or: we are client-centered. By other-vision, I mean the conceptions that others have of the public administration discipline, theory, and practice. Examples about the public administration discipline might be: PA is not rigorous. Or: PA is reactive. Examples about public administration theory might be: PA theory is irrelevant. Or: PA theory must not be pointy-headed. Examples about public administration practice might be: Big Government. Or: a bunch of bureaucrats. Or: they couldn't organize a one-car parade.

Couldn't such self-examination (or other-examination) benefit from understanding, say, Freud's *Interpretation of Dreams*? Freud's analysis is that dreams are meaningful. He claims that a dream is a fulfillment of a wish (in his chapter 2), that it is a disguised fulfillment of a repressed wish (in his chapter 4), and that wish which is represented in a dream must be an infantile one (in his chapter 7). Pick out, as examples, some features of Freudian understanding of dreams. In the manifest content, dreams (what about public administration visions?) disguise infantile wishes (attached to more recent adult wishes) to avoid censure, and they spring from what has been repressed. A dream's façade is built by dream work, a process of concealment. In terms of disguises, dreams (what about public administration visions?) relate to an unconscious that does not distinguish fantasy and reality; and the more verbal they are, the more disguised are the unconscious materials. In terms of content, it is clear that dreams (what about public administration visions?) have a language of their own—condensation, displacement, and symbolization. All this, and much more, is from Freud's *Interpretation of Dreams.*

Implication for Imaginative Creativity—Where Does Free Association Point?

The emphasis in psychoanalysis of the importance of free association suggests the value for public administration of thinking as play. Creative imagination, as noted earlier, is required not only in public administration–relevant analyses that involve the unconscious but also beyond.

By play at its highest level, I mean poetic contemplation that begins in imagination and that focuses on constitutive patterns of imaginative possibilities—contemplation for its own sake. At a lower level, it is a sort of questioning associated with Socrates's example of the gadfly—contemplation to right a wrong. See Farmer (2005a, pp. 3–11; 2009, pp. 388–390) for additional description. Contemplation is used in the usual sense of meditating about something deeply, focusing on being open to yet-unrecognized possibilities and yet-hidden nuances of meaning. Imagination in this context should not be confused with playing around, with playing with dolls, with being perky, or merely thinking out of the box. For one thing, I've noted that it includes Carl Jung's understanding of the play of the imagination as independent—as independent as is reflected in the Taoist system of meditation.

Recall Freud's analytical method for the archaeology of the mind—free association by the patient. Recall his self-analysis. Through strongly creative and imaginative listening to whatever the patient says, free association seeks access to hidden or forgotten feelings, memories, or wishes. Free association as a method is not beyond criticism (e.g., see Grunbaum 1998, pp. 187–192). But the emphasis on the method of free association does point public administration toward thinking as playing. It points public administration toward seeking, among other things, the benefits of the talking cure.

Epilogue

Shouldn't we recognize that psychoanalysis, if we are serious about it, can make us uncomfortable? Wrote Freud (1986, p. 147), "In psycho-analysis there is no choice for us but to assert that mental processes are in themselves unconscious. . . . Just as Kant warned us not to overlook the fact that our perceptions are subjectively conditioned and must not be regarded as identical with what is perceived though unknowable, so psycho-analysis warns us not to equate perceptions by means of consciousness with the unconscious mental processes, which are their object. Like the physical, the psychical is not necessarily in reality what it appears to us to be."

Suggested Readings

Castoriadis, Cornelius. 1997. *World in Fragments: Writings on Politics, Society, Psycho-analysis, and the Imagination*. Stanford, CA: Stanford University Press.
Diamond, Michael A. 1993. *The Unconscious Life of Organizations: Interpreting Organizational Identity*. Westport, CT: Quorum.
Freud, Sigmund. 1930. *Civilization and Its Discontents*. New York: J. Cape and H. Smith.
———. 1932 (1899). *The Interpretation of Dreams*. London: Allen and Unwin.

9

Public Administration from a Neuroscience Perspective

James Watson and E.O. Wilson, celebrated biologists, were surely right in claiming that the twenty-first century is the century of neurobiology. Neuroscience is producing spectacular results at an exponential rate. It is the coming language of the twenty-first century; it is part of the coming fabric of thinking and living. Yet, as Wilson and Watson would agree, and as we will explain, neuroscience implies more than *mere* biology.

Other social sciences and action studies have made some progress in embracing neuroscience (see below). Public administration trails toward the back of the pack. None of this is to claim that public administration hasn't dipped its toe into biology. Luther Gulick was among those who advised that "the new public administration, as a field of knowledge and operation, now requires specific attention not only to economics and psychology but also to relevant aspects of human biology" (Gulick 1984, p. xv).

From this general standpoint, this chapter begins by sketching the nature of a neuroscience perspective. The objective is to note what is critically important for PA theory and practice. The following five questions are discussed.

1. What is neuroscience? What, in a nutshell, is the neuroscientific?
2. What is neuroscience? What, in briefest terms, is the biology of the brain?
3. What is neuroscience? Does neuroscience imply biological determinism?
4. What is neuroscience? Are social sciences neuro-alert?
5. What is neuroscience? Are there related biology-inspired subjects?

The second part of the chapter discusses implications for public administration theory and practice.

6. Implication for planning—Shouldn't public administration recognize our emerging neurosociety?
7. Implication for managing—Who is the administrative person?

8. Implication for the underlying—Are administrative beliefs shaped within the brain?
9. Implication for the field—Will public administration become a subspecialty within neuro-gov?
10. Implication for creativity—Can neuroscience increase bureaucratic imagination?

In reading this chapter, readers are asked (per Reflection Exercise 1) to determine what insights about public administration theory and practice interest them from a perspective of neuroscience.

Sketching a Neuroscience Perspective

"Men ought to know that from nothing else but the brain come joys, delights, laughter and sports, and sorrows, griefs, despondency, and lamentations. And by this, in an especial manner, we acquire wisdom and knowledge, and see and hear what are foul and what are fair, what are bad and what are good, what are sweet and what are unsavory," wrote Hippocrates (460 B.C.E.–370 B.C.E.).

What Is Neuroscience? What, in a Nutshell, Is the Neuroscientific?

Neuroscience is the study of all aspects of the nervous system, consisting of the central and the peripheral nervous systems. All aspects include the relationship of the nervous system to such activities as behaving, thinking, remembering, feeling, deciding, and evaluating. The central nervous system includes the brain and the spinal cord. In a loose way, we can call it brain science.

Neuroscience consists of a host of specialties. These specialties are grouped into the humongous subject of neuroscience (as the Society for Neuroscience does, with its membership exceeding 38,000), rather than as distinct disciplines (on the Social Science Balkanized pattern). Levels of analysis within neuroscience include molecular neuroscience, cellular neuroscience, systems neuroscience, behavioral neuroscience, and cognitive neuroscience. Types of neuroscientists include computational neuroscientists, developmental neurobiologists, molecular neurobiologists, neuroanatomists, neurochemists, neuroethologists, neuropharmacologists, neuropsychologists, and so on. But this is to understate the range. Not mentioned, for instance, are medical specialties (like neurology and neurosurgery) and afflictions (like Alzheimer's disease, depression, stroke, and epilepsy). Not mentioned is genetics.

What Is Neuroscience? What, in Briefest Terms, Is the Biology of the Brain?

The average human brain consists of three pounds of matter. Yet it is probably the most complex structure in the universe. Its functioning is no less complicated. The structure consists of three major parts. A first part is the forebrain, which, divided into two hemispheres, covers the rest of the brain; the top, or cortex, is highly convoluted. It is implicated in most of the high-level functions that we assign to the mind; and some capabilities are localized, such as in the occipital lobes and motor cortex. A second part is the midbrain, which links to the thalamus (e.g., for information relaying) and the hypothalamus (e.g., for regulating drives). The latter is part of the limbic system, which features the hippocampus (involved in activities that include memory formation) and the amygdala (implicated in activities that include aggression). A third part is the hindbrain. It includes structures like the medulla (implicated in activities like breathing, digestion, and heart rate) and the cerebellum (involved in activities including coordination of muscle movement and senses).

For the functioning of the brain, a start can be made with the neuron; there are some 100 billion of them in the average central nervous system. There is other material in the brain, such as glia. A neuron or nerve cell consists of a soma, an axon, and the treelike dendrites. Many neurons are very short; some are long. They communicate across synapses (spaces) with other neurons. In this way, they establish patterns of connections. The communication between neurons is called action potential, a heavily studied part of neuroscience. An action potential is described by Baer, Connors, and Paradiso (2007, p. 794) as a "a brief fluctuation in membrane potential caused by the rapid opening and closing of voltage-gated ions channels; also known as spike, nerve impulse, or discharge. Action potentials sweep like a wave along axons to transfer information from one place to another in the nervous system."

But there is much more—for example, genes. We consist of trillions of cells, and inside each is a nucleus. Inside each nucleus are forty-six chromosomes. "Genes are recipes for making proteins. . . . The DNA language that makes up the gene recipes are four different chemicals—adeline, thymine, cytosine, and guanine" (Balkwell and Rolph 2003, pp. 6 and 8). And the story goes on.

For an introduction, see the suggested readings at the end of this chapter. There is no need for social scientists and others to be fearful of the content. It is true that it is not easy reading for some, but the excitement should compensate.

What Is Neuroscience? Does Neuroscience Imply Biological Determinism?

Embracing neuroscience means neither biological determinism nor even that biology trumps. Turning to neuroscience implies neither abandoning insights from the particular social sciences, nor rejecting epistemic pluralism. The brain is biological, of course; but it is not a mere matter of biology. By this, I mean that the biology of the brain is shaped by its experience. Social, political, economic, psychological, and poetic actions shape and reshape the structure and functioning of the brain. Neuroplasticity refers to the brain's capability, through developing or eliminating neural connections (rewiring, as it were), of adapting to its changing context. It implies the study of how the brain is shaped by its experience, and how the brain accommodates to experience.

Brain plasticity is lifelong. It's true that there are critical periods. For example, most of us know that the best time to learn languages is preteen. Use-it-or-lose-it is the brain's operating principle, even from the beginning. We are told that at seven months of age the typical child can hear sound differences in any language (she's a citizen of the world), and that at eleven months the typical child has lost this ability (she has lost her world citizenship). It is also true that brain functioning can be damaged (e.g., as through addiction, altering the level of neurotransmitters). It's true that brain connections follow rules from the genes. For instance, I read that Cynthia Kenyon "has increased the life span of tiny worms called Caenorhabditis elegans up to six times normal by suppressing a single gene" (Duncan 2005, pp. 57–58). Yet the brain is continually changing in response to cultural and other inputs until the moment of death. Even reading this book, as you read, is changing your physical brain.

What Is Neuroscience? Are Social Sciences Neuro-alert?

Yes, significant but limited advances have been made in social sciences and other subjects. For instance, there are neuroeconomics (see Glimcher et al. 2008), neuro-politics (see Alford 2006), and certainly varieties of neuropsychology (e.g., see Decety and Keenan 2006, on social neuroscience). It has extended to other subjects, like social work (see R. Farmer 2009). Let's focus here on neuroeconomics, which has been developed within behavioral economics, as an example.

Neuroeconomics provides a model for public administration, suggesting the possibility of public administration learning from neuroscience and also of public administration theory contributing to neuroscience. That this bidirectionality is not merely fanciful (as a second step, after public administration becomes more involved with neuroscience) is suggested by achievements toward the circumference of economic theory. The Society for Neuroeconomics in 2009 held its seventh "annual meeting." Neuroeconomics has been working on two-way trading. On the demand side, neuroeconomics aims to obtain neuroscientific results for the benefit of economic theory. On the supply side, the aim is to provide economics results of benefit to neuroscience, for example, to computational neuroscience. The Society for Neuroeconomics has begun each of its annual meetings emphasizing this bi-directionality. Behavioral economics—with applications reported in finance, game theory, labor economics, public finance, and macroeconomics—obtains upgrades from neuroscience that are described as informing this brand of economics. Neuroscience points to "an entirely new set of constructs to understand economic decision making" (Camerer, Loewenstein, and Prelec 2005, p. 10). Our "behavior is strongly influenced by finely attuned affective [emotion] systems whose basic design is common to humans and many animals" (Camerer,

Loewenstein, and Prelec 2005, p. 11). For Camerer and other neuroeconomists, the brain is no longer the ultimate black box.

What Is Neuroscience? Are There Related Biology-Inspired Subjects?

Yes. Evolutionary psychology and evolutionary biology are examples of subjects inspired by biology that are relevant to public administration—although disciplinary names themselves sometimes evolve. Evolutionary psychology has been described as the combination of evolutionary biology and cognitive psychology. Evolutionary biology is the study of the descent of living things from common ancestors—when living entities started during the some 4.5 billion years of the earth's history.

For example, turn to evolutionary psychology—as described by cognitive scientist Steven Pinker (1998), and as summarized in Evans and Zarate (2005). First, a prominent view is that the brain/mind consists of many specific-purpose modules, rather than a general-purpose problem-solving program. These modules implicate multiple neural pathways. These programs, having evolved by natural selection, are designed to solve a particular adaptive problem in a particular context. Examples are the problems of avoiding predators, eating the right food, forming alliances, helping children and other relatives, reading other people's minds, selecting mates (Evans and Zarate 2005, pp. 48–49). Second, another prominent view is that these mind modules were developed 100,000 or more years ago when the context was different (e.g., group size was smaller)—on the African savannah or elsewhere, where our adapting ancestors lived. In a sense, we are *out-of-date* creatures—in all things and no less in public administration.

Implications

Neuroscience promises obvious and powerful explanations and understandings that are relevant for public administration theorizing and practice. It can give traditional public administration—not a growth action subject—a needed shot in the arm.

Implication for Planning—Shouldn't Public Administration Recognize Our Emerging Neurosociety?

Neurosociety may well emerge, and public administration planning and policy making should come to terms with such brain-based prospects and developments. First, turn to Richard Restak's claim that neurosociety will emerge in the first half of the twenty-first century. Restak (2006, p. 1) writes that "our understanding of the human brain will revolutionize how we think about ourselves and our interactions with other people." Second, whether or not Restak's timing is right, consider how fundamental the change will be in the very language of public administration. Yes, neuro-developments can be relevant as inputs for program planning, for example, the relevance of the finding that 1 in 500 babies are born with afflictions like an-encephaly if their mothers don't ingest folic acid within the first three weeks of pregnancy (Baer, Connors, and Paradiso 2007, pp. 182–183). But, in two ways, the claim is that the relevance for public administration planning goes further than good input.

First, public administration should plan to contribute to the shaping of any such emergence of a neurosociety. The subtitle of Restak's book is *How the Emerging Neurosociety Is Changing How We Live, Work, and Love*. Restak lists what he considers to be seven brain-based developments that provide new societal capa-bilities. They are:

1. Tests that reveal our private thoughts and tendencies;
2. Brain scans that evaluate suitability for certain jobs;
3. Tests explaining interpersonal attractions and repulsions;
4. Advertising campaigns that use brain scans to predict likely purchases;
5. Chemical enhancers to stimulate wants;
6. Brain imaging to predict voting probabilities; and
7. Brain image patterning to reveal emotional reactions to movies and televi-sion shows.

Some of these refer directly to planning for public administration (e.g., evaluat-ing personnel for jobs); others refer to the context of public administration planning. Restak argues that developments like these "will become part of our everyday life during the first quarter of the twenty-first century" (Restak 2006, p. 2). He adds other neuroscientific features, like recognition of the neuoscientific unconscious (discussed later). If it wants to look forward to the future, public administration's strategic plan-ning should be in a position to evaluate whether such claims are exaggerated and what they might entail. This ability to look forward should not be confined to neuroscience. (For instance, it has been claimed that mid-century will see wide deployment of driverless cars, humanoid robots, intelligent surveillance systems, longer lives, and smart clothing—*smart* being not merely cool *threads*.) But Restak is saying that the neuroscientific capabilities of the emerging neurosociety are central.

Second, the advent of such a society promises to change the very language game needed for effective public administration planning and thinking. Neuro-science as a perspective, among others, has the momentum and the substance perhaps even to "muscle" a different way of thinking for governance. I'll limit myself here to the single example of a fresh public administration language that privileges deconstruction and that recognizes social construction. Recall what is meant by a language game. Ludwig Wittgenstein explained language games in terms of the manner of the discourses of a community, such as the discourses of public administration practitioners, political scientists, or biologists. Wittgenstein explained that language is an activity or a form of life, and that people participate in a variety of language games.

Neuroscience is itself a language, but typically all the dialects share the feature of encouraging deconstruction. The first journal issue of *Social Neuroscience* claims that common sense language does not match what is going on at one or the other neuroscientific levels. Common sense ways of conceptualizing X are not reflected in X's neural signature. For instance, if a single concept like empathy (if it is viewed as a single concept) has two neuroscientific manifestations (two neural signatures), perhaps the concept should be deconstructed.

Neuroscience can be another perspective that tips the balance against the constraints of what counts as public administration common sense. (Recall that common sense is not necessarily the same as good sense.) This parallels the way that most paradigm shifts in hard science show the hollowness of the common sense language game, for example, space-time understandings show the hollowness of talking about "ascending" into Heaven, understandings about subatomic particles is at variance with _____ (fill in the blank). Hard science has the big momentum. My favorite example is about heart and brain. Before William Hervey's seventeenth-century discovery of the circulation of the blood, it was not widely recognized that the heart is a mere pumping station. It is claimed that Aristotle, the first biologist as he is often called, concluded—unlike others such as Hippocrates—that the brain is a cooling system, while the heart is the seat and source of sensation. The Ancient Egyptian "common sense" idea was that the brain is mere stuffing. The language point is that we still misspeak about the heart. I love you with all my heart; no, I love you with all my stuffing. Our common sense language is, in this as in other respects, misleading.

Rosemary Farmer and Ananda Pandurangi (1997) add support to the deconstruction of the concept of schizophrenia, as another example. They suggest that it's not a unitary concept. That study had used functional magnetic resonance imaging to compare two classes of persons with schizophrenia—those with, and those without, brain abnormalities.

Should public administration's aim be less than the aim in neuropolitics, an academic movement on the circumference of political science? The languages of decision making, motivation, emotion, and stereotyping can be investigated profitably from a neuroscientific perspective. Such a claim was made by political scientists leading a training session on "What neuroscience has to offer political science," a short course preceding the 2006 annual conference of the American Political Science Association (APSA). The idea here is that what counts as common sense political science talk is problematized by neuroscientific results; and so it should surely be no less for public administration. At that same training session, George Marcus (then president of the International Association of Political Psychology) described neuroscientific results as showing that it is false to suppose that perceptions yield understandings that are "veridical, comprehensive, capable of instantaneous representation, and able to provide mindful control" (McDermott et al., 2006). As he explained it, perceptions are preceded by values and are necessary for motivations like survival. Assume that this claim is itself veridical. If so, wouldn't this claim be consistent with Michel Foucault's "deconstructive" observations on normalization and on the connection between truth and power—fundamentally significant for thinkers about bureaucracy? Doesn't this suggest the desirability of deconstructing the traditional urge for definite, easy-to-understand public administration and other answers? Doesn't this encourage us to recognize the value of "authentic hesitation" in our pronouncements? Doesn't it suggest the value of appreciating that, in public administration no less than in political science, rarely do we have ready access to the Truth, the whole Truth, and nothing but the Truth?

Don't underestimate the catalytic power of neuroscience, and don't suppose that the impact will be less for the language of a public administration that wants to remain relevant to the future of society. Within neuroeconomics, for instance, studies have been done on the neural basis of discounting future gains. Doesn't this encourage us to deconstruct the traditional overemphasis on the short term and the micro in the traditional language of public administration? Even perception of space is socially constructed. With damage to both sides of the posterior portions of the cortex, some people can see objects—but they cannot see space. As Lynn Robertson (2004) puts it, for them there is no "there" there. Rare people with "Balint's syndrome lose explicit spatial awareness but retain spatial information at an implicit level" (Robertson, 2004, p. 236). Others see only part of a space, such as one side of a picture—parallel to the short-run overemphasis just described for the traditional public administration language game.

Yet the issues to be addressed can be expected to present new challenges and controversies. For instance, Steven Pinker (2002, p. 2) argues against the Blank Slate conviction—the "theory" of human nature in which "the human mind has no inherent structure and can be inscribed at will by society or ourselves." This conviction has become "the secular religion of modern intellectual life" (p. 3). It is supported by the fears Pinker describes—the fear of inequality, the fear of imperfectability, the fear of determinism, and the fear of nihilism. The counterclaim that people have different genetic capabilities at birth inevitably encounters political correctness charges on both the left and the right. Yet Pinker can say that "brain tissue is not some genie that can grant its owner any power that would come in handy" (p. 75).

Implication for Managing—Who Is the Administrative Person?

The administrative self—the administrative person—is at the center of public administration managing. Neuroscience changes understandings about how and why the self thinks, feels, and behaves; it promises to inform psychology and psychotherapy. That public administration managing (concerned with getting things done through people) should embrace the brain seems a no-brainer. What is the neural nature of the unified self? First, consider emotions. Second, turn to fear. Third, consider movement.

This is a complex subject. For a demonstration of how conceptions of the self have changed over time and for a non-neurological view of the development of modern identity, a useful publication is Charles Taylor's *Sources of the Self: The Making of the Modern Identity* (1989).

First, is the unified administrative self a rational or an emotional being? Joseph LeDoux (1996) reports that neuroscience makes it clear that it is false to think that humans are thinking beings who have emotions. Rather, we are emotional beings who have thoughts. Barring brain injury or malformation, a nonemotional human moment is a fiction. This doesn't entail the unavailability of purely rational, purely objective judgments. But the implication for managing seems beyond a mere system upgrade.

Antonio Damasio argues that an emotional feeling is identical to the bodily sensations that express it; that emotions do not cause bodily symptoms, but vice versa; and that his theory of emotions can be generalized to all mental states. He wants to reconstruct the word "feelings"—whose principal meaning, he says, refers "to some variant of the experience of pain or pleasure as it occurs in emotions and related phenomena" (Damasio 2003, p. 3). For him, "all the mental phenomena we can describe, feelings and their essential ingredients—pain and pleasure—are the least understood in biological and specifically neurobiological terms" (p. 3). For criticisms of Damasio's ideas, see McGinn (2003).

Second, how does an emotion like fear work in the self? Here is an example, from the neurobiology of fear. Consider two neural pathways for fear alarums (see LeDoux 1996) to avoid, for example, a dangerous situation. On seeing the situation, the stimulus arrives at the brain's thalamus. The pathway in the brain leads from the thalamus to the amygdala, and the body freezes with fear at the sight of the situation, which might be either dangerous or safe. Another pathway leads milliseconds later through the sensory cortex to awareness. Faced with fears, for instance, the amygdala is involved in immediate feelings and action below the level of consciousness—until modified by later signals from the cerebral cortex. Francois Ansermet and Pierre Magistretti (2007) describe, for instance, how traces (physical modifications in the brain) that result from experience have a homeostatic function. There is what is called the somatic marker hypothesis. As Tancredi (2005, p. 77) explains it, "This hypothesis addresses the way in which specific feelings (somatic, i.e., bodily ones), no doubt associated with past experiences and stored in our memory, act as a signal, a type of marker that informs us and guides our reasoning about a situation and our decisions to act in a certain way."

There is relevance here to managing. Recall the functioning of fear in bureaucratic life, that is, fear of reductions in force (RIFs), fear of being found out to be wrong, fear of criticism from the powerful, and so on. Yet doesn't traditional public administration tend to assume rational administrative man, a self not unduly laden with fear? Traditional public administration takes little real account of fearful administrative man. There is also relevance beyond managing. To the extent that it wants to make policy and to plan (e.g., making decisions about police or homeland security), for instance, public administration should surely care about the upgrades that are facilitated by examining the neurobiology of fear.

Third, turn to movement. Note the place of movement in the neurobiological contribution to the construction of the self. (Some might speculate that, in its sense of "true" identity, public administration also privileges practical movement.) There is literature on the neural substrates of (say) my image of my body, for example, in Goldenberg (2005). On the construction of the self, Patricia Churchland (2002, p. 70) reminds us that "The key to figuring out how a brain builds representations of 'me' lies in the fact that, first and foremost, animals are in the *moving* business; they feed, flee, fight, and reproduce by moving their body parts in accord with bodily needs. This *modus vivendi* is strikingly different from plants, which take life as it comes."

Aggression, ideology, individual differences, and stereotyping are among other topics of relevance to the construction of the self. There are literatures in neuroscience on each of these. All are relevant to managing. On neuroscience and aggression, for instance, there is Nelson and his edited *Handbook of Biology of Aggression* (2006). On neuroscience and ideology, there is Bruce Wexler's *Brain and Culture: Neurobiology, Ideology, and Social Change* (2006). On human differences, start with Robert Sapolsky's *Biology and Human Behavior* (2005). Stereotyping is a topic much discussed in social neuroscience (e.g., Ito et al. 2006). There is much more on neuroscience and self-identity, for example, Todd Feinberg and Julian Keenan's *Lost Self: Pathologies of the Brain and Identity* (2005).

Implication for the Underlying—Are Administrative Beliefs Shaped Within the Brain?

To a significant extent, administrative beliefs and other beliefs impacting public administration are shaped within the brain. On the plus side, the unconscious is a neurobiological "reality," and, as Camerer, Loewenstein, and Prelec (2005, p. 11) put it, the "brain implements 'automatic' processes which are faster than conscious deliberations and which occur with little or no awareness of feeling of effort." On the other side, brain plasticity indicates that unconscious biological processes are not beyond any conscious influence.

On the plus side, Laurence Tancredi's discussion of neuroscience and moral beliefs suggests the significance of the unconscious. He writes about the hardwiring associated with the brain's limbic structures, producing emotional responses—fear, disgust, and guilt—in response to the environment. He describes these structures working with the prefrontal lobe to attach emotions to specific behavior (like incest, premarital sex, gluttony, and so on); emotional response can be internalized. Claims Tancredi, "We are getting a handle on brain biology as it relates to specific moral precepts, and in time all of them will be seen as originating, to some degree, in biology" (Tancredi 2005, p. 9). Also, note views about the brain's sensory systems being "narcissistic" (e.g., see Atkins 1996) and about the brain being wired to lie in, for instance, the anterior cingulate gyrus (e.g., see Tancredi 2005, pp. 119–121). Tancredi's book is entitled *Hardwired Behavior: What Neuroscience Reveals About Morality*.

The significance of the unconscious is also exemplified in the effect of mirror neurons on beliefs. Protect yourself against your mirror neurons; they operate unconsciously. The mirror neuron mechanism is central in learning by imitation. Largely through this mechanism, the brain learns by observing how others behave morally in different situations; for example, it learns whether it's the norm to believe (or to do) X or Y. Laurence Tancredi (2005, p. 40) explains that "These [mirror] neurons in humans involve a network which is formed by the temporal, occipital, and parietal visual areas, as well as two additional cortical regions that are predominantly motor. . . ." Imagine a public administration thinker exposed to other thinkers who believe common sense idea X, rather than idea Y. "The mirror neuron system, among other functions, is pivotal to the representation of sequential information, and to imitation" (p. 40). With repeated exposure, the norm becomes increasingly and unconsciously hardwired in the brain. Most of us forget the context within which we first came to believe X or Y. As Richard Restak explains, "In an attempt to compensate for this loss of context, the brain unconsciously assumes that familiar information is true information . . . 'I've heard that before, so there must be something to it'" (Restak 2006, p. 77). There is a sort of illusion-of-truth effect.

On the other side, Richard Dawkins in *The Selfish Gene* underscores the limits of our strong biological dispositions. "Our genes may instruct us to be selfish, but we are not necessarily compelled to obey them all our lives. It may just be more difficult to learn altruism than it would be if we were genetically programmed to be altruistic. Among animals, man is uniquely dominated by culture, by influences learned and handed down" (Dawkins 1989, p. 3). Again, there is (mentioned above) plasticity. The subtitle of Ansermet and Magistretti's *Biology of Freedom* (2007) is *Neural Plasticity, Experience and the Unconscious*. Yet we should not underestimate the strengths of the unconscious.

Implication for the Field—Will Public Administration Become a Subspecialty Within Neuro-Gov?

Neuroscience can be expected to act as a catalyst, in the longer run, in facilitating reunification of the fragmented social sciences (e.g., including political science and economics) and social action subjects (including public administration and business administration) that concern governance. Along the lines noted in Question 6, neuroscience can achieve this because it reveals that taken-for-granted concepts, and the language used to express them, should be challenged. Such a movement toward reunification of the fragmented social science and social action subjects is consistent with the tradition since Bacon and Comte. It is in the tradition of the work of the U.S. Social Science Research Council in the 1920s, the 1948 Foundation for Integrative Education, and the National Science Foundation's programs (discussed in chapter 16). On the downside, these movements toward unification have so far failed.

One possible disciplinary outcome is neuro-gov; another is organizational cognitive neuroscience. Neuro-gov, the broadest outcome, would include govern-mentality, referring to whatever systems and arrangements shape individuals—including not only public and private and nonprofit enterprises but also agencies like churches, nonprofits, schools, and families. This marriage between neuroscience and governance is termed neuro-gov, as I (2007b) have suggested. It is consistent with the argument of the biologist E.O. Wilson when, going even further, he wrote about consilience and the unity of knowledge—uniting the sciences and ultimately uniting the sciences and the humanities. Wilson defined concilience as "literally a lumping together of knowledge by the linking of facts and fact-based theory across disciplines to create a common groundwork for explanation" (Wilson 1998, p. 11). But neuro-gov does not entail a massive top-down reorganization. It could utilize epistemic pluralism.

Organizational cognitive neuroscience, applied to the public administration situation, is a narrower disciplinary aim. Michael Butler and Carl Senior describe organizational cognitive neuroscience as a connecting together of "two different discourses and the ideas, methods and outputs they contain—these being cognitive neuroscience and organization theory" (Butler and Senior 2007, p. 1). They define it as "applying neuroscientific methods to analyze and understand human behavior within the applied setting of organizations" (p. 8). The application, as they explain, can be at the individual, group, organizational, and interorganizational levels.

Implication for Creativity—Can Neuroscience Increase Bureaucratic Imagination?

How can neuroscience be relevant in understanding and promoting extraordinary creativity in public administration? This understanding can operate at the micro and macro levels.

On the micro level, we will turn in chapter 18 to Nancy Andreasen and her rec-ommendations for cultivating extraordinary creativity. Suggestions will be included for readers to adapt those recommendations as part of Exercise 3.

On the macro level, there are such questions as that about public administration and trauma. Start with Arnold Modell (2003) explaining how trauma can foreclose on the imaginative. For one thing, Modell claims that metaphors—at the center of the imaginative—are not merely figures of speech. They are neural features, the way that the brain yields meaning. Modell (2003, p. 9) emphasizes that "the construction of meaning is very different from the processing of information." He discusses how metaphor is the brain's primary mode of understanding and remembering the world. He writes of metaphor in corporeal imagination in terms of transferring between dissimilar domains, for example, between past and pres-ent, and—as in synesthesia—"hearing" colors and "seeing" sounds. For another thing, Modell (pp. 40 and 41) claims that "the metaphoric process [in a brain can be] foreclosed or frozen" by trauma. An example he gives is of a person who, having experienced a childhood trauma, experiences great stress as an adult when encountering a parallel kind of activity; in respect to this particular experience—as Modell puts it—"the distinction between past and present was obliterated." Is it far-fetched to wonder (on a macro level) if any parallel process occurred in public administration? I'm referring to the trauma in public administration's earlier years (and perhaps continuing), for example, its survival fears, its mocking by political science, and any associated desperation to placate mid-level practitioners. Did that early experience foreclose or freeze any of the metaphoric process in traditional public administration?

Epilogue

Do you remember Emily Dickinson's lines—those that begin like this?

> *The Brain—is wider than the Sky—*
> *For—put them side by side—*
> *The one the other will contain*
> *With ease—and you—beside*

Suggested Readings

Baer, M.F., B.W. Conners, and M.A. Paradiso. 2007. *Neuroscience: Exploring the Brain.* 3rd ed. New York: Lippincott, Williams, and Wilkins.

Damasio, Antonio. 2003. *Looking for Spinoza: Joy, Sorrow, and the Feeling Brain.* New York: Harcourt.

Farmer, Rosemary L. 2009. *Neuroscience and Social Work Practice: The Missing Link.* Thousand Oaks, CA: Sage.

Senior, Carl, and Michael Butler, eds. 2007. *The Social Cognitive Neuroscience of Organizations.* Vol. 1118. Boston, MA: Blackwell Publishing, on behalf of the New York Academy of Sciences.

10

Public Administration from a
Feminist Perspective

"Otherness is a fundamental category of thought," asserts Simone de Beauvoir (1933 [1952], p. xv), explaining that woman is "established" as an *Other*. In *The Second Sex* (p. xx), she first explains that the "category of the *Other* is as primordial as consciousness itself. In the most primitive societies, in the most ancient mythologies, one finds the expression of a duality—that of the Self and the Other. This duality was not originally attached to the division of the sexes. . . ." Famously and secondly, Simone de Beauvoir explains that one "is not born, but rather becomes, a woman. No biological, psychological, or economic fate determines the figure that the human female presents to society; it is civilization as a whole that produces this creature, intermediate between male and eunuch, which is described as feminine. Only the intervention of someone else can establish an individual as an *Other*"(p. xv).

On the one hand, traditional public administration does practice *othering*. I'll explain later that public administration tends to *other* people and ideas that do not fit into its way of seeing the world, for example, bosses typically tending to *other* dissenting subordinates, bureaucracies typically tending to *other* noncomplying clients, and so forth. On the other hand, public administration is *othered*. Aren't public administration theorists *othered* by theorists in disciplines like political science and economics, and aren't public administration practitioners *othered* by business practitioners? What insights are available from a feminist perspective for public administration practice and theory, especially about the *other*?

The first part of this chapter sketches the nature of feminism. The objective is to note what is significant for public administration practice and theory. Five questions are discussed:

1. What is feminism? In a nutshell, what's a description?
2. What is feminism? When did it start, and what were its historical waves?

3. What is feminism? What are major varieties?
4. What is feminism? Are there more categories, like womanism?
5. What is feminism? To what extent has feminism impacted public administration theorizing?

The second part of this chapter discusses implications for public administration of a feminist perspective. The following questions are discussed:

6. Implication for planning—Shouldn't public administration stop *othering* people?
7. Implication for managing—Doesn't mere efficiency *other*?
8. Implication for the underlying—Do sex and gender alert public administration to the unconscious?
9. Implication for the field—Doesn't public administration need a new language?
10. Implication for creativity—Is public administration's imagination socially constructed?

Readers are asked (per Reflection Exercise 1) to determine what insight or insights about public administration theory and practice interest them from a feminist perspective.

Sketching Feminism

"For a long time I hesitated to write . . . on woman. The subject is irritating, especially to women, and it is not new" (de Beauvoir 1993 [1952], p. xv). In this way Simone de Beauvoir opened her ground-breaking book that heralded the second wave of feminism.

Special to women are many problems of which men cannot have first-person experience, and not just giving birth. Yet especially through postmodern feminism, which deconstructs binary oppositions like woman and man, some French feminists are encouraging. Distinguishing between speaking *like* a woman and *as* a woman, for example, Luce Irigaray claims that both men and women can speak like a woman—as she puts it, not to assert mastery, not to be in control of meaning, and not to claim truth, objectivity, and knowledge.

What Is Feminism? In a Nutshell, What's a Description?

Feminism is the investigation of both the oppression of women and the liberation of women. Let's say this as a first cut, recognizing that refinements and qualifications are inevitably needed in such a one-liner. Consider oppression and, then, liberation.

"Women are oppressed, *as women*," argues Marilyn Frye (1983, p. 16). "Members of certain racial and/or economic groups and classes, both the males and the females, are oppressed as members of those races and/or classes. But men are not oppressed *as men*."

There are different feminist views on the nature and sources of oppression. The nature and sources of the oppression are seen variously, for instance, in such ways as a matter of justice, equality, and right, as a matter of the logic of capitalism, or as a matter of the cultural.

Feminism is a liberation movement. It looks forward to the realization of women's liberation from oppression. The character of this liberation is also variously understood. There are equality and difference feminists, for example. The former might seek either equality in such terms as jobs, education, law, pay, and political participation, or equality of opportunity. Difference feminists might argue for equal evaluation of the masculine and the feminine. To put it like this, however, is not to indicate the creativity and power of some of the understandings. Drucilla Cornell (1998, p. ix), as only one example, speaks of the ideal of freedom of what she terms the "imaginary domain," with freedom to create ourselves as "sexed beings, as feeling and reasoning persons."

What Is Feminism? When Did It Start, and What Were Its Historical Waves?

Consider start dates and waves, also in a nutshell.

When did feminism start? There are at least four possibilities, depending in part on the variety of feminism favored. A first possibility is at the beginning of humanity, when at a minimum the concept would have preceded the term. This choice might appeal to ecofeminists like Susan Griffin (1978), who argue that women are closer to nature than men.

A second possibility (missing out on Plato's *Republic*, which contemplates both philosopher queens and philosopher kings) is to go back to the early fifteenth century to Christine de Pizan and her 1405 work, *The Book of the City of Ladies* (where the feminism is veiled, necessarily, with the religious).

A third is the 1660s, with the playwright and novelist Aphra Ben. One of her plays was the two-part *The Rover* (1677) and one of her novels was *Oroonoko* (1688).

A fourth possibility is the late 1700s, after the French Revolution. Here the example is Mary Wollstonecraft and her *Vindication of the Rights of Women*. Asserted Wollstonecraft (1792, p. 21), "Would men but generously snap our chains, and be content with rational fellowship instead of slavish obedience. They would find us more observant daughters, more affectionate sisters, more faithful wives, more reasonable mothers—in a word, better citizens."

Have there been waves in the history of feminism? Wave or paradigm talk has its limitations (see chapter 2). But yes, many say that there have been three (some say two) feminist waves, as follows.

First Wave: 1830–1920

This wave includes the liberal and the socialist varieties. Consider the liberal perspective. The wave included such events as the Alternative Declaration of Rights at the American Seneca Falls Convention (1848) associated with Elizabeth Cady Stanton and Lucretia Mott. It included such powerful thinkers as husband John Stuart Mill and wife Harriet Taylor, and such activists as Sylvia Pankhurst. The movement was variously aligned with the temperance movement and the National American Women's Suffrage Association (obtaining the vote in 1920). This wave petered out in view of the material and military events that were faced.

Second Wave: 1960–1980 and Later

Following Simone de Beauvoir's *Second Sex* (1993 [1952]) and Betty Friedan's *Feminine Mystique* (1997 [1963]), there was an explosion of women's organization, as in the National Organization for Women (NOW). In England, more familiar names were Germaine Greer and Juliet Mitchell. In the United States, there was a growth of liberal-based activity and radical feminism. Probably contributing to the latter in the United States was what we can call the "unavailability" of socialist feminism, resulting from general hostility toward socialism.

Third Wave: 1980 to the Present

Described has been a movement toward cultural, psychological, and linguistic issues, away from (say) the economic. Postmodern feminism includes the French feminists, as noted below.

What Is Feminism? What Are Major Varieties?

There are varieties and subvarieties of feminism. I know of no political train of thought, no political ideology, that fails to proliferate and overlap with others (see chapter 5); feminism as a train of thought is no exception. From among these varieties and subvarities, let's consider four major categories—liberal feminism, socialist feminism, radical feminism, and postmodern feminism.

Liberal Feminism

Liberal feminism opposes the "monopoly power" of men. Such monopolies exclude women from equal access to such resources as pay and political power and education. Classical liberalism opposes all monopolies, whether public or private or sexual. So does liberal feminism. This way of viewing the opposition is in spite of the fact that some feminists associate competition (a nonmonopoly situation) and individualism with masculinity. The reasoning justifying this opposition to monopolies is based, variously, on natural rights arguments (e.g., Wollstonecraft), or on utility arguments (e.g., John Stuart Mill), or on Rawlsian-type considerations (e.g., Susan Okun).

Socialist Feminism

Socialist feminism comes in subvarieties. This is unsurprising as socialism, and indeed Marxism, also come in varieties. Note three subvarieties: First, early in the nineteenth century, there were the utopian socialists—e.g., Charles Fourier, Henri de Saint-Simon, and Robert Owen. They supported equality for women. They regarded marriage as outmoded. Fourier, for instance, encouraged free love, bisexuality, lesbianism, polygamy, communal kitchens, and communal child rearing. Second, there were the scientific socialists, as Karl Marx and Friedrich Engels called themselves. They considered oppression to be rooted in capitalism, and they thought that women would be liberated along with men. Engels, however, spoke of the division of labor in the bourgeois family, with the husband as the capitalist and the woman as the proletarian. Third, there has been a more recent attempt to develop socialist feminism based on understanding the economic and the cultural sources of the oppression of women. As a poster woman for this attempt, many would nominate Rosa Luxemburg (1871–1919).

Radical Feminism

Radical feminism opposes the roots of gender discrimination. The opposition is directed against patriarchy as a root feature deep within societal consciousness and thus institutions, rather than aiming for piecemeal improvements within the existing societal structure. Writes Shulamith Firestone (1979, p. 79), even "when they don't know it, feminists are talking about changing a fundamental biological condition. . . . That so profound a change cannot easily be fitted into traditional categories of thought, e.g., 'political,' is not because these categories do not apply but because they are not big enough: radical feminism bursts through them." She adds, "Until a certain level of evolution had been reached and technology had achieved its present sophistication, to question fundamental biological conditions was insanity. . . . But, for the first time in some countries, the preconditions for feminist revolution exist." Firestone looks to new technologies for liberation— artificial insemination, test-tube babies, domestic cybernetics. In an androgynous or unisex future, gender and sex will become redundant. There is a multiplicity of forms in radical feminism. Some are rooted in biology and psychology, for instance; others are not. For a long list, see Alice Echols (1989).

Postmodern Feminism

Postmodern feminism holds that the problem is cultural, no less. French postmodern feminists like Hélène Cixous, Luce Irigaray, and Julia Kristeva use approaches familiar in the postmodern literature to elucidate the oppression and liberation of woman. Supported is the idea that women need a language of their own. As indicated above, this language contrasts with the dominant male language—a male language that asserts mastery, being in control of meaning, and claiming truth, objectivity, and knowledge. It is a form of writing open to both female and male. But such feminine forms of discourse are threatening because (Kristeva argues) they cannot be contained within the rational structure of the symbolic order. Of course, there is more; for example, Irigaray seeks to psychoanalyze Western culture, looking for what underpins its fragile rationality.

What Is Feminism? Are There More Categories, Like Womanism?

Are there feminisms outside these major categories? Yes, there are feminisms like womanism, anarchist feminism, and ecofeminism. Consider womanism.

Start with the symbolic significance of bell hooks's (1984, p. 1) complaint about Betty Friedan: "Betty Friedan's *The Feminine Mystique* is still heralded as having paved the way for the contemporary feminist movement." Yet, bell hooks continues, "Freidan's famous phrase, 'the problem that has no name,' often quoted to describe the condition of women in this society, actually referred to a select group of college-educated, middle and upper-class, white women—housewives bored with leisure, with the home, with children, with buying products, who wanted more out of life" (p. 1). Friedan "ignored the existence of all nonwhite women and poor white women. . . . [She] deflected attention away from her classism, her racism, her sexist attitudes towards the masses of American women" (p. 2).

"Womanist is to feminist as purple is to lavender" (Walker 1983, p. xii). The term *womanist* was coined by Alice Walker (1983) in *In Search of Our Mothers' Gardens*. As she wrote, it is "the black folk expression of mothers to female children, 'You acting womanish,' i.e., like a woman . . . usually referring to outrageous, audacious, courageous, or *willful* behavior. Wanting to know more and in greater depth than is considered 'good' for one . . . a woman who loves other women sexually and/or nonsexually. Appreciates and prefers women's culture . . . and women's strength . . . committed to survival and wholeness of entire people, male and female. Not a separatist . . ." (pp. xi–xii). Womanism, the purple, includes talking back to lavender.

What Is Feminism? To What Extent Has Feminism Impacted Public Administration Theorizing?

In an article entitled "Sex, Gender, Feminism, and the Study of Public Administration," Kathy McGinn and Patricia Patterson (2005, p. 941) state, "[w]e are encouraged by the existence of work overcoming our field's self-imposed boundaries by questioning its time-honored practices and beliefs. . . ."

McGinn and Patterson propose a series of six interacting categories applicable to the study of gender in public administration. This was based on phase or stage theories across disciplines. Like the categorization of hurricanes, the smaller numbers represent the least disruptive winds. As one ascends the numbers, one would expect fewer and fewer feminist works in PA. The six categories are:

1. Fully androcentric public administration;
2. Women exist? exemplars and exceptions;
3. Woman as independent variable;
4. Woman as scholarly problem;
5. Feminism and serious questioning; and
6. Multifocal and inclusive public administration scholarship.

Of Category Six, they state that "While our search of the PA literature did turn up a small number of examples of what we would categorize as Category Six work, of the six categories this is the most difficult to illustrate" (McGinn and Patterson 2005, p. 940). They cite two Category Six articles—on reason as a homosocial construct (White 2003) and on work-family balance and job satisfaction (Saltzstein, Ting, and Saltzstein 2001).

However, as McGinn and Patterson (2005, p. 941) add, "By basing our claims on bodies of knowledge that leave out women, let alone sophisticated applications of gender, how can we [in PA] say that this knowledge is anything other than grossly inaccurate?"

Implications

Start with implications for public administration planning and management, seeking to overcome *othering*. Let's focus on the strategic, the long run.

The term *othering* means *marginalizing, putting outside of the main text, recognizing as on the edge.* In other words, it implies treating as of little or no account, as of little or no importance, as of second or no class. People and ideas can be *othered* by public administration, as noted toward the beginning of this chapter. Woman is a people category that can be *othered* in public administration, as suggested by the feminist perspective. bell hooks is quoted below as saying that ideas of love are *othered*, marginalized, by being considered basically a matter for women.

The term *othering* is not widely used in public administration practice. To make it more familiar, reflect on any experience you may have had with a career civil servant who disagrees consistently with her boss. In my experience in government, such a person in all earnestness would be called crazy or stupid. Not a team player. Such names mean that the person is treated as an *other*.

Implication for Planning—Shouldn't Public Administration Stop "Othering" People?

Macro planning seeking to overcome *othering* can seek inspiration from feminist aims and ideas. Strategic planning for public administration as a whole may well wish to extend feminist insights, applying the concept of *othering* to the bureaucratic treatment of its customers (clients, citizens) and seeking to remedy the problem. Focus on one form of such *othering*, what we'll explain as reducing a client to her bureaucratic pigeonhole. Re-expressed, this is *othering* of the nonadministrative.

Despite protestations to the contrary, most of us have seen bureaucracies *other* those who are the clients of that particular bureaucracy (customers, citizens), for example, as visa applicants are *othered* by the immigration service (or not), as welfare clients are *othered* by welfare agencies (or not), as taxpayers are *othered* by taxing authorities (or not), as patients are *othered* by hospitals (or not), as grant applicants are *othered* by granting agencies (or not), as the young are *othered* by the old (or not), and as the old-timers are *othered* by the newcomers (or not). And so on, ad nauseam. The point is not that visa applicants, welfare clients, taxpayers and so forth should not be treated like visa applicants, welfare clients, and taxpayers. The point is that there are different ways of so treating them, and some ways do *other* them while some ways do not.

We're choosing here to focus on only one form of this general category of *othering*, that is, reducing a client to her bureaucratic pigeonhole. This is the reduction of a whole person to the presenting problem. By *whole person*, I mean a whole person-in-herself in-her-difference. A whole person is one who enjoys (to a greater or lesser extent) biological, psychological, social, spiritual, and other dimensions. A whole person is one who has been developing a distinctive identity since childhood, including some features that are unfortunate and some that are fortunate. It is a living being who is fully human.

By *presenting problem* (a term adapted from psychoanalysis), I mean the reason or reasons, determined by bureaucratic rules and decisions, why that full human being is being processed by that particular bureaucracy. The first element of a presenting problem may be being a welfare applicant, a social security applicant, a prisoner entering the system, a military recruit, a patient seeking treatment for X. The second element is falling into the requisite bureaucratic category that shapes the action. For instance, a welfare applicant with more than the allowed income is in a different category than one with less than the allowable cutoff.

A whole person is not merely a thing with a presenting problem. A person is more than her problem. So, it is *othering* (demeaning, belittling) to call a person by her problem, such as her illness. For instance, a person who has a bad cold is not a mere cold. Most of us wouldn't mind that designation. But it becomes serious if we call a person with schizophrenia a schizophrenic, reducing her to her malady. Examples can be multiplied. A whole person is not merely a welfare applicant of a certain bureaucratically defined kind, for instance. She may also be a . . .

Why is this form of *othering* suggested by the feminist perspective? A reason is that this form of *othering* has been experienced for centuries by females, typically unconsciously. First and last, women have tended to be seen as sex objects by men who, in a patriarchal society, have relative power. A man can simply be a tinker, tailor, cabinetmaker, lawyer, and so on. Isn't the complaint that a woman can only be a woman tinker, a woman tailor, a woman cabinetmaker, a woman lawyer? In other words, she is seen and treated as the presenting problem by the power person. Recall what Mary Wollstonecraft identified as (for her) central. The woman tinker (tailor, etc.) is treated primarily as a sexual being rather than as a whole human being—as a person-in-herself in-her-difference. Wollstonecraft wanted women to be identified as human beings, not as mere sexual beings.

A caveat should be entered here. In such strategic planning, an option is to supplement the planning with attempting to achieve short-run gains for women. Few of us would want the planning to exclude that, if (repeat *if*) such a supplement is possible. There is much legal machinery now in government and in other workplace situations that ostensibly seeks to help women and others who seek protection against discrimination. Long ago in 1964 the Equal Employment Opportunities Commission was established in the federal government. In 1986 there was the Affirmative Action (Equal Employment Opportunities for Women) Act. More recently, in 1999 there was the Equal Employment Opportunity for Women in the Workplace Act, renaming and updating the 1966 act. And so on. Yet a question for planning or management consideration is, to what extent does enforcement of such laws occur?

Implication for Managing—Doesn't Mere Efficiency **Other?**

Traditionally, management aims at efficiency. The business and the economic perspectives invite increased attention to efficiency, and there is understandable complaint that public bureaucracy is failing to secure optimal return from its investment in employees—from its investment in what is called human capital. The feminist perspective, on the other hand, encourages public administrative management to consider what this aim of efficiency *others*. In other words, it invites consideration of what the aim of efficiency denigrates, obstructs, demeans, pushes to the edge. Consider (first) loving and (second) caring; consider, correspondingly, bell hooks and Carol Gilligan.

First, on love. "Patriarchy has always seen love as women's work, degraded and devalued labor" (hooks 2002, p. xviii). What bell hooks is saying is that love is *othered*. By implication, it is put outside the parameters of commonsense public administration, especially if you see public administration as anxious to "prove" its virility in a world where it is frequently attacked (frequently *othered*). In her third book on love, hooks writes that in "the patriarchal male imagination, the subject of love was relegated to the realm of the weak and was replaced by narratives of power and domination. . . . Love becomes solely women's work" (hooks 2002, p. 77).

Asking employees to work in a way that expresses love for the client is a very tall and long-run order. It means relating to a citizen who is a whole person-in-herself in-her-difference, to a whole person in her uniqueness. It means a being-with, a caring-for, the individual whole person (citizen, client, customer), even if that person turns out to be uncooperative with bureaucratic processes. It means a shift away from viewing government as rule-making-for-groups and rule-application-for-groups. It means moving toward symbols like unengineering, understood as knowing and embracing love. As I have noted before (Farmer 2005a), unengineering stands *against* such notions as reengineering or total quality management (TQM). It does so to the extent that the latter stand *for* techniques motivated inward toward the needs and functioning of the organization. Reengineering, successor to TQM and ancestor to whatever is the latest inward-looking management fad, has been described as "a multidisciplinary approach to implementing fundamental change in the way work is performed across the organization with the goal of dramatically improving performance and stakeholder value" (Loh 1997, p. xiv). Rather, while professing to look outward to the customer (client, citizen), such unloving aims primarily have an inward aim.

Shifting toward an aim of love is what happens now in some bureaucratic contexts—by exception. We have all encountered them. Recall the "gifting" examples given earlier by Robert Cunningham and Robert Schneider (2001). A gifting example is a police officer who goes out of her way to help a delinquent kid, a welfare officer who goes out of her way to help a wayward parent, a teacher who goes out of her way to inspire an unblossoming student. Some do this on their own time—and with no recognition. Dear reader, please think of more examples from your own experience, for example, a nurse in the intensive care unit, an official in . . . To repeat, individual-focused love can pop up or pop down in a bureaucracy. And one way to kill it is to prescribe it administratively.

Second, let's turn to caring. Some may find it more palatable than "love," and yet it is clearly implicated in loving. Let's turn to Carol Gilligan and her discussion of an ethic of care—and then to Joan Tronto.

Gilligan proposes an ethic of care, which she contrasts with a male-dominated voice about justice and with Lawrence Kohlberg's stages of moral development. Gilligan (1982) writes of three stages of morality as caring—care of self, care of others, and care of self and others. Kohlberg's three stages of moral development are preconventional, conventional, and postconventional, with the highest form of postconventional being understanding the universal principles that constitute systems of justice. Gilligan (1982) describes her ethic of care and an ethic of justice (like Kohlberg's) as "totally incompatible." As she writes, her conception revolves around understanding of responsibility and relationships, as contrasted with a conception of morality as fairness [which] "ties moral development to the understanding of rights and rules" (p. 19). Understanding ethics as including concern with what an agency or a manager "ought to do," clearly we haven't changed the subject from reflecting on implications of feminism for the traditional public administration ethic of efficiency.

Tronto (1993) advances the conversation about an ethic of care (and also argues against Gilligan and Kohlberg). In turn, the analysis was carried forward by Patricia

Patterson (1999). By care, Tronto is discussing practices, rather than dispositions or sentiments. She distinguishes between four integrated phases of the practice of care. The first is *caring about* (paying enough attention to recognize a need and believing it should be met). The second is *taking care of* (assuming responsibility to act on that need). The third is *care giving* (directly meeting the need, and by this she does not mean giving money). The fourth is being attentive to *care receiving*. Tronto holds that the first two phases are culturally masculine, and the last two are gendered. It's the difference between researching diseases and bathing patients. Isn't this more helpful than thinking about mere efficiency?

Implication for the Underlying—Do Sex and Gender Alert Public Administration to the Unconscious?

The feminine perspective alerts the public administration reader to the underlying societal consciousness that co-shapes what is constructed on the surface, as illustrated by feminist views on gender and sex. The radical feminist perspective brings up the question of whether central reforms, like long-term strategic reforms, have a consequential root character. Public administration can surely learn from the feminist perspective.

For the importance of the underlying, recall feminist views on sex and gender. Asked whether the nature of women is biologically determined or socially constructed, a usual feminist response is that gender is socially constructed and sex is biologically determined. (Note that, as feminism doesn't entail any particular view of human nature, different thinkers can be expected to present differing accounts.) John Stuart Mill considered the nature of woman to be an artificial thing, the result of forced oppression. Couldn't the nature of public administration be an artificial thing, the result of forces of power? Some such forces of power could be on the surface, as in political choices; others would lie underneath, as bureaucracy has a history that goes back beyond Woodrow Wilson to its royal origins. We'll wonder what the idea of the collective unconscious can add to the idea that bureaucracy has its origins in the closet of the king, a figure with (what else?) "royal" or heroic powers.

Do public administration reforms (e.g., for planning and managing) have a root character parallel to the root nature of radical feminist liberation? Or not? Or, is there any need to give an either/or answer? (I think not.) In other words, is a particular public administration problem so rooted in societal consciousness that piecemeal adjustments are bound to be fruitless—or of limited benefit? Let's adapt the quote (in Question 3, above) from Shulamith Firestone, writing about radical feminism. With apologies to Firestone, let's change it so that it speaks of public administration planning and management. "Even when they don't know it, public administration strategic planners and managers are talking about changing fundamental bureaucratic conditions. . . . That such profound changes cannot easily be fitted into traditional categories of thought, e.g., in public administration, is not because these categories do not apply but because they are not big enough: planning and management on these points may have to burst through them. . . . But, for the first time in some countries, the preconditions for a bureaucratic revolution might exist."

Implication for the Field—Doesn't Public Administration Need a New Language?

Doesn't public administration need a fresh language? This is a question prompted by an argument (offered by Hélène Cixous and by other French feminists) that women need feminine writing, a language of their own. See the introduction for Luce Irigaray's comment that this feminine language should be where mastery is refused, where meaning is allowed to shift, and where the writer is not in control of meaning or in possession of truth or knowledge. By contrast, isn't public administration governed by a language that wants to (appears to) assert mastery, to be in control of meaning, and to claim truth, objectivity, and knowledge? Reflect on your own experience of a bureaucracy in crisis. Bureaucracy seeks at least to master and control the situation. Such a language is inconsistent with a language of anti-administration. Attention should be paid to the way that socially constructed symbols and symbolic systems shape surface understandings in public administration's ordinary language. It is suggested that such claims are "illustrated" by feminist discussions, such as of the social construction, typically unconscious, of gender.

Hélène Cixous shares the postmodern objection to dualistic thinking based on unrecognized oppositions and hierarchies and to un-deconstructed metaphors and myths. Public administration appears dominated by dualistic thinking. It is infected with dualities that Cixous believes to dominate Western thought—dualities like heart and head, culture and nature, and man and woman—where one term is always privileged. Metaphors are part and parcel of any writing. They are present at various levels in public administration, like the machinery of government metaphor that underlies public administration and politics (e.g., see Farmer 2005a). Myths abound, as suggested by the discussion of New Rhetoric in chapter 12. Cixous and other postmodern feminists provide examples of how texts and symbols (e.g., Sleeping Beauty) indoctrinate individuals with beliefs that require deconstruction.

"Write yourself! Writing is for you, you are for you: your body is yours. Take it!" exclaims Hélène Cixous. At first sight, Cixous's writing on feminine language may seem far from public administration. The feminine language that Cixous recommends is first-person writing that involves "a transformation of our relationship to our body [and to other bodies]" (Cixous 1980, p. 97). Like somatic writing, it is writing from within our own lived experience, from within our guts. There is neither a special method nor special data. Rather it involves attention to bodiliness "even in purely verbal data." Cixous writes of a "world of searching, the elaboration of a knowledge, on the basis of systematic experimentation with the bodily functions, a passionate and precise interrogation of her eterogeneity . . ." (p. 246). Feminine writing is a form that she considers (as does Irigaray, noted earlier) open to both men and women. Yet, at second glance, for those wanting to assess in public administration terms such a call for a fresh language, think of the restraining effect of bureaucratic language, of bureaucrat-speak. Years ago I (1995, pp. 160–163) was struck by the thirty-two-page specification whereby the U.S. Department of Defense governed the purchase of chilled and frozen hot dogs. For example, "The container shall be a fiber-board box, constructed, closed and strapped in accordance with type I or II, class 2, grade 3, style RSC, of PPP-D-636." The example is not an isolated exception.

Implication for Creativity—Is Public Administration's Imagination Socially Constructed?

The range and role of imagination in public administration and in society are socially constructed. Isn't this implied by the feminist perspective, for example, by such views as that the genders of women and men are socially constructed? It is also clear that our public administration imaginations can be schooled to be sensitive to, and to understand, not only the *other* but also the extent to which our public administration context is male-dominated in such terms as fostering heroic leadership and unhesitant action.

Here's a parable about how the imagination is socially constructed in the education process and in society. The parable is about a stranger (a jolly authority figure) who visited a first-grade class and asked, "Who can sing? Who can dance? Who can play a musical instrument?" All the hands shot up. Visiting a high school, the stranger found that fewer hands went up. In college, far fewer hands shot up. Why? "Because we haven't been trained how to do that!" Among the general public, I wonder how many hands would be raised. In the bureaucracy, it would be a brave— or a drunken—hand that would be raised.

Here's an example about the social construction of the imagination in organizations. Do managers under different organizational or time pressures, for example, have different spaces to listen (and to speak) imaginatively? For instance, remember Richard Clarke (2004), who tried to gain the attention of the national security advisor and her boss. I would imagine that imaginative listening by the latter was limited by the "need" to be the boss and by competing pressures of other business.

Epilogue

More than two centuries ago, Mary Wollstonecraft (1792, p. 102) wrote: "Men and women must be educated, in a great degree, by the opinions and manners of the society they live in. In every age there has been a stream of popular opinion that has carried all before it, and given a family character, as it were, to the century. It may then fairly be inferred, that, till society be differently constituted, much cannot be expected from education."

Suggested Readings

Beauvoir, Simone de. 1993 (1952). *The Second Sex*. Trans. H.M. Parshley. New York: Alfred A. Knopf.

hooks, bell. 2002. *Communion: The Female Search for Love*. New York: HarperCollins.

Marks, Elaine, and Isabelle de Courtivron. 1980. *New French Feminisms: An Anthology*. Amherst: University of Massachusetts.

11

Public Administration from an Ethical Perspective

Doing the right thing is a motivation in shaping public administration thinking and practice. Therein lie problems. What is the right thing? How can we know? How can it be done?

If it chooses to think within its disciplinary area, traditional public administration is limited to applied ethics. Excluded from its specialty area are the broader branches of moral philosophy, like meta-ethics. This can be expected to lead to limitations in understanding. Let's give examples, and not all will agree with them. Misunderstandings are understandable to the extent that traditional public administration does not recognize, for instance, that each of the major alternative ethical systems (see Question 2, below) enjoys excellent supporting arguments and suffers from excellent opposing arguments. It is understandable to the extent that, confined within applied ethics, traditional public administration confuses "foundational" indecisiveness for relativism.

Public administration's applied ethics itself is still largely limited geographically and culturally. American public administration ethics, with exceptions, has been outstandingly nationalistic—limited within national borders. Such geographically constrained and culturally limited discussions of morality have probably sacrificed the inspiration and ideas of others. Also, arguably, some would add that such limited ethical thinking is unethical, especially in view of the fact that the circle of ethical coverage has expanded over the centuries from its limits to a clan or kingdom to worldwide human coverage—and even beyond to animals and ecological concerns.

This chapter on ethics is written from the perspective of moral philosophy. This is both a strength and weakness. The strength is that the literature of moral philosophy is wide and deep, including the writings of the greatest thinkers like Plato and Aristotle and Kant and others. No short chapter could substitute for the original literature of moral philosophy. A weakness is reflected in the fact that a discussion of ethics is shaped by its disciplinary context, and discussion may have different parameters when the ethics is seen not from a philosophical but from another perspective, like the political. The nature of freedom is discussed in moral philosophy, for example. But the political context (recall political theory from chapter 5) will include parameters such as the public administration–relevant claims that the idea of freedom tends to have been appropriated by the political right and to be expressed in terms of laissez-faire (e.g., Levy 2008).

From this general standpoint, let us sketch the nature of an ethical perspective. The following five questions are discussed:

1. What is an ethical perspective? What is ethics?
2. What is an ethical perspective? What are ethical systems?
3. What is an ethical perspective? Do ideologies function like ethics?
4. What is an ethical perspective? Is moral philosophy parochial?
5. What is an ethical perspective? What is the relation of ethics to power?

The second part of this chapter goes on to discuss selected implications of an ethical perspective. The five questions discussed are as follows:

6. Implication for planning—Should administrative input be technical or moral?
7. Implication for managing—Is efficiency the best regulative ideal?
8. Implication for the underlying—Should public administration ethics be certain or authentically hesitant?
9. Implication for the field—Should ethics be applied more deeply to macro public administration issues?
10. Implication for public administration creativity—Is ethics related to the spiritual?

Readers are asked (per Reflection Exercise 1) to determine what insights about public administration theory and practice interest them from an ethical perspective.

Sketching an Ethical Perspective

Should public administration agencies always act ethically? Should public administration officials, as a matter of rightness, always act ethically?

Is it unethical not to examine public administration theory and practice from an ethical perspective? Or, is that a nonsense question?

Ethics and morality can evoke negative connotations unjustifiably, because they are often unfairly linked in the mind to what seem like mere prohibitions and the mere evaluation of acts—often about sex. It is not that such prohibitions and evaluations are unimportant; it is that more "content" may be expected by the reader.

For the reader so bothered, recall that the ethical question need not be limited to "What about this act?" or "What is prohibited?" It can become "How ought I to go on with the rest of my life?" It can become what G.J. Warnock (1971, p. 26) describes when he writes that "the 'general object' of morality . . . is to contribute to betterment—or nondeterioration—of the human predicament, primarily and essentially by seeking to countervail 'limited sympathies' and their potentially more damaging effects. It is the proper business of morality . . . to expand our sympathies, or, better, to reduce the liability to damage inherent in their natural tendency to be narrowly restricted."

What Is an Ethical Perspective? What Is Ethics?

Ought prescriptions and ought questions are central to ethics. For individuals and for groups, ethics is about how we *ought* to live. Ethics is about what we *should* do. This is to be distinguished from how individuals and groups actually do live and what we actually do; in other words, what is customary and usual may or may not be ethical. It is also to be distinguished from what the law provides or prohibits; that is, a legal provision may or may not be ethical. To put it in the style of the philosopher David Hume, an "ought" cannot be derived from an "is." To put it in the more contemporary words of John Searle (who thought the opposite), "no set of descriptive statements can entail an evaluative statement without the addition of at least one evaluative statement" (Searle 1964, p. 44). The world of ethics can be understood as the world of what ought to be.

Ditto for public agencies! Ought an agency to tell the truth, the whole truth, and nothing but the truth at all times? To reformulate the question, is it ethical or unethical (right or wrong) for an agency to make a practice of lying in order to protect itself—or, is it ethical for an agency to make a practice of conducting misleading and deceitful public relations? Is it ethical or unethical (right or wrong) for an agency to make it a general practice to favor the rich and the powerful? And so on. Ditto for individuals who are employed in public agencies!

To suggest what ethics is, we also should note that the status of such ought prescriptions and questions has been variously interpreted by moral philosophers and others. There is a wide spectrum of views. The spectrum includes the views that such prescriptions have no rational foundation, have a rational foundation, and need no rational foundation. Making an informed judgment on such matters does require some familiarity with meta-ethics.

No rational foundation is the view in, say, logical positivism (once in fashion) that Herbert Simon accepted when he wrote his well-known *Administrative Behavior: A Study of Decision-making Processes in Administrative Organization*. The view was that ethical preferences are emotional expressions, claims to be distinguished sharply from factual statements (statements capable of being true or false). That ethics has a rational foundation was a claim advanced by Plato and others since. That ethics needs no rational foundation was advanced, for instance, by Emmanuel

Levinas (1906–1995) and others. Levinas held that the ethical relation is a foundation and not a superstructure. He regarded ethics as "first philosophy."

What Is an Ethical Perspective? What Are Ethical Systems?

Ethical systems include the deonotological, the consequentialist, the intuitional, the ethical egoist, the cultural relativist, the subjectivist, and the religious. Each system contains varieties and subvarieties. Ethical systems are indecisive in two senses. First, and as been noted, each system has excellent pro arguments, and each system is also subject to excellent con arguments. Second, considering the existence of so many alternative systems, the ethical is indecisive when considered as a whole.

The deontological is one class of ethical systems, deontological being derived from the Greek and designating *duty*. This system holds that moral prescriptions should be made as a matter of duty—without regard to assessment of consequences. An example of a celebrated philosopher who embraced such an ethical system was Immanuel Kant (1724–1804). The consequentialist is another category of ethical system, where the rightness or wrongness of an action or set of actions is judged according to consequences. John Stuart Mill (1806–1873), a utilitarian philosopher, advanced a sophisticated ethics that evaluated prescriptions in terms of a calculus of human happiness. The philosopher G.E. Moore (1873–1958) evaluated the consequences in terms of goodness. The intuitional is another category of ethical system, basing prescription on intuition. Ethical egoism is a category that differs again in describing as ethical what promotes best the greatest enduring benefit for me. Cultural relativism appeals to what is done in a society. Subjectivism is a class of systems that counts as ethical what I prefer. A religious system counts as ethical what is considered to be divinely commanded, even though various religions can offer different accounts of divine commands.

For examples of how each ethical system is supported by pro and con considerations, consider the deontological. It is a pro consideration that a deontological duty (e.g., an action, like truth telling, being obligatory) is a rational prescription supported by Kant's argumentation. Yet it is a con consideration that the consequences can be harmful to (say) innocent bystanders. Consider the intuitional. We do have intuitions that X is wrong (or right) when we encounter it. But, on the other hand, it is not clear how to resolve differences when one person has an intuition that X is right and another has an intuition that X is wrong.

The indecisiveness as a whole can be illustrated by recalling the variety of views about the nature of justice. Throughout history, views have diverged on the material and formal natures of justice. Justice has been understood, variously, in such ways as retribution, revenge, social harmony, mercy, desert, impartiality, mutual advantage, reciprocity, fittingness, fair distribution, and exchange. There are also conflicts (see Farmer 2005a, pp. 85–86) between recent views of justice developed by John Rawls, Robert Nozick, and J.J. Smart. Rawls analyzed a liberal theory of justice; Nozick advanced a libertarian theory of justice; and Smart, although denying justice to be a fundamental moral concept, evaluated justice claims on a utilitarian basis.

What Is an Ethical Perspective? Do Ideologies Function Like Ethics?

Ideologies act like moral imperatives in shaping not merely understanding of what should be done and what should be counted as right. They also serve as motivating forces. Isn't it arbitrary to limit consideration of ethics to the narrower class that philosophers consider to be ethical?

Examples of such ideologies in the United States include the political, like conservatism and liberalism. They also include beliefs about the inherent value of the free market (e.g., market fundamentalism) and about patriotism (e.g., American exceptionalism, shored by positive attitudes toward the Constitution). Such ideologies are supported by cultural beliefs that can be expressed in positive attitudes toward what is called (again) the American dream.

What Is an Ethical Perspective? Is Moral Philosophy Parochial?

On the one hand, yes. Until the past two centuries, moral philosophy throughout both West and East has been predominantly parochial, excluding the other. Even now, it is still largely limited geographically and culturally. (American public administration ethics, like public administration, has been markedly nationalistic—limited within national borders.) See the next paragraph for the claims that geographically constrained and culturally limited discussions of morality sacrifice the inspiration and ideas of others—and may well be unethical.

On the other hand, powerful thinkers have contributed to moral philosophy. As Richard Rorty explained (referring to philosophy in general), "Whatever happens, however, there is no danger of philosophy's 'coming to an end.' . . . [P]eople will still read Plato, Aristotle, Descartes, Kant, Hegel, Wittgenstein, and Heidegger" (Rorty 1980, p. 394). But then, making a useful point about philosophy as a conversation, Rorty excluded the East. "The only point on which I would insist is that philosophers' moral concern should be with continuing the conversation of the West, rather than with insisting upon a place for the traditional problems of modern philosophy within that conversation" (p. 394).

What Is an Ethical Perspective? What Is the Relation of Ethics to Power?

What counts as ethics has been interpreted, in an important respect, as an expression of power. Some might want to add that it can be interpreted as a check on power. This can be reexamined in terms of, say, Plato and Michel Foucault.

The power argument against justice was famously advanced, and allegedly refuted, in Plato's *Republic*. In Section 3 of Book 1, Thrasymachus—a character in the dialogue—defines what is right or just. He indicates that justice is what is in the interests of the stronger party. That is, a ruler, the stronger party makes ethical prescriptions (and laws) in his own interests. What is right for the weaker party is obedience to these laws. Readers should make up their own minds about the replies that Socrates offers in Book 1 of the *Republic*. I think that in this case they will not be convinced by Socrates' counterarguments.

A different form of Thrasymachus's argument can be constructed using Foucault's ideas about the connection of truth and power. For Foucault, what-counts-as-truth is shaped by power. He writes that power "produces knowledge (and not simply by encouraging it because it serves power or by applying it because it is useful); power and knowledge directly imply one another" (Foucault 1977a, p. 131). That is, what is accepted as knowledge is determined by interacting sets of strategic power considerations, although Foucault denies that such considerations can be reduced exactly to interests. He holds that the marks of what is counted as knowledge are set by power relationships, and knowledge as truth is embedded with power relations. Return to Foucault's idea of normalizing. What-counts-as-true in such fields as education, social work, psychiatry, and politics is what produces a normalized person—that is, what produces the right kind of person and the right kind of behavior. The point for Foucault is that what is normal is what reflects the power relations in a particular society. Same for public administration ethics.

Implications

Niccolo Machiavelli (1469–1527) gave advice to the ruler in his book *The Prince*. In chapter 18, he wrote that "it is well [for a ruler] to seem merciful, humane, sincere, religious, and also to be so; but you must have the mind so disposed that when it is needful to be otherwise you may be able to change to the opposite qualities. And it must be understood that a prince, and especially a new prince, cannot observe all those things which are considered good in men, being often obliged, in order to maintain the state, to act against faith, against charity, against humanity, and against religion" (Machiavelli [1532] 2008, p. 62). In other words, Machiavelli is saying that a ruler cannot be bound by what counts as morality; he or she must also be prepared to act contrary to the provisions of that morality. Putting it another way, the ruler must have his or her own morality, which may well run contrary to what surrounding society counts as moral. Machiavelli could have been speaking of the elected official, and that official's public administration subordinates.

Implication for Planning—Should Administrative Input Be Technical or Moral?

Should ethical considerations be primary in any planning input from any administrator? (Further, should ethical considerations be primary in each and every planner's actions?) More precisely, should the regulative ideal be that each and every planning input from an administrator (or from a planner) be primarily moral, with a technical subtext—or should actions be primarily technical, with a moral subtext?

As an example, should any anti-terrorism planning be primarily technical, with the moral secondary? Or, should such decisions be primarily moral, with the technical secondary? As another example, should planning connected with developing regulations for coping with hollow legislation be primarily technical, with the moral secondary? Or, vice versa? (Recall that hollow legislation consists of congressional acts that contain deliberate ambiguities requiring resolution in the form of bureaucratic regulations.) In view of what some pundits describe as an increased interest in values in American politics, such questions may seem timely.

Both pro and con arguments can be identified. Shouldn't public administration thinking be involved in deciding (or making a contribution to answering) such questions?

On the pro side, arguments can be advanced (1) from the nature of the human, (2) from the nature of decision making, and (3) from the nature of the system. The first argument centers on the idea that, unless she is a person who privileges the moral over the technical, a manager should not be considered to be acting as a complete human being. This claim runs counter to the oft-repeated statement "I am just doing my job" or "I am just doing what I was trained to do," in other words, moral input is not part of how the job is defined. It is a claim of some poignancy when bureaucrats are considered to be too apt to privilege being team players at all costs. The second argument focuses on the idea that public officials should take the fullest (even infinite) responsibility for their actions. Should a planner who believes that euthanasia is immoral participate in designing a program that contains provisions for mercy killing? For more on infinite responsibility, see Drucilla Cornell and coauthors (1992); Cornell writes of the infinite responsibility for bloodless bureaucratic violence, claiming that an administrator cannot appeal to legal or other prescriptions or to a superior's orders. The third argument is the claim, valid or not, that such a moral change would upgrade the system.

On the con side, arguments can be advanced (1) from the multiplicity of values, including regrettable values, (2) from impracticality, and (3) from inadvisability. The first argument refers to the multiplicity of values, often conflicting and sometimes anti-social, for example, right to life versus right to choose; right to bear arms versus right to control guns. The second argument focuses on the claim that it is too hard for a bureaucracy to switch from the technical to privileging the moral. The third argument claims that privileging individual ethics would open a Pandora's box, allowing individuals to inflict their personal moral preferences on others (e.g., allowing those who oppose X to deny X to clients and customers).

Implication for Managing—Is Efficiency the Best Regulative Ideal?

Efficiency as the "ethic" of public administration (or "ideology that functions as the ethic" of public administration) is a mechanism for helping to achieve what

Machiavelli describes. That is, the ruler prescribes, and (subject to certain constraints, like the law and the Constitution) the public servant carries out the ruler's will efficiently. This account can be made more agreeable by substituting "the people" for "the ruler." Efficiency as public administration's "ethic" facilitates what (as noted above) Thrasymachus and Foucault describe. The stronger party, the elected official, prescribes. An ethic of efficiency encourages public officials to execute the ruler's prescriptions. Those opposed to the efficiency ethic can make the claim that it has a poor grip in the face of such "natural" tendencies as othering. They could suggest that only those who have never worked in a large bureaucracy would be naïve enough to expect efficiency to dominate; they could say that efficiency has too weak a motivation. Others would deny this characterization.

Should planners seek what is ethical (ethics as seeking) in a fresh way? There are alternatives to an "ethic" or "ideology" of efficiency. Are they better? Among these options are the Categorical Imperative and (again) love.

Efficiency and these alternatives are regulative ideals. That is, they are visions or benchmarks of what should be done even though, on a consistent or frequent basis, they might be impossible. Note that "always be efficient" is a regulative ideal that is hard (impossible?) to achieve at all times. Is it more or less hard (impossible?) to achieve a regulative ideal like "love your enemies as you love yourself"? The regulative ideal of efficiency and the alternative ideals have such a disadvantage; but oddly, what counts as common sense in traditional public administration is that efficiency is more "natural."

The categorical imperative offers a viable alternative to the efficiency ethic. Immanuel Kant's categorical imperative distinguishes between persons as means and persons as ends, and it prescribes that a person should not be treated as a means only. Customers or clients of a bureaucratic (or political or economic) system are not ends, to the extent that their primary role is to exist for the benefits of that organization or system. That is, they are not humans, unreduced. Clients of a department of taxation (or transportation) exist for the purpose of paying their taxes (or using transportation). For the political system, clients or customers exist for the benefits of governmental service. For the automobile sales agency, customers exist for the purpose of buying cars. And so on. Try applying Kant's categorical imperative on your next visit to the Department of Motor Vehicles or to a fast food outlet, treating the clerk as an end and not as a means only. Then, try it on a client.

The utilitarian prescription offers another alternative. The aim is the greatest happiness or good for the greatest number. Some may wish to argue that efficiency achieves this aim, perhaps employing arguments like the pro-technical claims earlier in this chapter. It would be easier to argue in this way if the efficiency calculus also included, as it typically does not, concern for extra-systemic side effects. It is unlikely that John Stuart Mill would accept that his sophisticated utilitarian view reduces to *efficiency all round*. As Mill ([1869] 1978, p. 224) comments in his *On Liberty*, "I regard utility as the ultimate appeal on all ethical questions; but it must be utility in the largest sense, grounded on the permanent interests of a man as a progressive being." Substituting goodness for happiness in the utilitarian calculus, clearly G.E. Moore would not buy the efficiency argument. However, there are difficulties with utilitarianism that mere efficiency avoids, for example, that the happiness of minorities in a utilitarian calculus can be sacrificed for the numerically superior units of happiness registered by majorities.

Love is yet another alternative for strategic planning. The prescription is that planners should be fueled by the regulative ideal of love for the whole person-in-herself in-her-difference (to use a phrase borrowed from French feminist thinking—see chapter 10). I (2005a, pp. 177–182) have also advocated love as a regulative ideal for public administrators. Remember the warning label, however. There may be more than one kind of love, and some readers may want something short of the extreme form they have in mind. In that case, consider relabeling this regulative ideal.

Other alternatives could have been discussed, such as caring. For example, see Catlaw (2009, pp. 318–332). See also Cunningham, 2009, pp. 300–302, and Kouzmin, Witt, and Thorne 2009, pp. 341–372.

Readers are invited to develop their own planning examples of the relevance of alternatives as regulative ideals. Should planning for the education of children with autism be based on efficiency, or on one of the other alternative regulative ideals when providing services to a particular child with autism (in the particular situation that exists for that child, e.g., poverty)? Should planning for welfare assistance be motivated by efficiency, or by one of the alternative regulative ideals for relating to the temporarily disadvantaged—in their particular circumstances? And so on.

Let's continue with love as an example, and perhaps the reader would want to reflect on parallel comments for the other alternative ideals. There are different forms or manifestations of love, as has been illustrated in the literature (e.g., Ackerman 1995). A distinction can be drawn between loving a mate and loving a neighbor, for example. Both sorts of love seem different from loving chess (although former world champion Bobby Fischer had an erotic attachment to the 64 squares) and from loving champagne (although an alcoholic might have that always on his mind): the love of a preying mantis (biting the head off its mate) must be different from that of a Persian cat.

Let's illustrate what is meant by individual differences. I can see, for instance, that some public sector jobs require more love than others, for example, a public school kindergarten teacher versus a garbage collector. Some tasks are more erotic than others, for example, a therapist in an old persons' nursing home (if you agree that therapy requires a kind of caring, a kind of individual loving) versus a lawn keeper at a public war memorial. But even within categories, there are individual differences. For instance, has a good professor never loved some students (and I don't mean sexually); or, has she had a loveless teaching career? I cherish the memory that some professors, now dead, loved me—just as others despised me. Even within these apparently loveless categories, there can be love that passes (escapes) my understanding, for example, the public war memorial tender who may love the dead soldiers. Oh dear, we are in unfamiliar territory, and it is so easy to poke fun! But parallel fun could be poked at the efficiency criterion, such as seeking efficiency when developing programs that could result in ecological catastrophe, seeking efficiency when developing doomsday weapons for use in space, and so forth.

Implication for the Underlying—Should Public Administration Ethics Be Certain or Authentically Hesitant?

On the one hand, some would argue for bold and certain action to combat (say) practices that seem clearly immoral. This is not at all a weak claim. There are some ethical principles that seem essential to a claim to be a full human. For example, it is inhuman, in my view, to enslave humans; in my view, it is inhuman to torture. Some would argue for such bold and certain action to combat (say) corruption. They might point to the advantages of curbing the corrupt aspects of lobbying, as one example (e.g., see Berry 1997). Large U.S. police departments, for instance, typically maintain anti-corruption units, and it is at least arguable that such programs cannot function well if they are not conducted boldly and with assurance. Obligingly (as it were), ethics in traditional public administration is typically understood as a matter of applying certain definite moral prescriptions, such as, "do not accept kickbacks."

On the other hand, others might point to the uncertainty of moral prescriptions. It is not necessary to go as far as arguing that ethics is an empty subject, dealing in wishful thinking, but that is not an untenable argument (as the logical positivists, celebrated in accounts of public administration's history, and others have held). Instead, an appeal can be made to the diversity of ethical systems and to the indecisiveness (noted above) of truth claims adjudicating between such systems. An appeal can be made to the interconnection between ethical prescriptions and their contamination with power considerations, noted in Question 5. Many a reflective person would confess that he had been normalized at his grandmother's knees into whatever moral truth claims he supports. Others would not.

Those like the philosopher John Caputo would declare themselves to be "against ethics." For Caputo, moral prescriptions are empty: "I have for some time now entertained certain opinions that I have been reluctant to make public. . . . I am against ethics. Here I stand, I cannot do otherwise" (Caputo 1993, p. 1). He concludes that the grounds for ethical claims are groundless; there is nowhere solid to stand. But Caputo is conscious of the practical problem of having to combat immorality in the world. "[S]urely, there is enough immorality in the world, enough unethical conduct in public and private life, without the philosophers coming out against ethics? Would it not be a better and more salutary undertaking, and certainly more in the public interest, to defend ethics against the detractor instead of implicating oneself in damaging its good name?" (p. 1). So we are back to whether it is desirable to tell (in Plato's Socrates' phrase) a noble lie. Those like Caputo prefer not to be unethical (as they see it) about ethics.

Standing against an arrogant "I know best" or "my system is right" attitude on the part of governing bureaucracies and persons in power, a better argument may be for the superiority of authentic hesitation. The hesitation can be authentic, without denying (as opposed to asserting) one's own convictions. Among the arguments for authentic hesitation are (1) the uncertainty or indecisiveness that surrounds moral claims, and (2) the advantages of being open to the Other—other persons and other perspectives. Such authentic hesitation has a long history in Western and Eastern philosophies, under such names as trust, toleration, mutual respect, mutual recognition, sympathy, public reason, and giving full consideration to the arguments of others.

Ethics as seeking is a form of authentic hesitation, laying primary emphasis on the seeking of the ethical rather than on claiming a definite conclusion. The seeking recognizes that something is wrong in justice thinking/acting as we have inherited it. I (2005a) have argued that what's wrong includes justice seeking that is too constrained in self-consciousness, too limited in considering philosophical style and lived experiences, too confined in a single disciplinary tradition, and stopping too short in its recognition of the complexities of concrete historical and cultural situations. Justice-as-seeking searches into the self (difficult, and thus hesitantly) and into the Other (equally hesitantly). Agencies should also search into themselves and into the other. Valuable for this are both reflecting on open-ended traditional insights (like the Golden Rule) and pondering literatures in "other" traditions (like the Confucian).

A rationale for such a shift can be formulated by appealing (again) to the paradox that it is not possible to live a fully human life without ethical principles—and, at the same time it is rationally impossible to be certain about the Truth of a particular perspective. To repeat this in public administration agency terms, one arm is that it is impossible for an agency to be all it can be if it operates without ethical principles—and at the same time another arm is that it is rationally impossible, especially in a society that values diversity, to be absolutely certain about the Truth (again) of a particular set of prescriptions. The grip of the paradox is that neither arm is weak.

Implication for the Field—Should Ethics Be Applied More Deeply to Macro Public Administration Issues?

Among the implications is that the public administration field should be adjusted to gain deeper ethical understandings in analyzing macro issues. Others may suggest other implications, for example, public administration specialists becoming more at home with meta-ethics, public administration specialists becoming more philosophical (more reflective, more open to argumentation, and more familiar with varieties of philosophical positions—as opposed to the ethos of an action subject like public administration or even political science) in their consideration of moral philosophical issues.

In speaking of deeper understanding in applying ethics to macro public administration issues, the contrast being drawn is between issues of concern to the individual public administration agency and those of concern to the public administration system as a whole—again, parallel to the distinction in economics. The claim here is not that micro moral issues are unimportant; it is that public administration macro moral issues frequently receive short or no shrift, being treated primarily by exception.

The traditional demarcation of the public administration field steers the thinker away from digging deep enough into the nature of macro public administration, and that in turn limits moral analysis of the macro. The achievements of Robert Moses, responsible for so many public works in New York State from the 1930s to the 1960s, provide an example of this. They provide a clearer example of a macro issue requiring applied moral examination. Robert Caro (1974), Moses's biographer, notes the bridges and underpasses on the parkways that were intentionally designed to be low—to permit only private cars. The bridges and underpasses were designed to exclude buses, and the intention was to prevent the poor and minorities from using the parks. The policy was being implemented, it is said, without knowledge of the public. The public administration thinker of that time would have been performing a macro service if she identified that this political, social, and administrative policy was being implemented by technological means, and if she had then gone further and subjected the "hidden" policy to moral analysis.

Technology in general is another *macro* example. The macro political, social, and administrative aspects of technology constitute a relatively neglected subject matter in traditional public administration. To be fair, they are relatively neglected in the social sciences. This has been expressed cogently by Ursula Franklin (1990). She explains the difference between a holistic technology and a prescriptive technology. Holistic technologies are normally associated with crafts, for example, cooking and weaving, and the artisan is in control, making decisions as the work proceeds. Prescriptive technologies are production processes that require precision, control, and (as the name implies) prescription, such as the production processes seen long ago in the Chinese Shang Dynasty's massive metallurgical production activity and, more recently, those production processes seen in the British industrial revolution. Such prescriptive technologies are used not only in materials production but also "in administrative and economic activities and in many aspects of governance" (Franklin 1990, p. 17). These prescriptive technologies have brought many benefits, such as higher living standards. They have also brought, in Franklin's view, "a culture of compliance. The acculturation to compliance and conformity has, in turn, accelerated the use of prescriptive technologies in administration, government and social services. The same development has diminished resistance to the programming of people" (p. 19).

Is Franklin right or wrong about (say) such a trade-off between productive technology and compliance? What can moral analysis (applied ethics) say about the current balance of such a trade-off? For the public administration field to answer the second question requires that the field be broad enough to answer the first question.

Implication for Public Administration Creativity—Is Ethics Related to the Spiritual?

Extraordinary imaginative creativity is required in expanding applied ethics to include the spiritual—as well as to correct the insularity of the subtopic of public administration ethics. By spiritual, I mean the kind of contrast that Robert Fogel describes between the spiritual and the material. It is neither intended to include, nor to exclude, religion.

Fogel, winner of the 1993 Nobel Prize in Economics, argues that the greatest mal-distribution in the rich countries is in terms of spiritual, not material, assets. The following indicates what he meant by the spiritual. He believes that it is necessary "to address such postmodern concerns as the struggle for self-realization, the desire to find deeper meaning in life than the endless accumulation of consumer durables and the pursuit of pleasure, access to the miracles of modern medicine, education not only for careers but also for spiritual values . . ." (Fogel 2000, pp. 176–177). He holds that self-realization should be understood in terms of fifteen spiritual resources; these include a sense of purpose, a vision of opportunity, a sense of mainstream life and work, a capacity to engage with diverse groups, an ethic of benevolence, the capacity to resist the lure of hedonism, the capacity for self-education, an appreciation for quality, and self-esteem.

Public administration ethics should embrace what Fogel calls the spiritual.

Epilogue

If he had been thinking of the PA context, would Lord Shaftesbury (1671–1713) have been right in his claim that there is no real love of virtue without the knowledge of public good?

Suggested Readings

Ehrenreich, Barbara. 2001. *Nickel and Dimed: On (Not) Getting By in America.* New York: Metropolitan Books. (The relevance of such observations to public administration was discussed at the 2008 annual meeting of the Public Administration Theory Network, following a reading from a play based on this book.)
Fogel, Robert. 2000. *The Fourth Great Awakening and the Future of Egalitarianism.* Chicago: University of Chicago Press.
Solomon, Robert C., and Jennifer K. Green. 2004. *Morality and the Good Life: An Introduction to Ethics Through Classical Sources.* New York: McGraw-Hill.

12

Public Administration from a Data Perspective

Data relevant to public administration can come (and do come) from positivist inquiries, and such positivist studies should be encouraged to continue even by those who consider hermeneutic analyses more hopeful and helpful. And vice versa. Data relevant to public administration can come (and do come) from hermeneutic interpretations, and such hermeneutic studies should be encouraged even by those who consider positivist data more helpful and hopeful. There is no inevitable clash between smart science and smart hermeneutics, contrary to what many say; they can coexist.

The first part of this chapter sketches the nature of public administration data. Five questions are discussed.

1. What are data? Aren't empirical data basic especially the quantitative??
2. What are data? What are scientific data?
3. What are data? What is a scientific proposition?
4. What are data? Can data come from hermeneutics?
5. What are data? Can data come from discourse theory?

The second part of this chapter goes on to discuss implications of a data perspective. The five questions discussed are as follows:

6. Implication for planning—Should public administration use both positivist and hermeneutic data?
7. Implication for managing—Is organization science feasible?
8. Implication for the underlying—Should public administration face up to rhetoric and symbols?
9. Implication for the field—Is the scope of the public administration field adequate?
10. Implication for imaginative creativity—Are life-changing data to be expected?

Sketching Data

It is unreasonable to ignore what positivism provides. It is unreasonable to ignore what hermeneutics provides. Let more than one flower bloom!

What Are Data? Aren't Empirical Data Basic, Especially the Quantitative?

Empirical data surely are important, e.g., for settling questions by the test of experience, and public administration should continue—and extend—its search for empirical data. But, as Martin Hollis explains, two difficulties arise. Human minds "are finite and . . . direct experience extends only to a small stretch of space and time." The other kind of "ignorance concerns the idea that the inner workings of nature are hidden from the five senses" (Hollis 1994, p. 4).

Statistics provides a quantitative technology for empirical science; it is a logic and methodology for the measurement of uncertainty and for an examination of the consequences of that uncertainty in the planning and interpretation of experimentation and observation" (Stigler 1986, p. 3). Note also that "Modern statistics is much more than a toolbox, a bag of tricks, or a miscellany of isolated techniques useful in individual sciences. There is a unity to the methods of statistics" (Stigler 1986, p. 4). Statistics has been recognized as an independent field only in the last century, although it existed before then.

Two features common in scientific and other disciplines can be found in statistics. First, and correctly, Leonard Savage begins his study of the foundations of statistics by noting that "the foundations are the most controversial parts of many, if not all, sciences." He observes in a striking passage that, "as to what probability is and how it is connected with statistics, there has seldom been such complete disagreement and breakdown of communications since the Tower of Babel" (Savage 1972, p. 4). In his view, this does not concern the mathematical properties, but the extra-mathematical properties, of probability. However, he reports that there is relative calm about foundations, probably due to the domination of statistics "by a vigorous school relatively well agreed within itself about the foundations" (p. 3). Second, there is a tendency for specialties to be parochial in denigrating alternative methodological perspectives. Savage notes that statisticians "have an understandable penchant for viewing the whole of the history of science as revolving around measurement and statistical reasoning" (p. 3).

What Are Data? What Are Scientific Data?

Deirdre McClosky offers what she calls the "ten commandments and golden rule of modernism in economic and other sciences." Earlier (1995) I listed them, and they state:

1. Prediction and control is the point of science.
2. Only the observable implications (or predictions) of a theory matter to its truth.
3. Observability entails objective, reproducible experiments; mere questionnaires interrogating human subjects are useless, because humans might lie.
4. If and only if an experimental implication of a theory proves false is the theory proved false.
5. Objectivity is to be treasured; subjective "observation" (introspection) is not scientific knowledge, because the objective and the subjective cannot be linked.
6. Kelvin's Dictum: "When you cannot express it in numbers, your knowledge is of a meager and unsatisfactory kind."
7. Introspection, metaphysical belief, aesthetics, and the like may well figure in the discovery of an hypothesis but cannot figure in its justification; justifications are timeless, and the surrounding community of science irrelevant to their truth.
8. It is the business of methodology to demarcate scientific reasoning from nonscientific, positive from normative.
9. A scientific explanation of an event brings the event under a covering law.
10. Scientists . . . ought not to have anything to say as scientists about the oughts of value, whether of morality or art (McClosky 1985, pp. 7–8).

Public administration has not done well in what passes as administrative science; consider item 9, for example. Reader, how well do you think that public administration has done on the basis of McClosky's criteria?

What Are Data? What Is a Scientific Proposition?

The nature of a scientific fact is contested. More generally, the nature of a fact (what is referred to in a true proposition) is a contested fact. For some, a scientific proposition is epistemologically privileged. That is, a proposition like "two bodies attract one another in direct proportion to their masses and indirect proportion to their distance from one another" (a general proposition that is independent of a particular time and place) offers greater assurance of being true than a nonscientific proposition. A scientific proposition is more worthy of being believed. For others, a scientific proposition is just like any other proposition—no more privileged than my report (if it is raining) that it is raining. For some, facts are independent of interpretation. For others, there are no facts, only interpretations; see Friedrich Nietzsche, for example.

Estimates of the status of a fact range, it can be said, from minimal to large. At one end of the range, there are no uninterpreted facts. At the other, facts are as plain as the end of your nose. The latter claim is that what we count as facts are really real. Claims to know the really real take us to the realm of metaphysics, and we encounter difficulties of the kind that can be illustrated by physics attempting to cope with the ultimately real—from a period when atoms were considered the smallest indivisible particles of matter, to a period when some spoke about sub-atomic particles as if they were arranged like billiard balls, to a period when people speak about quarks, and beyond.

The idea that facts emerge by themselves is simplistic, of course. For those who want to say that all that is needed on the science side is good observation, recall philosopher of science Karl Popper. Famously, Popper used to challenge audiences to "observe." They would then wonder, "observe what?" His point was that a proper science should begin with theorizing, not with observation: for him, all observations are theory-laden. As Paul Diesing (1991, p. 31) explains Popper, a "proper science ought to begin with theorizing, not with observation. If we begin by looking around, we will not know what to look for and will not notice much. We should begin by inventing a hypothesis."

Scientific data are enough for causal explanations of behavior, and positivist data should be sought. Use of the data should not be discouraged by the fact that there is no consensus in the philosophy of science about the nature of a scientific proposition. In the strong terms of John Wisdom (1987, p. 69), "hardly anyone in this scientific age knows what the nature of science is." This could be supported by reading about the puzzles in philosophy of science, such as the puzzling problem of induction. Philosophy of science has a huge literature. It is also very exciting; just read Karl Popper, Thomas Kuhn, Imre Lakatos, or Paul Feyerabend.

What Are Data? Can Data Come from Hermeneutics?

Yes. Hermeneutics provides understandings about human action, compared against explanations of behavior. It provides reasons for such action, compared against causes of behavior. It interprets meanings and values. It can interpret the story, the text, behind a wink. It is not limited to a blink. Hermeneutics aims to interpret (clarify, bring out) the meaning of any such text. Text would include any governmental or bureaucratic action, any societal action, any citizen group's or individual citizen's action.

"We are now under the aegis of the hermeneutic or interpretive tradition in social theory and its governing imperative that the social world must be interpreted from within," writes Martin Hollis (1994, p. 143). He continues, "In its full splendor it is a very grand tradition, with as strong a sense of the underlying movement of history as rationalists or realists have ever had of the hidden order of nature. In this aspect it is often termed 'historicist' and its tutelary genius is Georg Wilhelm Friedrich Hegel (1770–1831)."

A difficulty with hermeneutics is that one interpretation can be replaced with another interpretation. Karl Apel and Jürgen Habermas argue that successive interpretations (e.g., of history) lead to better understandings. Hans-Georg Gadamer disagrees; his view is that each successive understanding is different.

What Are Data? Can Data Come from Discourse Theory?

Yes. Discourse theory (which, of course, is hermeneutic and which also includes nonverbal discourse) has achieved important results in non–public administration disciplines such as philosophy, sociology, linguistics, psychology, critical theory, postcolonial studies, and postmodern feminisms. Discourse theory arrived later in public administration. The account of discourse theory offered in *Language of Public Administration* (Farmer 1995) relied on theorists like Ludwig Wittgenstein and Michel Foucault. But there are others, such as Mikhail Bakhtin and his concept of a voice within a text. Most discourse theorists would agree that all discourses—all claims about meaning—are located within constraints that are mainly unconscious. These constraints include the institutional, the social, and other contexts within which we do our thinking: they limit our thinking.

The constraints of our discursive practices structure our sense of reality. Recall a contrast between police officers and social workers. Police officers typically think of the world as tending to consist of good guys and bad guys, for instance, while social workers typically see the world as tending to consist of needy clients and others. "To give a trivial example from the surface level, an NYPD police inspector, in 1972, faced with a secretary who was habitually late for work, threatened that he would lock her up 'for theft of services'; . . . a social worker is unlikely to see the world in such terms" (Farmer 2002, p. 274). Large police departments, as mentioned in chapter 11, typically have internal affairs units, whereas social work departments that do would be exceptional. The creative administrator—police or social work or any other kind—should seek data not only about things "out there," but also about the functioning of her own consciousness—and her own unconscious. Discursive practices can limit us to perceiving as real only a certain portion of total reality. They can limit the admissibility of linking one set of statements with others, blocking possible claims.

Implications

"The status of social science is seriously in doubt," writes Andrew Sayer (1992, p. 1) in the first sentence of his book, *Method in Social Science*. He continues, "Outsiders' attitudes towards it are often suspicious or even hostile, and social scientists themselves are deeply divided over what constitutes a proper approach to social research. The uncertainty has been heightened by increasing doubts in philosophy about traditional views of scientific objectivity and progress."

Implication for Planning—Should Public Administration Use Both Positivist and Hermeneutic Data?

Both positivist and hermeneutic data can enrich planning. For examples on both sides, consider police planning. Police administration is a specialty independent

..c public administration field but clearly a conceptual element within public ..ministration practice.

On the positivist side, the Kansas City Response Time Study (Bieck 1977, 1979, 1980) was a positivist experiment that showed the need to reconceptualize police response time. It led to other positivist experiments in, say, differential response time systems and in management of demand. It indicated the need to revamp the planning of police services, which since the 1967 President's Commission on Law Enforcement and Administration of Justice had centered much effort and money on response time reduction, for example, in operations research, in computer-aided dispatch systems, and in using average response times as performance criteria. The Kansas City study, later replicated in other jurisdictions, showed that rapid response is important in only a minority of incidents. It reported, for example, that 62 percent of the Part 1 crimes and 51 percent of all crimes are not discovered until after the perpetrators have left the scene, and rapid response to effect arrests or locate witnesses is largely irrelevant. Also, even where "witnesses are involved while the crime is occurring, the impact of rapid police response is often nullified by delays in citizen reporting. The number of "arrests attributable to rapid response is small—in this study in only 3–7 percent of the Part 1 and 5–6 percent of the Part 2 crimes. Many on-scene arrests could have been made regardless of police response . . ." (Farmer 1981, p. 25). How could response time be reconceptualized? Rather than thinking of response time merely as the interval between the moment the police agency receives a call for service and the arrival time of the squad car, it is necessary to include the citizen mobilization interval—the time it takes a citizen to report the incident. "The citizen mobilization interval, the forgotten element in response time, [was] large in Kansas City—48.1 percent of the total response time for Part 1, 51.7 percent for Part 2, and 49.3 percent for noncrime incidents" (p. 25).

The City of Wilmington Split Force and Management of Demand experiments discovered unrecognized relationships and fresh possibilities (Tien and Cahn 1980; Tien, Simon, and Larson 1979). On relationships, for instance, one result was recognition that "citizen satisfaction depended not on rapid response, but on the difference between observed and expected response" (Farmer 1981, p. 25). Wilmington found it possible to "manage" some 22.5 noncritical calls for police service. Noncritical calls were handled in one of four ways. The call "could be formally delayed up to thirty minutes, with the citizen being advised; it could be handled by telephone, with no further departmental action; the citizen could be asked to walk into police headquarters; or the caller could be advised that the department would return the call at a prearranged time" (p. 25). What is the situation now? I don't know; I have not followed it since 1990. (For more on police research, see, e.g., the Executive Session on Policing and Public Safety, Harvard's Kennedy School of Government and U.S. National Institute of Justice, NIJ, March 2009.)

On the hermeneutic side, consider another police planning example—a change in conceptualization developed by Elinor and Vincent Ostrom and the Workshop in

Political Theory and Policy Analysis at Indiana University at Bloomington. Note the reconceptualization whereby police departments are viewed as an industry rather than in organizational terms. In other words, the police text is reinterpreted. Now, no claim is being made that Vincent and Elinor Ostrom considered their work as hermeneutics; they considered it behavioral. Yet, in fact, this adjustment was hermeneutic or interpretivist. Vincent and Elinor Ostrom (1965) borrowed the concept of industry ("a set of interrelated public enterprises which makes common use of a common body of knowledge and methods in the production of similar goods or services") from their understanding of economics, and pointed out that "the concept of an industry can . . . be applied to the provision of police services by the many local, state and federal agencies [which] use closely related production methods to attempt to control similar sets of events in relation to similar objectives or intended outcomes." They describe the "police industry" in eighty standard metropolitan statistical areas. In doing so, they acknowledge what they describe as the crudity of the term, acknowledging that the precise boundaries for any industry cannot be specified. Police administration is typically treated as if it were confined to the administration of single public administrative entities. For one thing, this tends to marginalize consideration of private police, with its greater volume of manpower than exists in public policing. For another, it narrows the idea of a police manager to exclude mayors and other officials who are "police managers" in a wider sense. For yet another thing, and this was a main point for Elinor and Vincent Ostrom, application of the concept of police industry results (in their view) in overturning the idea of duplicative waste in the provision of police services.

For more examples of hermeneutic studies useful for police planning, consider those generated within police agencies. How much "science" is there in any "police science" in such reports? Favorite among my examples are reports on corruption in the New York City Police Department (NYPD). The Knapp Commission's *Report on Police Corruption* (1973) gives an excellent account of the forms of corruption then prevalent in the NYPD, surely important for any planning that was subsequently undertaken. So does the *City of New York Commission to Investigate Allegations of Police Corruption and the Anti-corruption Systems of the Police Department* (Mollen 1994).

Implication for Managing—Is Organization Science Feasible?

Yes, positivist organization theory presents conclusions that should be considered. But, it is unclear why other sources should be excluded, unless one holds the untenable view that all nonscientific data are unhelpful.

First, let's speak for positivist organization study. Positivist organization theory holds that organizations can be explained by scientific laws that relate organizations to material features in their contexts, and that conclusions from such positivist work yield laws that are invariant across all types of organizations and cultures. Such research is reported to have started in a series of works in the 1960s (Donaldson

1996), each relating the organizational features to their contexts. For example, Blau (1970) and Pugh, Hickson, and Hinings (1969) are reported to have shown that organizational size determines organizational structure, and Chandler (1962) showed that organizational strategy determines the required organizational structure. Situational "factors of environmental instability, technology, size and strategy came to be called contingency factors. Likewise, this body of work came to be called contingency theory" (Donaldson 1996, p. 2). Such theory is characterized as determinist "in that managers are seen as having to adapt the organizational structure that is required by the contingency factors, in order to gain organizational effectiveness" (Donaldson 1996, p. 3); it is methodologically positivist and informed by empirical research. It is also consciously scientific in style, seeking to emulate the natural sciences.

Such positivist organization theory has been challenged by anti-positivists. Also, as would be expected, particular results have been challenged; for example, Blau's theory about organizational size has been criticized as not recognizing that size is multidimensional, and Blau's view has been defended as well (e.g., see Donaldson 1996, pp. 147–158). On the general criticisms, Lex Donaldson (p. 159) concludes that "anti-positivism has fared poorly. The attempt to remove determinism has foundered. . . ." He also finds unsatisfactory the attempts to use types or configurations of organizations and the attempts to replace the "generalizing approach of positivism by the far more localized program of organizational systematics . . ." (p. 159).

Donaldson quotes the well-known poetic comment from the philosopher David Hume from Hume's *Enquiry Concerning Human Understanding*: "When we run over libraries, persuaded of these principles, what havoc must we make? If we take in our hand any volume; of divinity or school metaphysics, for instance; let us ask, Does it contain any abstract reasoning concerning quantity or number? No. Does it contain any experimental reasoning concerning matter of fact and existence? No. Commit it then to the flames: for it can contain nothing but sophistry and illusion" (Donaldson 1996, p. 163).

Second, let's speak for hermeneutic studies, such as insights offered by discourse theory (see Question 5 above) and, say, cultural studies. Ziauddin Sardar and Boris Van Loon tell us that "Cultural studies started as a dissenting intellectual tradition outside academia, dedicated to exposing power in all its cultural forms, but it has now become a discipline and a part of the academic establishment" (Sardar and Van Loon 1997, p. 168).

Think of the relevance, say, of Christopher Lasch (1979) in the *Culture of Narcissism*. To the extent that one supposes that the cultural constitution of managers conditions and shapes managing, why should such studies be neglected by managers? Wouldn't the kind of people available be of interest to (say) human resources managers—or human capital managers?

For the general drift of Lasch's argument, just look at some of his chapter headings. They include changing modes of making it, the degradation of sports, schooling and the new illiteracy, the socialization of reproduction and the collapse of authority, the flight from feeling, and the shattered faith in the regeneration of life.

Then there are relevant histories and even literature—and more. Reading histories is two-edged; some are soporific and mind closing, others are liberating. For the liberating histories, let Howard Zinn's *A People's History of the United States* (1999) be a broad-brush symbol. "These-Arawaks of the Bahama Islands were much like the Indians on the mainland, who were remarkable (European observers were to say over and over again) for their hospitality, and their belief in sharing. These beliefs did not stand out in the Europe of the Renaissance, dominated as it was by the religion of popes, the government of kings, the frenzy for money that marked Western civilization and its first messenger to the Americas, Christopher Columbus" (p. 1).

Reading and listening to literature and stories can provide useful public administration data. In the nineteenth century, Charles Dickens was helpful with his "exposés" of Victorian life (e.g., "Please sir, can I have some more?" said Oliver Twist). Now it has extended to few—very few—television shows. Let the HBO television show *The Wire* (a "cop show" in a sense) be a contemporary symbol for the liberating literary. The fifth and final season of the show addressed the media, portraying how the social, political, and economic realities of American cities cannot be solved without a reformed media. As series creator David Simon indicates, the problems of the modern American city "will not be solved until the depth and range of those problems is first acknowledged. And that won't happen without an intelligent, aggressive and well-funded press" (www.hbo.com/thewire/about/).

Stated Leo Strauss, the political philosopher, "a contemporary novelist with a reasonable degree of competence tells us much more about modern society than volumes of social science analysis" (Strauss 2001, p. 7).

Implication for the Underlying—Should Public Administration Face Up to Rhetoric and Symbols?

Both positivism and hermeneutics can contribute to understanding what underlies public administration. Re positivism, note what neuroscience (see chapter 9) can contribute to explaining the working of the unconscious. Re hermeneutics, see chapter 8 and Freud's account of the superego, the ego, and the id; also see Jung and Lacan.

Understanding what underlines public administration should also turn to the field of New Rhetoric, which focuses on the symbolic. On symbols, Kenneth Burke described New Rhetoric as rooted in . . . the use of language as a symbolic means of inducing cooperation in beings that by nature respond to symbols" (1969, p. 43). In politics, Murray Edelman (e.g., in his *Politics as Symbolic Action*) called attention to political symbolizing. In policy analysis, Deborah Stone is among those who have written about the centrality of symbols. In economics, Deidre McClosky has written about the rhetoric of economics. Symbols are a means of influence and control, and there is a strong connection between symbols and symbolic systems and what counts as true.

Symbols can be read as having a variety of meanings, conscious or unconscious, stable or flickering, obvious or obscure. That is why we need New Rhetoric to help us interpret public administration situations. As I've said before (e.g., 2005a), beware large flags behind the boss's desk, a commonplace in the U.S. government. They're not just to express the director's loyalty. Beware the elevated head table at a conference. It's not just elevated to make it easier for the plebs to see. Beware the fatherly talk from the agency head, reminding us that we are all members of a family. It's not just to reassure us that we should be brotherly (and sisterly) to one another. It's also to remind us that he is daddy. *Things* are certainly important, and they require attention. Yet so do *symbols*, which pile on other symbols—often giving mixed and subliminal messages.

Implication for the Field—Is the Scope of the Public Administration Field Adequate?

No. Outside the boundary walls of the public administration field are valuable public administration inputs. Public administration theory and practice should recognize that they lack not only data but also theories, techniques, and insights from an array of non-PA disciplines. This book emphasizes such a lack. Earlier, I (2005a, pp. 26–27) referred to the lack resulting from excluding political science, economics, political economy, moral philosophy, sociology, civil society, the complex of action subjects like business administration, social work—and beyond. An ideal turf would include subjects relating to the biological, the social, and the spiritual; it would include history and literature, and the history of political ideas and the history of economic ideas. It would also include all the administrative specializations—not only business administration but also hotel administration, police administration, sports administration, and so on.

A caveat. The contention is that public administration lacks enough such data and theories, techniques, and insights. It is not denied, however, that some traditional public administration specialists have taken pride in the osmosis whereby public administration ingested some data etc., from outside disciplines, like psychology.

Implication for Imaginative Creativity—Are Life-Changing Data to Be Expected?

Publications that are considered by successful and creative public administration thinkers to have changed their professional ways of thinking should be sought. Prominent public administration thinkers were asked what book, if any, changed their professional lives. The answers are reproduced in the Suggested Readings section below, and it is recommended that the reader limit herself (or himself) to reading what catches her (or his) eye in the long listing.

Most people don't expect books relating to public administration to be life changing. I'm not criticizing books relating to public administration any more than books relating to subjects like economics, political science, or other disciplines. Life confining is par throughout the gamut of such fields.

I agree with those who want to call into question what is typically counted as a "real" public administration book. Is it *The White Goddess* or *Budgeting for the Billions*? I don't think that any of the participants in this project would think that being interested in the hills outside our own public administration valley is a deficiency. What are offered are books that are described by successful public administration thinkers as public administration life changing.

Epilogue

And now to the next chapter and to Reflection Exercise 2.

Suggested Readings: Life-Changing Books

The following two questions were among those asked of the distinguished public administration thinkers.

1. What book, above all others, changed your professional life? (Book?)
2. What, in a sentence, is the book about? (About?)

Answers were published in *Administrative Theory and Praxis* (Farmer 2003).

From Robert Denhardt, Arizona State University

1. Book? Sheldon Wolin, *Politics and Vision.*
2. About? A great book throughout, *Politics and Vision* has a final chapter titled, "The Sublimation of the Political" that describes the rise of an organizational society in many ways displacing traditional political categories of membership and engagement. It suggested a political theory of organizations.

From Sandra Kensen, Tilburg University, Netherlands

1. Book? Bruno Latour, *Science in Action.*
2. About? The book shows how scientists make facts: facts are not there to be discovered. Latour writes as if he is telling an adventure. Latour is a true narrator.

From Gary Wamsley, Virginia Polytechnic Institute and State University

1. Book? Philip Selznick, *Leadership in Administration.*
2. About? Selznick [offers] ideas about institutions, missions, cultures, socialization processes, the creation and maintenance of cultures, elite cadre selection, language, myths, symbols, icons, etc. and their power and influence over behavior. . . .

From Louis Howe, State University of West Georgia

1. Book? Michel Foucault, *Discipline and Punish.*
2. About? The book is about a series of techniques of power—"the disciplines"—that, while they pervasively govern people in detail, they do so in ways that do not set off the alarm bells set by constitutional limits on power.

From Mohamad Alkadry, Old Dominion University

1. Book? Edward Said, *Orientalism.*
2. About? [The book is about] the colonial and postcolonial delineation of the cultural boundaries of the Orient.

From Peter Bogason, Roskilde University, Denmark

1. Book? Charles E. Lindblom, *The Intelligence of Democracy.*
2. About? The message of the book is that there are many other ways to coordinate than by hierarchy. And one thread that runs through my writings over the years is that although hierarchy is somewhere in the vicinity most of the time, people prefer to resort to other means. And Ed Lindblom has a wonderful description of such mechanisms—of what he calls mutual adjustment.

From Bob Cunningham, University of Tennessee

1. Book? Roger Fisher and William Ury, *Getting to Yes.*
2. About? [Re: Fisher and Ury], looking for creative ways to solve problems so that the whole is greater than the sum of the parts has become a way of life, challenging my previously held zero-sum assumptions. From the many bruises I had incurred before, I knew zero-sum was wrong: so adopting GTY was easy and comfortable. . . .

From Rupa Thadhani, Virginia Polytechnic Institute and State University

1. Book? Helene Cixous, *Vivre l'orange.*
2. About? What I gathered at the time from the book was about writing, about inspiration, and about Clarice Lispector's influence on Cixous's writing.

From Curt Ventriss, University of Vermont

1. Book? Alberto Ramos, *The New Science of Organizations*, and Karl Polanyi, *The Great Transformation.*
2. About? Both of these books, in their own unique way, have developed a critique of the underlying assumptions of modern public affairs—that is, they both raise the salient issue that a market-centered society is inexorably linked to a market orientation that rules so freely through our political, economic, and administrative veins.

From Patricia M. Patterson, Florida Atlantic University

1. Book? James C. Scott, *Domination and the Arts of Resistance: Hidden Transcripts.*

2. About? Scott brings a fascinating array of historical, literary, and anthropological understandings to a learned and cheerful study of off-the-record interactions between powerful and powerless people; he reveals disguised and unobtrusive forms of political struggle and resistance where other authors have revealed only despair.

From Richard Box, University of Nebraska, Omaha

1. Book? Herbert Marcuse, *One-Dimensional Man.*
2. About? Marcuse presents a description of society using his version of Frankfurt School political economy: it is powerful and disturbing.

From Camilla Stivers, Cleveland State University

1. Book? Dwight Waldo, *The Administrative State.*
2. About? Anyhow, you were probably looking for books that are much more unorthodox, but that's honestly the one that hit me like a ton of bricks and has never stopped.

From Mark Rutgers, Leiden University, Netherlands

1. Book? Peter Winch, *The Idea of a Social Science and Its Relation to Philosophy.*
2. About? What is social science about, i.e., how does the study of the social world differ from the physical world.

From Michael Spicer, Cleveland State University

1. Book? Friedrich Hayek, *Constitution of Liberty.*
2. About? Hayek's book is about the relevance of the limits of human reason in modern governance and public policy.

From Ricardo Schmukler, Independent, Argentina

1. Book? Robert Graves, *La Diosa Blanca* (*The White Goddess: A Historical Grammar of Poetic Myth*).
2. About? What, in a sentence, is the book about? It is about poiesis, poetic myth, the sacred and the profane in the poetic fabric of languaging and everyday life in a time [before] patriarchal domination. Then, it can be said that it is about musical comprehension—thinking and acting as gifted by the love of Muse, the White Goddess. In almost one sentence, at least.

From J.J. Hendricks, California State University, Stanilaus.

1. Book? Theodore Roszak, *Person/Planet.* That book introduced ideas that evolved and matured in his *Voice of the Earth.*
2. About? Roszak, historian and novelist . . . does a lot of things in the book on alienation in the environment and culture. . . .

From Gary Marshall, University of Nebraska, Omaha

1. Book? Robert Denhardt, *In the Shadow of Organization.*
2. About? The book is about the limits of instrumental rationality, the importance of

personal development and the need for an ontology of public administration that goes beyond economic exchange and power.

From Tansu Demir, University of Texas at San Antonio

1. Book? Paul Feyerabend, *Farewell to Reason.*
2. About? The book was about the critique of reason, as reason had been understood in Western civilization. In the book, Feyerabend was debunking Western civilization, the instrumental reason on which Western civilization is based, and was talking about the destructive and oppressive consequences of the reason [that] Western civilization employs.

From Frank Scott, California State University, Hayward

1. Book? M. Scott Peck, *The Road Less Traveled.*
2. About? The central theme of the book is the link between honesty, suffering, and growth, and specifically that our personal growth depends upon following the "road less traveled," the often painful path of personal growth that depends upon being honest with both ourselves and others.

From Michael Harmon, George Washington University

1. Book? Gibson Winter, *Elements for a Social Ethic: The Role of Social Science in Public Policy.*
2. About? In nutshell, what Winter did was explain, convincingly to me, how the then-preeminent "styles" (or, following Burrell and Morgan's later appropriation of Kuhn's term "paradigms") in American social science necessarily imply, while at the same time concealing, normative and ideological commitments. Winter labeled these styles Behavioralist, Functionalist, Voluntarist, and Intentionalist, the last of which (and, to him, the preferred style) served as his term for Schutzian phenomenology.

Part II

Synthesis for Theory and Practice

13

Synthesizing:
For Public Administration Planning

What can we learn about public administration planning? What should we learn about such planning, in its complexity, from synthesizing the implications of the multiple perspectives? Let's reflect on how all of the perspectives, taken together, relate to the selected public administration element—to planning. Recall Reflection Exercise 2, described toward the end of chapter 1. It invites readers to develop their own hermeneutic assessment. Reflection Exercise 2 consists of two steps— summarizing the implications of the various perspectives identified for planning, and synthesizing these summaries plus input from other implications (e.g., what underlies). This chapter offers my summaries and synthesis. Readers may want to use them as points of departure for their own assessments.

Uncover more of what is hidden. Be more open to the macro and longer term. Use epistemic pluralism. These are among elements of the synthesis offered. The synthesis includes the suggestion(s) that public administration should encourage policy, program, and administrative planning for agencies that aims to uncover more of what is hidden. It includes, for another thing, embracing a macro administrative plan for the public administration discipline that meets these aims. It includes fostering the use of epistemic pluralism. Such planning, it is recognized, is constricted by public administration's subordination to the political, for example, subordination of agencies to political appointees.

This chapter consists of three sections. The first section relates to step 1 of Reflection Exercise 2. It summarizes of the implications for public administration planning from each of the perspectives discussed in this book. The second section relates to step 2 of Reflection Exercise 2. It presents an account of a synthesis. Distinguished from a minimal synthesis (i.e., limited to one or two perspectives), this is a grand synthesis in that it encompasses a larger number of perspectives— including what may turn out to be dry holes. The third section speaks about the slogan *"more uncovering of what is hidden."*

Summarizing in a Context of Complexity

Readers should recall the complexity of planning. With such recognition, the summaries will be sharper—more to the point. My own summaries are offered here.

Recall that it is false to suppose that planning is planning is planning. The complexity of planning can be illustrated by recognition, as suggested in chapter 1, that planning has different levels and overlapping types. Public administration courses tend to focus on the midlevel bureaucrat, for instance; others can have a different slant. Some courses, as another example, have appropriated specific disciplinary approaches, such as those public policy courses that center on rational choice.

Take the matter of levels. Is the planning the same when it is done by a strategic planner or by a planner at the lower end of the ladder? At the highest rung of the ladder, Philip II of Spain was a royal bureaucrat. He presided over the "rise of what we might call the 'paper state' in the early modern period." Peter Burke (2000, p. 119) explains that Philip was nicknamed "the king of paper" because he spent so much time at his desk learning about and controlling his subjects. He adds that Louis XIV the Sun King, Frederick the Great of Prussia, Catherine the Great of Russia, and Maria Theresa of Austria were in the same mode. Such examples remind us to be less inclined to chop off levels—all levels of top—of the "paper state," for example, by such ideological moves as declaring political appointees to be beyond the scope of public administration practice. Being political doesn't preclude being also bureaucratic, and vice versa. We should be less inclined to leave political appointees like department and agency heads to political science, as if such officials played no part in planning.

On the lower rungs of the ladder, is planning in a research and planning unit the same as planning by a first-level supervisor? Is it the same as it is for a mail carrier or a firefighter? There have been studies of street-level bureaucrats. Yet we should remember from Barbara Ehrenreich (2002) and from Prioleau Alexander (2008) that white-collar workers like you and me do not readily understand the differences between blue- and white-collar situations. There can be a loss of practicality when the bottom is lumped in with the middle, as if differences make no difference.

Take the complexity of overlapping types of planning. It is a mistake to treat planning as a single term. Chapter 1 asked whether planning of one kind (e.g., administrative planning) could not be considered central in traditional public administration, while another kind (e.g., policy studies and policy analysis) is considered to be on the circumference. There I explained that I was borrowing a distinction made by Dwight Waldo (1956, p. 157) between activities in the center and at the circumference of public administration. The discourse, the world, of the policy analyst is distinctive. I quoted Spiker (2006, p. 1) speaking of policy analysis in practice as encompassing policy formation, public sector management, and policy analysis and review. Others write of the policy analysis field as "committed to science and its methods" (e.g., Heineman et al. 2002, p. 1), and still others point out that the "study of public policy is now a well-established component of several academic disciplines, as well as having a literature, professional association, and theories of is own" (Peters and Pierre 2006, p. 8). Then there is administrative planning of various levels and types. It is worth repeating that a particular discourse of planning should not dominate our reflection. We should avoid becoming entrapped in the specialist literatures of planning, although they are important.

Summarizing Implications

Here are the implications for planning from the selected perspectives discussed in the previous chapters (Question 6 in each chapter). The implications are as follows.

From a Business Perspective

Macro public administration should develop a strategic plan for public administration as a whole. It can select from among the ten-point list for an entrepreneurial model for government, offered by Osborne and Gaebler (1992). This entrepreneurial model is for catalytic, community-oriented, competitive, mission-driven, results-oriented, customer-driven, enterprising, anticipatory, decentralized, market-oriented government. For specifics, see chapter 3 (a business perspective).

From an Economic Perspective

For public administration strategic planning, adopt Vincent Ostrom's *Paradigm of Democratic Administration*. This paradigm stands against perfection of hierarchical ordering relating to a single center of power. It also stands against hierarchical ordering of a professionally trained public service. For planning, use the economic or rational choice model. For more of the propositions from Ostrom's paradigm, see chapter 4 (an economic perspective).

From a Political Perspective

For strategic planning for public administration, implications point the way to the more philosophical. A first implication for public administration planning is to embrace policy studies and policy analysis more thoroughly. A second implication is to embrace political philosophy in a genuine philosophical sense, as exemplified by thinkers like (say) Leo Strauss, applying such insights to public policy issues of relevance to bureaucracy. A third implication for such planning for public administration is to emphasize the sovereign and guiding character of the U.S. Constitution. For more explanation, see chapter 5 (a political perspective).

From a Critical Theory Perspective

Seek emancipation toward the lifeworld. For public administration planning, a principal aim should be to constrain the world of bureaucratic and other systems and to privilege the lifeworld. That is, emancipate self over system. Turn to the observation that discourse theory "is emerging in public administration as a way to recapture a sense of public administration outside the narrow confines of management technique and efficiency. It seeks to free citizens and administrators from reified, theoretical preconceptions and institutional constraints, allowing them to recreate themselves and their institutional arrangements in current discourse settings" (Box 2005, p. 91). Attention is also invited to genuine citizen participation. All this would seek to constrain the world of bureaucratic and other systems. For more on Jurgen Habermas's account of the lifeworld, see chapter 6 (a critical theory perspective).

From a Post-Structural Perspective

Recognize deconstruction as a significant resource for public administration planning. It can be valuable in coping with, for instance, the symbolic, metaphors, and binary oppositions. Recall that examples of important symbols in public administration include, for instance, big government, leader, balanced budget, and the American Dream. It is hard to penetrate, as it were, through symbolism to what otherwise could be considered the real. For further comment on deconstruction, see chapter 7 (a post-structural perspective).

From a Psychoanalytic Perspective

Macro and micro public administration strategic planning should recognize and "use" the unconscious in coping with what counts as public administration common sense. Recognize the ideas of Sigmund Freud, Carl Jung, Jacques Lacan, and others, such as Cornelius Castoriadis. See the latter's beautiful line, for instance: "Each society, like each living being or species, establishes, creates its own world, within which, of course, it includes itself" (Castoriadis 1995). For comments on the unconscious, see chapter 8 (a perspective of psychoanalysis).

From a Neuroscience Perspective

For public administration planning, recognize and evaluate Richard Restack's claim that neurosociety will emerge in the first half of the twenty-first century. Public administration should plan to contribute to the shaping of any such emergence; public administration planning and policy making should come to terms with such brain-based prospects and developments. Also, the advent of neurosociety promises to change the very language game needed for effective public administration planning and thinking. That is, neuroscience may join in tipping the balance against the constraints of what counts as administrative common sense. Should public administration's aim be less than the aim in neuropolitics and neuroeconomics, academic movements on the circumferences of (respectively) political science and economics? For a description of these claims, see chapter 9 (a perspective of neuroscience).

From a Feminist Perspective

For public administration planning, seek to overcome othering of customers, citizens, and diverse groups that are not-us. For example, a client should not be reduced to a mere bureaucratic pigeonhole or a mere presenting problem. This sort of othering is suggested by a feminist perspective because a parallel form of othering has been experienced for centuries by females. Women have tended to be seen as sex objects by men, who have relative power in a patriarchal society. As indicated, a man can simply be a tinker, tailor, cabinetmaker, lawyer, and so on. Isn't the constraint that a woman can only be a woman tinker, a woman tailor, a woman cabinetmaker, a woman lawyer? For a description of this and more on what is meant by treating each person as a whole person-in-herself in-her-difference, see chapter 10 (a feminist perspective).

From an Ethical Perspective

An ethical perspective raises the question (among others) of whether ethical considerations should be primary in any planning input from public administrators. More precisely, should the regulative ideal be that each and every planning input from an administrator (or from a planner) be primarily moral, with a technical subtext—or should actions be primarily technical, with a moral subtext? For more on this question, see chapter 11 (an ethical perspective).

From a Data Perspective

Both positivist explanations and hermeneutic understandings can be valuable for planning and policy making. For one thing, public administration planners and administrators should assist political appointees and other planners to learn what underlying explanations and understandings are relevant to policy and other planning questions. For more on this, see chapter 12 (a perspective of data).

From a Traditional Perspective

Is there help enough for planning? Planning has always been important for public administration, and it was noted that P (planning) was the first letter in the now-outdated POSDCORB acronym. Agency micro planning is a staple of administrative life, as is well known. From the early years of traditional American public administration, the discipline itself did have a macro plan—emphasizing budgeting, staffing, organizing, and generalist administering. Macro planning also was reflected in administrative histories. Yet arguably, public administration specialist interest in macro planning has been relatively lacking in the more recent years. Such diminishment has been encouraged by a variety of factors, like the public administration context of lack of confidence in government. Such diminishment is unsurprising, however, to the extent that traditional public administration is primarily concerned with (to repeat the point) middle-level management and with the shortterm, and to the extent that macro planning is considered within the provinces of the political, of specialist programs (like urban studies, criminal justice, etc.), and of policy analysis.

Synthesizing

Five claims are used to synthesize the implications for public administration planning of the multiplicity of perspectives. As part of Exercise 2, readers are invited to substitute their own views. So we should first turn to methodology.

Readers should not lament the lack of a simple cookbook when undertaking a hermeneutic activity like synthesizing. But they should be aware of the complexity. The synthesizing should cope with, as will be explained, the facts that each of the five public administration elements are interrelated and that prejudices can distort.

The hermeneutic aim of synthesizing is to interpret the meaning of the implications. Hermeneutics refers (as discussed in chapter 12) to the interpretation of a text, elucidating the underlying meaning. A text is any kind of writing or situation or action that can be interpreted.

The hermeneutic approach that I prefer is that developed in the wake of Gadamer, Habermas, Apel, and Ricoeur, and it seeks the underlying meaning of a text by thinking of the overall story that best brings together the text's important elements. I should repeat that this approach thinks in terms of a hermeneutic circle that tries various interpretations until, considering all components, the "best fit" understanding is reached about the meaning. It is the best fit in that it takes account of all the specifics and does so in proportion to their importance. For a description of my use of the hermeneutic circle, see Farmer (1995, pp. 26–29). But two points should be stressed. First, the reader is not at all obligated to follow the hermeneutic circle, or the form of hermeneutics that I have used. Readers will recognize that there are good and bad and indifferent—and sometimes great—interpretations.

Complexity occurs in that planning in practice is co-embedded with other public administration functions. Reporting, budgeting, policy making, efficiency-seeking, privatizing, creating, managing symbolization, anti-corruption management, bureaucratic-speak, citizen participation in bureaucratic decisions, stereotyping, and human capital management are practices that are implicated in planning. Chapter 1 also mentioned that there is even planning for managing, for organizing, for staffing, for directing, for coordinating, and for each of the other functions. This makes synthesizing for planning more complicated in that the implications for managing, for what lies underneath, for the public administration field, and for imaginative creativity should also be recognized.

Complexity also occurs within the synthesizer's conscious and unconscious prejudices, and we return to this in chapter 18 when discussing work and lived experience. In retrospect, the most impressive (to me) part of my planning experience is what I did not know. I was excited when functioning as a budget analyst, for instance, to see the logic of connecting planning with budgeting and then programming—and then to evaluation, looping back to planning. It all seemed so logical. It was only many years later that I came to understand about lobbying— ironically, about the connection of money (in such forms as campaign money) and budgeting and planning, and so forth. It is significant for readers (and me) to attempt honest self-reflection. As we all know, such honesty is not easy; it is often blocked by unconscious drives.

Synthesis and Public Administration Planning

The implications for public administration planning can be synthesized—in my view—in the following five suggestions. These suggestions are intended for emphasis both when public administration is able to plan independently and when it has a role that is subordinate to political officers charged with policy-making responsibility.

1. When advising political superiors and when conducting their own independent planning, public administration thinkers and practitioners should excel in uncovering more of what is hidden. They should include uncovering relevant scientific and hermeneutic results, including those about forces that underlie public administration. Policy, program, and administrative planning in public administration should include uncovering more of the longer run and the macro.
2. The public administration discipline should develop its own strategic plan for good governance.
3. The public administration plan should use epistemic pluralism in order to reflect more on public administration as a discipline. This reflection should include the aim of reflection for its own sake, critical reflection, and seeking what is just and right. It should include putting administration and policy and programs, as it were, on the analytic couch.
4. Public administration thinkers and practitioners should aim to advocate (both when advising political superiors on planning and when conducting their own independent planning) policies, and programs and administrative arrangements that would seek societal emancipation toward the lifeworld.
5. When advising political superiors and when planning independently, public administration thinkers and practitioners should aim to exceed a regulative ideal confined to mere efficiency; alternatives include, for instance, caring and loving. This should include aiming to overcome othering, by

seeking administrative action that recognizes the whole person-in-herself in-her-difference.

Public Administration Planning as Uncovering

Readers should aim to push the envelope in their reflecting, in identifying their own synthesis. The envelope, it will be recalled, refers to the artificial constraints of habit that inhibit counterintuitive ideas.

The thoughts here are intended to help this process. They concern point 1, that public administration thinkers should seek to excel in uncovering. Let Martin Heidegger be an inspiration, if you like, in his description of truth as an uncovering, as unveiling! Truth or aletheia, for him, is disclosedness.

Point 1 states that when advising political superiors and when conducting their own independent planning, public administration thinkers and practitioners should excel in uncovering more of what is hidden. They should include uncovering relevant scientific and hermeneutic results, including those about forces that underlie public administration. Policy, program, and administrative planning in public administration should include uncovering more of the longer run and the macro.

Four examples are offered here. They concern police planning, ideology, the spirit of our age, and the concept of democracy. The first example uncovers a false assumption about the utility of police preventive patrol—and I start with this example because it is clearly down to where the rubber hits the road. The second refers to uncovering ideological roots in, say, policy evaluation. The third uncovers a feature purported to be a component of the spirit of our age. The fourth purports to uncover the false assumption that PA-think can stick with business as usual, without being transformed by the increasing influence of others. The point of the examples is to speak to the utility for planning of uncovering; the point is not the examples in themselves. If she disagrees with (or dislikes or resents or is offended by) the particular examples, the reader should feel free to substitute her own examples. To repeat, the aim is to help the reader's thinking about uncovering the counterintuitive.

Example 1: Police Planning

Scientific studies have uncovered some, and can produce more, valuable counterintuitive input for "practical and everyday" longer-term planning and programming in such specialty areas as police management. Hermeneutic and interpretive studies also have uncovered—and can uncover—valuable counterintuitive input. This point was already made in chapter 12. I want to re-emphasize it.

Examples include positivist studies conducted long ago on the utility of police preventive patrol, uncovering evidence that questions the utility of the huge investment of resources and attention into preventive patrolling. To assist in recognizing the practicality of such studies, recall that the financial cost of a patrol car in an assigned area 24 hours a day 365 days per year is not just the purchase price of a single patrol car. It also includes the total of the salaries of the five officers it takes to cover that one-officer beat for the year; the salary cost doubles when each car contains two officers.

A study was conducted in Kansas City, Missouri, on the effects of changes in preventive patrol levels. This study was different from the rapid response time study, also conducted in Kansas City and discussed in chapter 12. "Fifteen beats were used in the study. Beginning in October 1972, the number of marked police cars was increased by three times to five of these beats (the proactive beats); it was maintained at the same level in five matched (control) beats; and preventive patrol was eliminated, apart from that associated with police responding to calls for service, in five other matched (reactive) beats. Victimization, opinion and reported crime data were analyzed for the year-long duration of the study. 'What the experiment found is that the three experimental patrol conditions appeared not to affect crime, service delivery, and citizen feelings in ways the public and the police often assume they do'" (Kelling 1974, p. 3).

Most public administration planning—and most police planning—is not at all positivist, nor need it be. The 1972 Master Plan, which I prepared for the City of New York Police Department, is an example. The police commissioner stated that the plan "features efficiency, effectiveness and responsiveness to community needs." It provided for an effort to upgrade patrol services by introducing programs in ten major areas—the allocation of manpower, field operations, management practices, organization, personnel, patrol function, utilization of civilians, administrative procedures, equipment, and other departmental programs impacting on patrol. On field operations, for instance, plans were presented (and executive responsibilities assigned) for directed patrol, proximity patrol, model precincts, anti-crime patrol, precinct intelligence networking, optimal policing of details, crime apprehension and service cars, court alert system, arrest vans, scooters, park/walk/talk program, daily patrol log, and public assistance in crime prevention. A parallel comprehensive plan was developed for the detective bureau, which in those days was organizationally separate from the patrol.

Example 2: Ideology and Policy Evaluation

Policy evaluation and creation can be improved by uncovering what underlies in terms of rigid ideology. In his *Ideological Budgeting*, Steven Koven (1988, p. 26) tells us that policy "evaluation and creation will improve if rigid interpretation of dogma can be identified, controlled and replaced with more neutral analysis."

Koven observes, "In the extreme case, ideological budgeting reflects blatant irrationality justified on the basis of emotion and passion." He describes it as a threat to neutrality and intersubjectivity in the evaluation of public policies. He points out that such neutrality and intersubjectivity are "not realities today" because of the many abuses of policy analysis. Koven (1978, p. 169) goes on to explain that "Commonly cited policy abuses include the eyewash (looking only at good aspects of programs), the whitewash (covering up program failure), the submarine (destroying a program regardless of its worth), postponement (delaying necessary action), and substitution (shifting attention to the less relevant but defensible aspect of a program)."

Example 3: Spirit of Our Age

Turn to James Carroll (2006), although the author surely would be astonished to learn that he has made a contribution to public administration planning or to micro public administration. In homage to his father, Lieutenant General Joseph Carroll, James Carroll describes the more than sixty-year history of the Pentagon Building, and he tells the story—as he should—in the context of the rise of American world power and of the development of nuclear capability.

Carroll describes what he considers to have been the unconscious momentum that shaped not only the history of the Department of Defense but also public attitudes and government in the United States. The momentum remains a component of the dominant mindset (or set of mentalities) in society. This doesn't mean that all individuals in a society are equally infected by that mentality. But, for Carroll, it is the driving dynamic, co-shaping thinking and action. There are positive components in society's mentality, such as ingenuity, energy, and competitiveness. But Carroll wants to alert his readers to the negative features that he considers more important. I am not in a position to say whether all his interpretations are correct. I'm not concerned whether his "meta-narrative" could be bettered by, say, a Freud or an Althusser, and I don't know whether Carroll's story contains all relevant elements—the changing consciousness, the flickering "reality" of rhetoric, and so forth. The reader will wish to reflect on whether the negative dynamic is significant in planning related to nondefense areas like, say, prison administration.

A stunning political claim: Carroll claims that, with the establishment of the Pentagon, the center of power in the United States shifted to the other side of the Potomac River. For example, he analyzes how the building came to "symbolize, and to promote, a massive bureaucratic power center broken loose from the checks and balances of the government across the river . . . and apparently broken loose from the constraints of human will" (Carroll 2006, p. 27). Starting with the devastating bombing of cities in World War II, he describes how the marriage of traditional martial destructiveness and unlimited technological capacity set in train a virtually unstoppable momentum. Of course, this is not totally new information. Carroll quotes Defense Secretary William Cohen as comparing the building with Moby Dick, for instance, with Cohen casting himself as Ahab strapped (at least in the movie) to the back of the whale. Many have discussed the perils of nuclear weaponry; Helen Caldicott (2002), for example, has much to say of importance to public administration. Carroll speaks of the shift in the meaning of "military objectives" from an insistence on military targeting to include "any living thing that moves" (p. 99). As he explains, what "the population of the Pentagon had in common was not the warrior's ethos but the functionary's" (p. 29). I can relate to this, as I recall my experience in the headquarters of the NYPD; we lived within the tunnel view of a poor man's Vatican, where ranking police officers—like bishops—were a dime a dozen. Previously, I have quoted Gulick as saying that "Students of administration do not need to be concerned about the 'next war'—the military planners will take care of that—but they do need to be concerned with extracting from recent experience its rich harvest for the immediate management problems of a chaotic world" (Gulick 1948, p. viii).

The momentum that Carroll describes is made up of a variety of components. Here are three, the last of which underscores an important reason for public administration planning attention. First, there's the "self-fulfilling paranoia." It's a mindset that expects "the worst from enemies—and the rest of the world as well. The 'paranoid style,' when adopted by the defense intellectuals, was not only justified but made to seem the height of rationality, able to be articulated even by the formulas of hard science" (Carroll 2006, p. 213). Carroll is using the term "paranoia" in a usual sense, indicating a "psychiatric disorder involving systematized delusion, usually of persecution" (p. 137). A delusion is defined in Kaplan and Sadock (Sadock and Sadock 2003, p. 283) as "a false belief, based on incorrect inference, about external reality, not consistent with patient's intelligence and cultural background"; I specially note Kaplan and Sadock's additional statement that a delusion "cannot be corrected by reasoning." In terms of international relations, it's the kind of dynamic that can make it difficult to distinguish the normal pushiness of large countries (or communities) and the desire that no "other" country (or community) should injure us. It is paranoia that can make us blind to the effects of our own actions in shaping the actions of others (Carroll gives Soviet actions as his example), and that can prevent us from accurate interpretation of intelligence (Carroll illustrates with the West's failure to understand the political significance of Stalin's death). To give a more recent example, Stephen Cohen (2006), in his article entitled "The New American Cold War," points to conditions in Russia as constituting what he considers the gravest threat to American security, and he comments that "The dangerous fallacies underlying U.S. policy are expressions of an unbridled triumphalism, treating Russia as a defeated nation" (2006, p. 16). On the domestic front, the attitude can be illustrated by the passage in ten U.S. states of legislation making it easier to use deadly force in self-defense. "Supporters have dubbed the new measures 'stand your ground' laws, while critics offered nicknames like the 'shoot first,' 'shoot the Avon lady' or 'right to commit murder' laws" (Tanner 2006). Carroll describes how, oddly, the first U.S. secretary of defense, James Forrestal, is said to have yelled, "The Russians are coming!" a few days before hurling himself to his death from the fourteenth floor of the Bethesda Naval Hospital, where he suffered from a private problem of paranoia.

Second, Carroll describes the momentum as privileging revenge, discussing the revenge implications of Pearl Harbor. He claims that the momentum includes nuclear amnesia and military eagerness to launch a nuclear strike (2006, p. 212). Impulses like revenge can be complex, as perhaps Shakespeare's revenge play *Hamlet* is telling us. Exclaims Hamlet, "What a piece of work is a man, how noble in reason, how infinite in faculties, in form and moving how express and admirable, in action how like an angel, in apprehension how like a god?" (*Hamlet*, II.ii.304–308). Harold Bloom (2003, p. 87) describes this utterance by Hamlet as coming closest to being "a central statement." Yet the play ends with the stage piled with corpses, from both sides.

Third, there's a twin dynamic. As Carroll (2006, p. 138) puts it, "fear of an enemy outside is accompanied by fear of an enemy inside." He traces this back to 1789, with the Alien and Sedition Acts. For that matter, recall the history of the un-American activities investigations. The point is that the delusional spirit of militarism and paranoid revenge is not a mere "military" thing. The existence of the mindset has an impact on nonmilitary bureaucracies, like such inhumanity as is in the immigration service, and what Carroll calls the militarization of the State Department. To make this clearer, "They Deserve It" is the title of one article, with the subtitle "Male prison rape is still not taken seriously, despite the huge number of victims" (Bell 2006, p. 18). Public administration planning should pursue other possibilities, determining whether this mentality infects, for instance, the internal revenue and welfare services.

The negative momentum, described by Carroll, deserves attention for public administration planning interested in grasping the spirit of the times. Carroll's inter-pretation raises unpleasant "facts" about which many are happy to have amnesia, for example, the effects of the accumulation of nuclear weaponry. Yet, I disagree with Carroll on lesser points. Three small examples: First, Carroll does not emphasize the momentum in terms of growing nationalism, which John Lukacs says is difficult to separate from patriotism. "Patriotism is defensive; nationalism is aggressive" (Lukacs 2005, p. 36). Second, Carroll does point to antecedent incidents of revenge, giving the example of the revenge of starting Arlington Cemetery in General Lee's garden. Arguably, he should have made more of the pre-Pentagon violence that has reportedly been a factor in national history since the not-so-gentle Puritans first landed (see Philbrick 2006), such as the violence reflected in high crime rates, gun ownership, the slaughter of native Americans, and the scar of slavery. Third, there is the economic. Carroll does recognize the effect of the momentum on the economic system. He makes the claim that "Because of Red Scare activities, Americans would accept the maturing of an economic system that, in its effects if not its structure, condemned most of the world to crushing impoverishment" (2006, p. 214). But he could have made more of the role of the economic in nourishing the momentum, when segments of the economy have become so dependent on defense juice.

Public administration planning should not buy a helmet and go military; that is not my point about false assumptions. Rather, public administration planning should be open to the totality of the government (and governance) range—including the military—so that it can gain better understanding of the dominant mindset of our society and our age. Public administration planning should be alert to the positives—and the negatives—of the spirit of our age.

Example 4: Social Science and East Asian Input

"I firmly believe that the entry of East Asians into the social sciences is going to transform how we think about human thought and behavior across the board" (Nisbett 2005, p. 226). Relevant to public administration's false assumptions, this is a striking sentence about public administration thinking as business-as-usual.

On business as unusual, there is the false assumption that the Western "mentality" is the *only* way of thinking and acting about public administration and its planning, that is, that PA-think should stop at the water's edge of Western mentality (or mentalities). Differences have been claimed between Asian and Westerner by writers like psychologist Richard Nisbett (2005), who does not intend to stereotype entire continents or to deny individual variations. Nisbett depicts and analyzes contrasting orientations, as self-reinforcing homeostatic systems, between Asian thinking (which he defines, rightly or wrongly, as influenced by China) and Western thinking. My interest is in illustrating that it is false to claim that the habits of mind with which public administration is familiar are the only ones available. I'm not concerned whether each of Nisbett's particular contrasts are correct, although others have offered some similar contrasts (e.g., Graham 1992, on the attitudes toward the law of noncontradiction). I'll pick out only a sample of Nisbett's other examples. The mentality dominant in the West, as opposed to the Asian, classes objects in terms of attributes, rather than resonance; it sees the world as a collection of diverse objects (after Aristotle), rather than substances. Paralleling such differences, one chapter title in Nisbett (2005, pp. 137–163) asks, "Is the world made up of nouns or verbs?" Nisbett holds that the Western mentality views societies as aggregates of individuals, while there is no word for "individualism" in Chinese. (The "closest one can come is 'selfishness'"— p. 51.) The Western mindset concerns itself more with the control of others and the environment, rather than self-control.

False Assumptions in Other Social Sciences

Don't all the mainstream social sciences and action subjects include false assumptions relevant to public administration and planning? Here is an example from political science. A similar case is available for yet other disciplines, such as economics, history, and philosophy.

Political science as-it-is—rather than as it is *ideally*—tends to attract false assumptions. One such assumption may be the genealogy of democracy, falsely seen as simply a Western gift. Amartya Sen (2005, pp. 13–14) notes in his book *The Argumentative Indian*, "Even though it is very often repeated that democracy is a quintessentially Western idea and practice, that view is extremely limited because of its neglect of the intimate connections between public reasoning and the development of democracy. . . . Balloting can be seen as only one of the ways—albeit a very important way—to make public discussions effective, when the opportunity to vote is combined with the opportunity to speak and listen, without fear." Sen shows that "traditions of public discussion exist across the world, not just in the West" (p. 13). He gives illustrations from the histories of parts of Asia, Africa, and Europe (Sen 2003). In a recent class, an African doctoral student repeatedly made a similar claim about the prevalence of "palaver" throughout Africa. (I notice the ethnocentric definition of palaver in the *Oxford English Dictionary* as "a talk, a conference, a parley, especially between African tribes' people and traders or travelers." It also offers some unflattering descriptions, like "unnecessary, profuse, or idle talk.") Sunil Khilnani (1999, p. 59) analyzes how democracy is "today at the very center of the Indian political imagination." On the other hand and still excluding the one billion Indians, Nisbett claims that "the whole rhetoric of argumentation that is second nature to Westerners is largely absent in Asia" (Nisbett 2006, p. 73). Yet, I notice the scare word "largely," and I recall that argumentation can take various forms. Also, notice Nisbett's later comment that "we all function in some respects more like Easterners some of the time and more like Westerners some of the time" (Nisbett 2005, p. 229).

Epilogue

Public administration and planning should include focusing on uncovering false assumptions, even if the unveiling is unpleasant. It should do so even if the other disciplines don't. This requires some courage.

Suggested Readings

Berry, Jeffrey. 1997. *The Interest Group Society.* 3rd ed. Boston, MA: Longman.
Jun, Jong S. 2006. *The Social Construction of Public Administration.* Albany: State University of New York.
Pinker, Steven. 2002. *The Blank Slate: The Modern Denial of Human Nature.* New York: Penguin.
Rabin, Jack. 1992. *Handbook of Public Budgeting.* New York: Marcel Dekker.
Weimer, David L., and Aiden R. Vining. 1992. *Policy Analysis: Concepts and Practice.* 2nd ed. Englewood Cliffs, NJ: Prentice Hall.

14

Synthesizing:
For Public Administration Managing

What can we learn about public administration management? What should we learn about public administration managing, in its complexity, from synthesizing the implications of the multiple perspectives?

More visioning, less *othering*! Public administration should embrace a visionary management style that at least seeks to avoid *othering*. This style seeks to avoid *othering* perspectives, employees, clients, and other institutions. It seeks this aim, for instance, in its expectations from subordinates and from educational programs, for example, from MPA programs. These expectations include ensuring that subordinate managers also embrace the visionary and reject *othering* in managing budgeting, personnel, and other areas. Avoiding *othering* perspectives implies epistemic pluralism and including capabilities within agencies, such as employing staff competent in sets of disciplinary perspectives.

Reflection Exercise 2 (described in chapter 1) asks readers to think through the contents of such management style using the suggestions that are offered in this chapter on implications and synthesis. The approach is parallel to that indicated in the previous chapter for planning. Identifying implications (Step 1 of Reflection Exercise 2) includes recognizing complexities in conceptualizing managing. Synthesizing (Step 2) requires recognizing related implications from the other public administration functions, for example, visionary management is interconnected with imaginative creativity.

This chapter is divided into three sections. The first section (relating to Step 1) summarizes the implications for public administration management from each of the various perspectives. The second (Step 2) offers a synthesis for management. The third section speaks about the slogan *more visioning, less othering.*

Summarizing in a Context of Complexity

Complexities in understanding *managing* exist in terms of level and kind and context. It is indeed a mistake to think that managing is managing is managing. See chapter 1. On level and kind, are the level and kind of managing in the Treasury Department the same as managing a wastewater treatment plant? On context, the orthodox period thought of seven management functions—POSDCORB (planning, organizing, staffing, directing, coordinating, reporting, and budgeting). Later this came to include others, such as managing external relations and public relations.

Complexities arise also from the fact that the meanings of managing change as the boundaries of managing vary. The "boundaries" for understanding *managing* can be drawn more or less narrowly, as explained in chapter 1. Included or excluded can be this or that terrain, for example, nonprofit or military administration.

Implications for management from the selected perspectives are as follows. They are described in each chapter under Question 7.

From a Business Perspective

For management, an implication is to explore the business management literature for useful techniques. Supply chain management (SCM), which over time should make a larger appearance in public administration, is a clear example. SCM has a large and growing literature, and it is described as becoming increasingly prominent in business management. For more on supply chain management, see chapter 3 (a business perspective).

From an Economic Perspective

For managing, seek the powerful insights available from public choice economics. For the inside of bureaucracies, public administration management should engage such ideas as the budget-maximizing bureaucrat and the "rational" tendency of bureaus to overproduce. For the outside of bureaus, management should take advantage of economic analyses of such PA-relevant topics as lobbying, interest groups, and the conditions required for optimal outsourcing. For more on these items, see chapter 4 (an economic perspective).

From a Political Perspective

Bureaucracy should be managed consistent with a democracy, and not just like a business. More visionary and reflective management analysis is needed that focuses on the longer run. Public administration theorizing should contribute to refining understanding of the basis of such democratic-bureaucratic policy (e.g., in political philosophy) and to shaping specific policies for such a democratic purpose. This will speak, for example, to appropriate citizen participation. It should speak to obstacles (again) like lobbying. This implication is consistent with what Janet and Robert Denhardt call new public service, speaking of seven lessons for public administration. Among these lessons are to serve citizens, not customers; to value citizenship over entrepreneurship; to recognize that accountability is not simple;

to serve rather than steer; and to value people, not just productivity. For more on these claims, see chapter 5 (a political perspective).

From a Critical Theory Perspective

For managing, seek to emancipate clients and subordinates and ideas. Seek to administer anti-administratively. Anti-administration is described as aiming to include not only mainstream ideas and people, but also ideas and people that are other. It also seeks to include nonmechanical, as well as mechanical, understandings. For more about anti-administration (nature, examples, rationale, and history), see chapter 6 (a critical theory perspective).

From a Post-Structural Perspective

For managing, post-structuralism also points toward the value of anti-administration. This is the same implication that was identified from the critical theory perspective. For an explanation in terms of imaginization, deconstruction, deterritorialization, and alterity, and for references to writers like Foucault, Lyotard, and Deleuze and Guatarri, see chapter 7 (a post-structural perspective).

From a Psychoanalytic Perspective

For managing, turn more fully to psychoanalytic theory. More psycho-storying and re-storying are implied. Traditional public administration already includes psycho-elements, like human relations theory and psychological organization theory. More valuable results can be anticipated from managing that makes greater use of Freudian, Jungian, and Lacanian theories. For more details, see chapter 8 (a psychoanalytic perspective).

From a Neuroscientific Perspective

For public administration managing, seek powerful neuroscientific understandings of how and why the self (including the administrative self) thinks, feels, and behaves. For examples such as that a self is primarily an emotional being who thinks (rather than primarily a thinking being who has emotions), and for the neurobiology of fear, see chapter 9. For commentary on how the self constructs its own image in such terms as movement, aggression, ideology, individual differences, and stereotyping, see the same chapter (a neuroscientific perspective).

From a Feminist Perspective

Public administration management should adopt better alternatives than mere efficiency as a regulative ideal. This perspective invites consideration of what the ideal of efficiency denigrates, obstructs, demeans, pushes to the edge. Love and caring have been suggested as alternative regulative ideals for managing, and there is a valuable literature on each. The practice of love includes the ideas of caring-for, being-with, the individual whole person (citizen, client, customer), even if that person is uncooperative with the bureaucratic process. The practice of caring has been described by Tronto in terms of four integrated phases. These are *caring about, taking care of, care giving,* and *care receiving.* For more on these claims, see chapter 10 (a feminist perspective).

From an Ethical Perspective

This also suggests that managing should seek better alternatives than mere efficiency as a regulative ideal. Alternatives include a regulative ideal based on the ethics of the categorical imperative, utilitarian ethics, and an ethics of love. For more, see chapter 11 (an ethical perspective).

From a Data Perspective

For public administration managing, seek data from positivist organization theory, without supposing that all nonscientific data are subjective and unhelpful. Also use hermeneutic data without supposing that all scientific data are unhelpful. For more commentary (including that on positivist organization theory), see chapter 12 (a perspective of data).

From a Traditional Perspective

More profound and more visionary upgrades could be expected if public administration management thinking could focus more on the longer run, and if the fact that there are different levels of managing could be more keenly appreciated. Traditional public administration has been in hot pursuit of what practitioners and the public are supposed to deem to be practical—and that has been the shorter run. Yet it is in the longer run that what is socially constructed can be adjusted.

There has been a limiting tendency to regard short-term public administration practice as a given or natural kind, rather than to recognize it as socially constructed. Jon Jung describes seven limitations of modern public administration practice. These include vertical governing (hierarchical administration), professional dominance (so much reliance on experts), instrumental-technical rationality, complexity, placating citizens, dualistic thinking, and reification (mistaking socially constructed entities for natural kinds). For more of each of these points, see chapter 2 (a traditional perspective).

Synthesizing

More visioning, less *othering.* Five claims synthesize the implications for public administration managing, giving appropriate weight to relative importance of the implications. Step 2 of Reflection Exercise 2 invites readers to substitute their own views, using the suggested claims as a springboard.

Complexity means that the synthesizing must recognize the implications identified not only for managing but also those indicated for the other public administration features. This chapter speaks of visioning, for instance; but an implication discussed in chapter 8, question 9, for the public administration field discusses the relevance of Freud to understanding visioning. Managing, planning, what lies underneath, the PA field, and imaginative creativity are, as suggested, interrelated. It is through managing (and planning) that features like imaginative creativity can be expressed.

Complexity during the synthesizing process also means recognizing our own prejudices. When I was a public administration manager, what I saw was conditioned by my context. Common biases are to equate the good of the customer with the good of the program, the good of the program with the good of the agency, and the good of the agency with the good of me (the manager).

The following prescriptions are suggested as synthesizing the array of implications:

1. Embrace a visionary management style that seeks to avoid *othering*. This style seeks to avoid *othering* perspectives, employees, and clients.
2. Seek nonhierarchical management arrangements and practices. Manage in ways consistent with nonhierarchical democracy, honest transparency (rather than mainly public relations agency-justifying talk), genuine citizen participation (rather than mainly "sham" participation). Adopt a less hierarchical regulative ideal than mere efficiency.
3. Aim to administer anti-administratively, seeking the ethical.
4. Develop deeper understandings of the administrative self (e.g., through more extensive use of psychoanalytic and neuroscientific insights). Pursue deeper understandings of the agency (e.g., storying and re-storying, with such aims as deconstructing what is socially constructed yet what appears given).
5. Emphasize understanding management at the macro and longer-run levels, without neglecting the micro and shorter run.

Public Administration Managing as More Visioning, Less *Othering*

Readers should aim to push the envelope in identifying their own synthesis. Speaking about *more visioning and less othering*, these thoughts are intended to help this process. The thoughts concern point 1. That point reads: *Embrace a visionary management style that seeks to avoid* othering. *This style seeks to avoid* othering *perspectives, employees, and clients.*

In visioning that seeks to avoid *othering*, shouldn't managers aim for more self-consciousness about the features of their visioning by considering four sets of options? Let's call these options the descriptive versus normative, the visceral versus academic, the process versus end-state, and the comprehensive versus partial options.

Shouldn't managers play with possibilities to identify what their imaginations can tell them about these features? They may also reach down to the unconscious. Recall chapter 8 and the suggestion that analyses of dreams can be applied to public administration visioning, distinguishing between self-visioning and other-visioning. It described self-visioning as referring to the public administration discipline's or an agency's or a manager's self-conception. It described other-visioning as referring to conceptions that others have of public administration.

A start could be made by considering:

- Herbert Simon for the descriptive versus normative option (at the American Political Science Association in Washington, D.C. in September 2000)
- Aung San Suu Kyi for the visceral versus academic option (at the International Political Science Association in Quebec, Canada, in August 2000)
- Francois Delesse for the process versus end-state option (at a rally of the Peasants' Confederation at Avignon, France, in June 2000)
- Jose Bove (accents omitted, as on all French words in this chapter) for the comprehensive versus partial option (at McDo's, August 1999, in Millau, also in France)

Think first about the *descriptive versus normative* option for a successful visionary public administration manager. Should a vision describe how things can be explained? Or, should it offer a picture of the ethical—the normative? Herbert Simon delivered the 2000 ASPA annual meeting's John Guas lecture, "Public Administration in Today's World of Organizations and Markets." Simon covered many points and he did so with panache; we will limit ourselves here to only two or three. For some, the most striking of his claims were that markets cannot operate without organizations; that the most significant event of the past several hundred years has not been the growth of markets but the growth of organizations; and that economic theory is in a troubled state. It seemed to me that the first two of these claims are essentially Economics 101/102; and the third requires the telling of the positive, as well as the negative, sides of the story. The most valuable feature of these claims, although what Simon said should not have been news to many, was that he said what he did—and he carries the weight of a 1978 Nobel Prize winner. The most astonishing indicator of our own political-economic discourse (and no criticism of Simon) is that he could be right that the Guas-attendees would appreciate to be reminded of the first two obvious facts. It is also that, even though there are cruel limits in rationalizing economics, the audience would not want to know both sides of the story about economic theory. Yes, we do tend to emote in binary terms—X is either completely true, or completely false. Let us go on to speak in binary terms, recalling that there can be value in binary terms as long as we remember that they are eventually deconstructible. Was the vision, represented by the three interesting points in Simon's lecture, descriptive or normative? It seems reasonable to ask this of Simon, as he could "jocularly" say that he still believed (sadly, he is now dead) in the fact-value distinction. What he said was clearly descriptive. Yet, there was a normative implication. But, as he would be the first to say, the normative implication has no force—no grip—without normative premises.

Turn next to the *visceral versus academic* option for the successful visionary manager. Should she speak with her body, her passions, her life experiences, her corporeal spirituality, her head, and all else that constitutes her—or should she use her academic or official voice? Aung San Suu Kyi, general secretary of the National League for Democracy in Burma, was a "speaker" at the 2000 International Political Science Association (IPSA) conference via a clandestine video tape. Winner of the 1991 Nobel Prize for Peace for her "non-violent struggle for democracy and human rights," she had become in 1988 the leader of Burma's democratic opposition. She and her party won the Burmese election in 1990. But the military regime ignored the election results and has since kept her under house arrest. As the Nobel Committee Chair said, Aung San Suu Kyi "unites a deep commitment and tenacity with a vision in which the ends and means form a single unit. Its most important elements are: democracy, respect for human rights, reconciliation between groups, non-violence and personal and collective discipline." (Shortly after the IPSA meeting, she spent many days trapped by the military in a car by the side of the road.) First the IPSA audience endured very long speeches by one official and two academics, delivered in impeccable officialese and academese. No disrespect intended. Then the smuggled videotape of General Secretary Kyi was introduced to the IPSA audience by a member in exile of her "shadow" government. He was Bo Hla-Tint, a man who (in the event of his return to his country) faces either death or twenty-five years in prison for having won in 1990 a parliamentary seat in Burma. Then, intermingled with the whirring on the tape's audio track of the machines intended to foil the dictatorship's listening devices, Aung San Suu Kyi on tape exposed her heart. At the end, we all applauded politely; after the shock had passed, many of us wept.

Turn now to the *process versus end-state* option. Should a visionary manager focus on procedures (say, in administration) or outcomes in people's lives? For instance, should there be a procedural vision, as if excellence in bureaucratic or political procedures can guarantee all one wants to guarantee? Or should one focus on the end-states? Francois Delesse, president of his town's section within the association, took me to a rally of the Peasants' Confederation just outside Avignon. Francois is a loveable and gregarious thinking man, and a man who never talks unless passionately and intelligently, a sparkling delight to be with. A retired teacher, he is a practitioner and convinced believer in the "way of life" of the rural people in Provence, the first Roman province in Gaul. He lives with Claude, his wife, in Vaison la Romaine in the Vaucluse, a Provençal region where (arguably) sublimity is everyday. Amid vineyards and cherry orchards, his house looks directly toward Mt. Ventoux, said to be in 1336 the first mountain climbed for personal "pleasure" (by the poet Petrarch). Nearby is Nyons, one of the world's premier-quality olive oil production areas; nearby are the justifiably famous wine areas of Gigondas and Chateauneuf du Pape. This is a way of life that includes attaching importance to putting people and community first, to the cultivation of good food and good rural living, and to the Provençal and French traditions that revolve around individual (e.g., walking, driving incredibly fast) and community activities (e.g., the weekly markets). Much of this runs counter to the imperatives of globalizing laissez-faire capitalism. For example, I was struck by the long "uneconomic" lunch breaks even at the Vaison la Romaine supermarkets. In other words, and rightly or wrongly, Francois shares with many in his area a vision of the good life; and those who experience it (or a similar life) infrequently and for short periods can feel/think/internalize that love of a valuable style of living. So, when he appears at the Avignon rally in his shepherd's rain hat, he is defending an end-state vision that comes from the time before Provence was even part of France. I am not sure that traditional public administration's attention to process (the efficiency of processes) is not also an end-state vision, albeit an indirect one. This is, and as just noted, making such assumptions as that our political structure and shenanigans always work out for the best.

Turn finally to the *comprehensive versus partial* option. Is a visionary public administration manager obligated to produce a comprehensive vision? Or, is it enough to produce partial visions, jigsaw parts, leaving the rest for dialogue by—or with—others? Jose Bove, a leader of the same Peasants' (or Farmers') Confederation to which Francois subscribes, has a comprehensive enough vision. Do those in public administration (which Bove is not) need to be similarly comprehensive in our visioning? Bove is an "agriculteur," a former Parisian turned sheep farmer. A mustached figure, he was prominent in turn-of-the-millenium World Trade Organization demonstrations. He is best known as a thinker/activist who led what the Agence France-Presse news story insisted on calling an "attack" on a McDonald's Restaurant that was then in process of being constructed in Millau. The alleged attack was immediately prompted by the American increase in import duties against items like Roquefort cheese (much produced in the Millau area), an increase that in turn was in retaliation against the European ban on American hormone-laced meat products. As far as I know, the alleged assault consisted of pelting the not-yet-constructed McDonald's with zillions of apples—which seems quite symbolic considering the role of the apple in the story of original sin. Jose Bove also wants to preserve the rural way of life and a just price for farmers (which the mainstream newspapers always tend to dismiss by including misleading remarks about French "culinary traditions"). He is opposed to *"la malbouffe,"* which as he explains (Bove and Dufour 2000) is a neologism he coined to avoid using the more vulgar description he wanted to use. He means what he sees as the soulless and characterless type of homogenized food produced by the giant globalizing corporations like McDonald's—as he sees it, bad to the taste and bad for the health of the body (*"sans gout ou immangeables"*). He is opposed to biotech food and genetically engineered crops produced by the large agricultural conglomerates and "uncontrolled globalization." In fact, he has been charged for destroying genetically modified maize seeds at the Novartis factory. (At his trial he said, "Yes. This action was illegal, but I lay claim to it because it was legitimate.") My examples may be giving the wrong impression that Jose Bove's vision is limited to immediate Provençal and southern French needs. That this is not true is made clear in the title of his book, *The World Is Not for Sale.*

Epilogue

What is an optimal vision(s) for public administration management visioning(s)? What is a practical vision(s)? The reader may have her own views about what is optimal and practical.

Which of the following are preferable? Managing sensitive to tradition or managing sensitive to the Other excluded by tradition? Managing confident that my vision is dead right or that even my vision can be dead wrong? Managing that is directed exclusively toward improving things or managing that privileges improving consciousness, for example, declining to treat people as mere things? Managing on the basis of a single perspective or managing on a multiperspectival basis?

Suggested Readings

Burrell, Gibson. 1997. *Pandemonium: Toward a Retro-organization Theory.* Thousand Oaks, CA: Sage.

Lynch, Thomas, D. 2006. *Handbook of Organization Theory and Management: The Philosophical Approach.* 2nd ed. New York: Taylor and Francis.

Taylor, Charles. 1992. *Sources of the Self: The Making of Modern Identity.* Cambridge, MA: Harvard University Press.

15
Synthesizing:
For What Underlies Public
Administration

What underlies public administration? What should we learn about *what underlies* from synthesizing the implications of the multiple perspectives?

Even more consciousness of the unconscious. The play of analysis.

Public administration should increase its recognition of the deleterious effects of unconscious rhetoric in our language and way of thinking, of symbolic systems that are at work under the surface of public administration's consciousness. It should increase its appreciation for the relevance of psychoanalytic understandings, which are currently pursued on public administration's circumference. It should indulge the play of analysis.

Reflection Exercise 2 asks readers to think through the contents of a strategy to liberate public administration from the distortions and constraints of its unconscious (our unconscious), using as a springboard the suggestions that are offered in this chapter on implications and synthesis. The approach is parallel to that indicated in the previous chapters for planning and managing.

This chapter is divided into three sections. The first section refers to Step 1 of Reflection Exercise 2. It summarizes the implications, from each of the various perspectives, for liberating PA from what underlies its thinking and practice. The second refers to Step 2. It offers a synthesis of a desirable strategy. The third section speaks to the prescription, *"Even more conscious of the unconscious."*

Summarizing in a Context of Complexity

Here are implications—from each of the selected perspectives (discussed in Question 8 in each chapter)—for recognizing what underlies public administration.

Complexity exists to the extent that shaping our knowing are such underlying and dynamic features as ideology, language and symbols, individual unconscious, and societal unconscious. Recall George Soros (2008, p. 3) claiming that our "understanding of the world in which we live is inherently imperfect because we are part of the world we seek to understand. There may be other facts that interfere with our ability to acquire knowledge of the natural world, but the fact that we are part of the world poses a formidable obstacle to the understanding of human affairs" (p. 3).

From a Business Perspective

Public administration should be more alert to the underlying rhetoric and assumptions, some positive and others negative, that are "bought" when a fresh approach or technique is imported. An example is leadership, over and above the idea of good management. Such an idea of leadership might well be a societal fetish, connected with conscious and unconscious deference to power. For more, see chapter 3 (a business perspective).

From an Economic Perspective

Public administration should be conscious of the role of economic rhetoric and symbolic systems. Commonplace are the translation of economic ideas into ideology and then indoctrination by such economic ideologies that (in part) link with the unconscious, such as the competing ideas of those like Harold Laski, John Maynard Keynes, and Friedrich Hayek growing into ideologies, respectively of socialism, a market requiring macro management, and market fundamentalism. The dominant ideology in the United States is the unfettered free market. Such ideology has many aspects, such as connecting with the American dream and with the celebration of rugged individualism. For commentary on the idea of indoctrination (overlapping with education), and for the role of standards of learning in encouraging market fundamentalism, see chapter 4 (an economic perspective).

From a Political Perspective

Public administration should improve on what is socially, and partly unconsciously, constructed as common sense. It should recognize that it shares this same problem with political science, which has been described as yoking itself to dubious assumptions implicit in ordinary language talk about politics, such as talk about big government as a single coherent phenomenon. The significance of clarifying the unconscious working of rhetoric and symbolic systems has been long recognized by a minority in political science, for example, Murray Edelman. Public administration should be more aware of what underlies and what counts as common sense, like American exceptionalism. For most of us, the primary aim would be to tweak, rather than to eliminate, such ideas. For more explanation, see chapter 5 (a political perspective).

From a Critical Theory Perspective

Traditional public administration should aim to emancipate itself and us from the one-dimensionality of its theorizing and practice. This is exemplified, for example, in the top-down—the hierarchical—character of public administration and in the effects on public administration of power. For reference to Herbert Marcuse's discussion of one-dimensionality and the Great Refusal, see chapter 6 (a critical theory perspective).

From a Post-Structuralist Perspective

Public administration should recognize the context of normalizing and hyperreality. Normalizing can be illustrated by describing different ways of seeing the world exhibited by, say, police and by social workers. It is also exemplified in the effect of standards of learning in "indoctrinating" a particular view of economics. Hyper-reality speaks to the blurring of distinctions between the real and the unreal. Public administration should be aware of Jean Baudrillard's claims about the implosion of meaning (in the media and prompted by technology) and about mass media and information systems constituting new forms of control that change government and living. For more (e.g., Baudrillard's assertion that we live in a world with more information and less meaning), see chapter 7 (a post-structuralist perspective).

From a Psychoanalytic Perspective

Public administration should recognize the importance of its unconscious work-place. The emphasis in psychoanalysis analysis on the importance of free association supports the suggestion that there is value for public administration in thinking as play. This should be applied more keenly, using the understandings available in (say) Freudian and Jungian and Lacanian theoretical systems, to the unconscious psychodynamics that underlie public administration. At its center, public administration soft-pedals the unconscious, which contains uncomfortable features. For more commentary and examples, see chapter 8 (a psychoanalytic perspective).

From a Neuroscientific Perspective

To a significant extent, administrative and related beliefs are shaped within the brain. Public administration should recognize that the unconscious has been described as a neuroscientific reality, providing explanations about (say) how human "automatic" processes operate. Yet brain plasticity indicates that unconscious biological processes are not, at least, beyond conscious influence. Laurence Tancredi (2005) discusses the significance of the brain's limbic structure for unconscious moral choices and the significance of mirror neurons for unconscious beliefs. Richard Dawkins (1976) underscores the limits of strong biological dispositions. For other examples, see chapter 9 (a neuroscientific perspective).

From a Feminist Perspective

The feminist perspective alerts the public administrative theorist and practitioner to the underlying societal consciousness that co-shapes what is constructed on the surface, as illustrated by feminist views on gender and sex. The radical feminist perspective brings up the question of whether reforms (e.g., for planning and managing) have a root character parallel to the root nature of radical feminist liberation. For more, see chapter 10 (a feminist perspective).

From an Ethical Perspective

Pros and cons are raised about being authentically hesitant in public administration's moral claiming. *Ethics as seeking* is a form of authentic hesitation, laying primary emphasis on the seeking of the ethical—rather than on claiming definite conclusions. For comments on the nature of authentic hesitation and on its relative advantages, see chapter 11 (an ethical perspective).

From a Data Perspective

Positivism can contribute to explanations of the unconscious dynamic of public administration. So we are not surprised to find explanations available from, say, neuroscience. Hermeneutics can contribute to understandings of the unconscious dynamic, for example, the meanings of actions, values. We should also be unsurprised that hermeneutic studies have practical utility in interpreting and laying bare the significance of, say, symbolic systems that are embedded in our language and our way of understanding. New rhetoric, not at all a mere matter of elegant chat, is an important resource in elucidating what underlies the language and the symbolic systems that are utilized. Symbols can be read as having a variety of meanings, conscious or unconscious, stable or flickering, obvious or obscure. For more, see chapter 12 (a perspective of data).

From a Traditional Perspective

Traditional public administration in practice tends toward regarding its theory and practice as dealing with administrative things basically independent of societal and individual consciousness, subconscious and unconscious. Clearly this claim does not apply to all traditional thinkers; think of Waldo, for example. Some nontraditional thinkers, by contrast, regard the unconscious as primary. Discussion of deeper levels is not central in traditional public administration, for example, acceptance of the role of market fundamentalism in the American culture, acceptance of belief in American exceptionalism, and acceptance of the modernist view of the world as a machine. For commentary on the fact that it appears natural to think that the entire ball game really consists of adjusting things like administrative structure and procedures, see chapter 2.

Synthesizing

Even more consciousness of the unconscious! The play of analysis!

Five claims synthesize the implications about what underlies public administration, giving appropriate weight to relative importance of the implications. Step 2 of Reflection Exercise 2 (toward the end of chapter 1) invites readers to substitute their own views, using the suggested claims as a point of departure.

The complexities described for planning and managing apply no less to what underlies public administration. See chapters 13 and 14. Complexity exists, for example, in synthesizing not only the implications identified for what underlies public administration but also those indicated for the other public administration elements, such as planning and managing.

The following synthesis is suggested:

1. Become more conscious of the unconscious workings of symbolic systems and rhetoric in shaping surface public administration. Recognize that this goes deep into culture, into beliefs like those in the American dream and in American exceptionalism.
2. Become more conscious of the dynamic unconscious, as elucidated in Freudian, Jungian, and Lacanian psychoanalysis. Recognize the significance of the unconscious in shaping human and public administration action and thinking.
3. Steer away from one-dimensionality. Also include understanding of new public administration insights, such as those of Jean Baudrillard.
4. Public administration should be concerned not only with mechanical things "out there." It should also focus on our own consciousness.
5. Adapt the play of analysis (informed by accounts of the dynamic unconscious), by emphasizing thinking in the form of contemplative play and free association.

More Conscious of the Unconscious

This discussion of being *even more conscious of the unconscious* is intended to help readers in reaching a more satisfying and helpful synthesis.

The thoughts here concern point 1 above, which urges: Become more conscious of the unconscious workings of symbolic systems and rhetoric in shaping surface public administration. Recognize that this goes deep into culture, into beliefs like those in the American dream and American exceptionalism.

It is not news that longstanding agencies have subcultures that shape surface actions; it is old news in the literature: see administrative histories. Agencies have a way of doing things; professions and trades have ways of doing things; agencies remember and repeat their histories.

This does make me wonder what underlies the emphasis in public administration on the smaller (the lower level) and the quick (the shorter term). Clearly, there are societal factors like historical and institutional conditions, and I wonder what underlies these elements in societal consciousness. I gave my own interpretation in *To Kill the King* (2005a) in terms of new rhetoric and of Sigmund Freud's specification of the three marks of civilization—beauty, order, and cleanliness. That spoke in terms of disciplines having as one of their functions to make clear that the corresponding practices are civilized (obviously, there are other functions, like upgrading efficiency in public administration's case). This has been recognized where the elegance of mainstream economic theory is described as suggesting that market practice is "civilized." Compare the mathematical elegance of economic theory (so beautiful, so orderly, and so clean) with the state of the marketplace. Of such a contrast, Kenneth Burke writes that the New Rhetoric helping us through the scramble, the wrangle, the give and take, the wars of nerves of the marketplace. O.C. McSwite comments, "What I like about [Burke's] poetic words is how effectively they evoke the buzzing blooming confusion of real life in government administration. As such they put in their place all the attempts we find in 'traditional public administration' to reduce the setting of public administration, as well as the work of it, to rational processes that can be applied mechanically" (McSwite 2009, p. 314). It is as if, unconsciously, the rationality of traditional public administration is aimed at persuading us of the beauty, orderliness, and cleanliness of public administration practice.

Free Association

I made a one-day visit to Cleveland in the very late 1970s, but—strange to say—it made the front page of the local newspaper. The news story was primarily about citizens upset about the lack of resources, upset about lack of resources for crime control and especially about police foot patrol. That day I was the visiting representative from the U.S. Department of Justice. The *Cleveland Plain Dealer* carried a photograph of one of the citizens holding up a shoe on a pole—symbolizing foot patrol. As explained (Farmer and Patterson 2003; Farmer 2003), citizen activists had driven me on a tour through parts of the city. They stopped about eight times; at each stop, citizens would chant and wave placards. I would walk up to the citizens, shake many hands, and touch as many people as I could. With no irony (thinking that the situation could get out of hand), I would say, "I'm from the Department of Justice, and I'm here to listen."

What had I been doing there? My mission had not been to find out, or to decide, anything. My bosses had told me to go; they wanted me to go. I had a naively rational and mechanistic view of bureaucracy, a hydraulic view. As explained, the rational and the mechanistic is "the kind of view criticized in politics by Murray Edelman (1971) and others and criticized in policy analysis by Deborah Stone (2001) and others" (Farmer 2005a, 57–61). In reflecting, I can recognize that a more helpful way to understand what I was doing is in terms of rhetoric and symbolic action.

Rhetoric is often misunderstood as nothing more than a way to improve prose composition. No, New Rhetoric doesn't mean empty rhetoric. Rather, Burke (1966, p. 4) suggests that New Rhetoric means "a study of misunderstanding and its remedies"—something clearly relevant to public administration. New Rhetoric means "rooted in . . . the use of language as a symbolic means of inducing coopera-tion in beings that by nature respond to symbols" (Burke 1969, p. 43).

There is a rhetoric of symbols, administrative or political. A symbol can tell a variety of stories, some meaning one thing to this group and another thing to other groups. Routine administrative actions exhibit subtle rhetoric—as well as obvious symbolic meanings. It bears repeating that symbols pile on symbols, rhetoric piles on rhetoric—just as metaphors pile on metaphors in language.

That the unconscious has been socially constructed is clearer in the case of economics; but it is no less present for public administration. To repeat a point made in chapter 4, a form of economics is now taught as early as in kindergarten in the United States. Many kids are being seduced, unconsciously and often even consciously, to lust for the market and market values. Ideology is being foisted, as the unfettered market is being privileged as natural. Individual success is being equated with financial success.

How could a public manager free associate? For the purpose of any reader un-familiar with New Rhetoric (or psychoanalysis), in the past I have offered a quick-and-dirty technique for rhetorical analysis. This is no substitute for the methods of New Rhetoric or for the power of the various psychoanalytical techniques, clearly. The elements of the technique are to:

1. Notice examples of rhetorical analysis in books on rhetoric in other dis-ciplines;
2. Start reading a dictionary of rhetorical terms;
3. Pick out from the dictionary whatever terms seem likely candidates;
4. Reflect on the chosen terms in relation to selected public administration texts, and let the imagination play;
5. Do the same for public administration practice.

Start with Deborah Stone (2001).

Let's return to sophisticated accounts of the dynamic unconscious of individuals, agencies, and societies—the personal and the collective. Emphasizing the pro-fundity of psychoanalysis, recall the Lacanian view that the human subject is the subject of the unconscious, rather than the conscious. Remember (from chapter 8) that O.C. McSwite uses this view to deny the utility of what counts as common sense in public administration. Recall that McSwite presents four implications from the Lacanian theory. The first is that truth is available only by "admitting the unconscious into the realm of consciousness" (McSwite 1997a, p. 57). The second is to deny economic epistemology for public administration. Administrative man is not economic man. Third, "the idea of administration as the rational attainment of goals [should] be abandoned" (p. 57). Fourth, public administration has unwittingly tied itself to the assumptions of modernism. Public administration should reflect on these four claims. Take the claim, for instance, that administrative man is not economic man. Is public administration planning not basically trapped in a commonsense and limited view of the human subject as fully rational economic man—more precisely as a man without the complexities of an unconscious?

The allure of psychoanalysis and New Rhetoric means the allure of increased public administration capability available from examining unexamined thinking and practice. It can be part of a liberation strategy for public administration, clearing away the psychoanalytic and rhetorical impediments that underlie public administration and that are unavoidably embedded in the warp and woof of administration.

Epilogue

On more reflective or philosophical days, I agree with Plato's Socrates that the unexamined life is not worth living. Shouldn't Socrates agree with me that unexamined public administration psychology and unexamined public administration rhetoric are not worth experiencing?

Suggested Readings

Burke, Kenneth. 1969. *A Rhetoric of Motives.* Berkeley: University of California Press.
Evans, Dylan. 1996. *An Introductory Dictionary of Lacanian Psychoanalysis.* London: Routledge.
Pinker, Steven. 1994. *The Language Instinct: How the Mind Creates Language.* New York: HarperCollins.
Stone, Deborah. 2001. *Public Paradox and Political Reason.* New York: HarperCollins.

16
Synthesizing:
For the Public Administration Field

What can we learn about public administration as a disciplinary field? What should we learn about the constitution of the public administration field from synthesizing, in its complexity, the implications of the multiple perspectives?

Deterritorialize = Tear down this disciplinary wall. The public administration field is too narrow. Its constricted scope excludes too much in terms of helpful insights and stimulation, not only from below (see chapter 15) but also from outside its disciplinary walls. Its pitch is too low, focusing not enough on higher-level problems. Harmful is its excessive focus on the short term and on the micro. Needed is a genuine and sophisticated macro public administration.

For those troubled by the mistaken ideas that public administration practice is a natural kind and that its nature is obvious, recall the human body and Karl Popper—and his argument that all observations are theory-based. It is true that the human body is the human body (parallel to public administration), but medical thinking divides up and shapes the terrain. Cardiologists focus on the heart, for example, and podiatrists think only below the knees. Some physicians might emphasize the mind or prevention; others not. Then there is holistic medicine. Public administration is parallel in this respect; it is sliver of what it could be, and its boundaries are eminently artificial.

Reflection Exercise 2 (page 15–16) asks readers to reflect on the scope and the limits of the public administration disciplinary field, using as a starting point the suggestions offered in this chapter on implications and synthesis. Step 1 is to summarize the implications for the selected perspective. Step 2 is to synthesize implications.

This chapter is divided in three sections. The first section (relating to Step 1) offers my summary of the implications for the public administration field as a discipline. The second (referring to Step 2) presents a synthesis. The third section discusses questions about deterritorialization.

Summarizing in a Context of Complexity

Tear down this wall. Here are the implications—from each of the selected perspectives (taken from Question 9 in each chapter)—for the public administration field as a discipline.

Complexity results from—among other things—changes in the context of administering, and this complicates any process of specifying implications for *the* field. On this basis, we can assert that it is false to say—without reservations—that PA is PA is PA. Chapter 1 noted changes in technology, changes in knowledge content, and changes in the helping context. Is managing that was pre–cell phone and precomputer the same as managing that is post–cell phone and postcomputer? Is pre-Twitter the same as post-Twitter? Can we identify changes not only in technologies but also in management-relevant social attitudes? Have there been changes in the scale of government and in related disciplines? Is what was needed or wanted to manage the Justice Department in 1910 the same as it is in 2010?

Complexity also runs to the different administrative levels. The impact of contextual change may have (and sometimes may not have) different consequences at the strategic, than at the first-line supervisory, levels.

The promised implications are as follows.

From a Business Perspective

The public administration field should include much more focus on a higher level of management, at least in the form of strategic management for the individual organization. Such strategic management decisions in business management are described as concerned with the entire environment in which the firm operates and with the whole of the resources and the people who constitute the company. This runs counter to a difficulty in government to the extent that departments act in ways to optimize the interests of that department but without doing so for the government as a whole. Strategic management in business management is well developed. It is not foreign to the public administration literature, however. For a comment on strategic management education in business schools, see chapter 3 (a business perspective).

From an Economic Perspective

The field should include macro public administration. To the extent that it exists now, macro public administration is an exception. Also, it is not as sophisticated as macroeconomics. The overlapping kinds of issues that "require" macro public administration are at least of two kinds—macro problem-focused and lens-focused. For examples on the availability of practical macro public administration issues, see chapter 4 (an economic perspective).

From a Political Perspective

Public administration should emulate what some see as the broadness of scope of political science. It should not take the political for granted, so, for example, it should include study of "broad issues of constitutionalism, politics and democratic theory" (Henry et al. 2008, p. 7). It should not limit itself mainly to a training role, inclining toward a skills core for lower-level and mid-level public officials. Public administration should seek to escape what is described as a Jeeves role, confined to that of a servant. Public policy studies and analysis can serve as a tonic for public administration. For more, see chapter 5 (a political perspective).

From a Critical Theory Perspective

The public administration field should seek to escape from its traditional boundary demarcations. For one thing, Jurgen Habermas is among those who imply that public administration's boundary lines are artificial or socially constructed. Habermas includes a description of the rise in the early years of modernity of the sphere of rational debate, mediating between the public and the private. It included the political club, the newspaper, and the journal. Habermas then describes the decline of this sphere, increasingly taken over by private corporations and the state. Recall the rise of public relations and advertising, and corporations becoming more dominant over culture. For another thing the public administration field should aim for the emancipation of people, and its disciplinary boundaries should be adjusted to support this aim. For more on Habermas's analysis, see chapter 6 (a critical theory perspective).

From a Post-Structural Perspective

The public administration field should be extended through deterritorialization, that is, circumventing the disciplinary limits that are imposed on studies—including professional public administration studies. One option is that the field can embrace what is described as *governance*, what Michel Foucault calls *governmentality*. For more comments, see chapter 7 (a post-structural perspective).

From a Psychoanalytic Perspective

The public administration field should be extended to pay more attention to the unconscious dynamics that underlie public administration practice and thinking. It should give higher priority to psychologically informed self-examination. An example given is the application of the psychoanalytic (again) to public administration visioning, that is, to self-visions and to other-visions. For more explanation, see chapter 8 (a psychoanalytic perspective).

From a Neuroscientific Perspective

The public administration field should adjust its boundaries to accommodate neuroscientific explanations. One alternative is the creation of neuro-gov, a term for the marriage of neuroscience and governance. This could be effected on a tailored and ad hoc basis, avoiding any massive restructuring. Another (probably less satisfying?) alternative is through *organizational cognitive neuroscience*, a term for the marriage of cognitive neuroscience and organization theory. For further description, see chapter 9 (a neuroscientific perspective).

From a Feminist Perspective

Public administration should pay attention to its language. Recall that Luce Irigaray and Hélène Cixous and others think that women need a language of their own. Irigaray argues for feminine writing or language—where mastery is refused, where meaning is allowed to shift, and where the writer is not in control of meaning or in possession of truth or knowledge. Such a language in public administration would be opposed to bureaucratese and would be consistent with anti-administration. Also it would recognize that its surface "reality" is shaped by underlying and unconscious dynamics. Attention should be paid to the way that socially constructed symbols and symbolic systems shape surface understandings in public administration's ordinary language. Such claims are "illustrated" by feminist discussions, such as that of the social construction of gender. Cixous and others provide examples of how texts and symbols (e.g., Sleeping Beauty) indoctrinate individuals with beliefs that require deconstruction. For more explanation, see chapter 10 (a feminist perspective).

From an Ethical Perspective

The field should be adjusted to gain deeper understandings in applying ethics to analyze macro public administration issues. Also, public administration specialists should become more philosophical (more reflective, more open to argumentation, and familiar with varieties of philosophical positions). For examples of macro public administration ethical concerns, see chapter 11 (an ethical perspective).

From a Data Perspective

Public administration theory and practice should recognize that they lack not only data but also theories, techniques, and insights from an array of non–public administration disciplines. This book emphasizes such a lack from business administration, economics, political science, critical theory, post-structuralism, psychoanalysis, neuroscience, feminism, and ethics. Earlier, I (2005a, p. 26–27) referred to the lack resulting from excluding so much from political science, economics, political economy, moral philosophy, sociology, civil society, the complex of action subjects like business administration, social work—and beyond. An ideal turf would include more from the biological, the social, and the spiritual; it would include more from history and literature, as well as the history of political ideas and the history of economic ideas. It would also include more from all the administrative specializations—not only business administration but also hotel administration, police administration, sports administration, and so on. For more, see chapter 12 (the perspective of data).

From a Traditional Perspective

Public administration should recognize that it has not itself generated a compelling strategy for upgrading its help to the public service—unless new public management incorrectly is counted as such. It lacks the equivalent to the orthodox period's macro and high-level administrative planning of public administration activities as a whole, taking into account the changed and changing context of administration. Is it fair to say that traditional public administration is committed to the rhetoric of change, while also being committed to the status quo within its own field? For comments on the character of public administration, see chapter 2 (a traditional perspective).

Synthesizing

Deterritorialize. Five claims synthesize the implications for the public administration field as a discipline, giving appropriate weight to relative importance of the implications. Step 2 of Exercise 2 invites readers to substitute their own views, using the suggested claims as a point of departure.

Complexity is reflected in the advisability that the synthesizing should recognize the implications identified not only for the public administration field but also those indicated for the other public administration features, for example, for managing. Complexity, as before, also extends to recognizing our own prejudices.

Here are the suggested five syntheses:

1. Deterritorialize. Public administration should recognize that it limits its effectiveness by its narrow boundaries, such as by excluding insights available from subjects and perspectives currently excluded or marginalized.
2. Public administration should expand to establish a sophisticated macro public administration subject, on the general pattern of the macro-micro split in economics.
3. Public administration should expand to emphasize and incorporate the kind of reflection contemplated in feminine language.
4. Public administration should expand to obviate its artificial boundary demarcations. Even within the public sector area, its exclusions are arbitrary, for example, excluding the military—and subspecialties are eating

farther away at the public administration body. Within the management area, excluding activities like business is arbitrary.

5. Public administration should expand to diminish its emphasis on the mechanics of administrative systems and to augment its emphasis on the lifeworld.

Deterritorializing

On the one hand, there's the prospect of deterritorialization through massive restructuring, via reorganization or via a catalyst like neuroscience. On the other hand, there's deterritorialization through epistemic pluralism. To facilitate the reflection required in synthesizing, here are some thoughts about this choice.

These thoughts concern point 1 above—deterritorialize. Public administration should recognize that its narrow boundaries limit its effectiveness by excluding insights available from subjects and perspectives currently excluded or marginalized, for example.

What Is It?

Deterritorialization refers to the desirability of circumventing the entrenched disciplinary divisions that present obstacles to seeing reality accurately. It means removal of the code or grid that is imposed on the study of issues by the way that the thinking is conducted and the way that the business of thinking is structured, as I (1995) described it more than a decade ago. For example, separating business administration from public administration—or separating politics from economics—can be described as distorting what we see. Arguments can be advanced for territorialization, that is, permitting greater specialist analysis. Looking at the condition of public administration and looking at the condition of the social sciences would be a counterargument.

Deterritorializing and territorializing were terms first used by Gilles Deleuze and Félix Guattari. They wrote (1977, p. 321) that it "should be said that one can never go far enough in the direction of deterritorialization: you haven't seen anything yet—an irreversible process." They argue that, in principle, territorializing is regrettable.

Looking at public administration, it would be valuable to decode the extent to which there has been exclusion of the perspectives discussed in this book. Removal of the grid would make for more robust engagement of the business, economic, political, post-structural, critical theory, psychoanalytic, neuroscientific, feminist, ethical, and other perspectives.

There is a kind of hyper-exclusion within public administration. One exclusionary feature—noted before—is the privileging of what is obviously practical in the short run and what concerns the mid-level and lower-level employee. This excludes consideration of long-run issues and more adventurous solutions that would materialize only in a longer run. It also excludes macro problems and solutions. Limiting subject matter and ideas to what yields a payoff only in the short run is a constraining grid that deterritorialization would remove. Same for the constraining grid of considering disproportionately concerns relating to the middle and lower levels of the bureaucracy!

Such exclusions in the business of public administration thinking occur within the setting of the increasing fragmentation of the social science and social action subjects. Social sciences are disciplines like economics, sociology, and social psychology; social action subjects are fields of study like public administration, business administration, criminal justice administration—and the proliferating subfields of study like human resources administration, hotel management, juvenile justice administration. Increasing specialization and proliferation have been characteristics of modernity, especially in the social sciences and social action subjects.

The problem is worsening. And every reform effort leads to even more fragmentation, it seems.

Julie Klein (1990, p. 21) has described the "modern connotation of disciplinarity" as a nineteenth-century product, for example, and she links it with the "evolution of the modern natural sciences, the general 'scientification' of knowledge, the industrial revolution, technological advancements, and agrarian agitation." She adds that, as modern universities developed, disciplinarity was encouraged by industries demanding specialists, by disciplines recruiting students, and by more expensive instrumentation in some fields.

Social science and social action subjects are now atomized, inhibiting the examination of cross-disciplinary issues and confining insights to limited perspectives. Hans Flexner (1979, p. 93) gives an example from the United States: the "history of the curriculum in American higher education has been one of increasing diversification and specialization." The social sciences are more liable to fragmentation than the physical sciences because (see chapter 2) they tend to be low-paradigm fields. This reflects a distinction that has been drawn between high paradigm (like physics) and low paradigm (like sociology).

Deterritorializing by Reorganization

Reversing the fragmentation of disciplines, especially—but not exclusively—in the social sciences and in social action subjects, can be sought through reorganization. The past century has seen a rich variety of attempts at reorganization in the form of interdisciplinarity (interaction between disciplines). For histories of these attempts, see Klein (1990) and Flexner (1979). Interdisciplinarity has been applied to the functional aspects of disciplines such as general education, professional education, the training of researchers, basic research, and applied research. An account of developments in the United States and elsewhere would include descriptions of national and other organizations (such as the Social Science Research Council in the 1920s, the 1948 Foundation for Integrative Education, and the National Science Foundation's programs). It would also include descriptions of externally driven developments (e.g., those resulting from World War II, such as the Manhattan

Project), and of internally driven developments (e.g., those resulting from synthetic theories, such as structuralism and general systems theory).

The proliferation continues. While there have been some successes at transdisciplinarity (a science crosscutting several disciplines), the attempts to achieve interdisciplinarity have mainly resulted in what has been called an "interdisciplinary archipelago" of new disciplines (Farmer 1995, pp. 218–225). Throughout the modern period, a long list of philosophers have expressed concerns about the fragmentation of knowledge and have made calls to restore the lost unity. Bacon and Comte come to mind, for example. Expressions of concern continue.

Deterritorializing by Catalyst

Neuroscience promises to act as a catalyst in seeking reunification in the longer run. The reason is that the study of neuroscience challenges taken-for-granted concepts of disciplinary orthodoxy in, say, the social science and social action disciplines (e.g., see Farmer 2007b, pp. 74–89).

Neuroscience, among others, has the momentum and the substance perhaps even to "muscle" a different way of thinking for post-traditional governance. For examples, see chapter 9.

But such a strategy aiming for a restoration of the lost unity can be expected to evolve only on a gradual or evolutionary basis. Through a catalyst like neuroscience, a reasonable long-term aim may well be to create a gathering together of, say, all the subjects connected with what I have called governance—all knowledge concerned with governing or being governed.

Deterritorializing by Epistemic Pluralism

Epistemic pluralism offers a workable remedy to such disciplinary concerns. It is workable because it does not involve a huge organizational restructuring of disciplines.

Rather than such a restructuring, it bears repeating that I (2005a) proposed a tailored and ad hoc approach. A model for such knowing (as Deleuze and Guattari explain) is not the "orderly" tree but the "disorderly" rhizome. The tree or arborescent metaphor refers to knowledge as hierarchical, as rooted and as a unity—with branches and sub-branches. The rhizome in botany is a rootlike and horizontal stem that grows along or under the ground, sending roots below and stems above. It really is a pipe dream to work toward a massive lumping together of fields and disciplines into the huge transdiscipline that would be appropriate for public administration.

Complexity is represented in the conflict between the "rationality" of a broad social science (that includes public administration as a component) and the apparent "political" impracticality of a massive structural readjustment (disturbing powerful vested interests). This is a conflict which is sidestepped by epistemic pluralism.

Epilogue

"I remember very well the time when I was captured by the dream of unified learning. It was in the early fall of 1947. . ." (Wilson 1998, p. 3). Thus E.O. Wilson, the distinguished biologist and friend of ants, begins his book on the unity of knowledge. Wilson reports how he had been enthralled when he recognized the implications of evolution for biology and for science. "And for philosophy. And for just about everything. Static pattern slid into fluid process" (p. 4). He borrows a phrase for unity of sciences, calling it the Ionian Enchantment. Wilson (p. 5) saw this enchantment as extending through the sciences, and "in the minds of a few it reaches beyond into the social sciences, and still further, as I will explain later, to touch the humanities."

Suggested Readings

Rabin, Jack, W. Bartley Hildreth, and Gerald J. Miller. 2007. *Handbook of Public Administration.* 3rd ed. New York: Taylor and Francis.
Wilson, Edward O. 1998. *Consilience: The Unity of Knowledge.* New York: Alfred Knopf.

17

Synthesizing:
For Imaginative Creativity

What can we learn about imaginative creativity? What should we learn about imaginative creativity in public administration from synthesizing, in its complexity, the implications of the multiple perspectives?

Imagine. Public administration should adopt a strategy to seek and to use imaginative creativity, both extraordinary and ordinary, in both theorizing and practice. Two levels of creativity are distinguished in creativity studies in neuroscience and elsewhere. In my view, a helpful way of making the distinction can be in terms of Thomas Kuhn (see chapter 9). Extraordinary creativity can be understood as the imaginative activity that is required for the equivalent of paradigm shifting. Ordinary creativity can be described as the imaginative activity that is required for problem solving capable of resolving puzzles within an orthodox framework.

Imagine, and imaginize. Public administration theorizing and practice should aim for imagination to have a pervasive effect on public administration and on society. Public administration managers should be held accountable for their imaginative creativity, and they should expect others in their agencies to privilege imagination. Recall that imaginization was earlier described in terms of rationalization, the dominant idea of the Enlightenment. Rationalization was the dynamic idea that more and more reason can be expected to yield more and more human happiness and more and more moral behavior. In a parallel fashion, imaginization is the dynamic idea that more and more imagination can be expected to yield more and more human happiness and more and more moral behavior.

Reflection Exercise 2 for imaginative creativity is parallel to that for the previous public administration elements, for example, for planning and management. Step 1 of this exercise asks readers to identify the implications of the perspectives already discussed. Step 2 asks readers to synthesize implications. Recognition of the complexities is also required, as for the previous elements.

211

This chapter is divided into three sections. The first section refers to Step 1 of Reflection Exercise 2. It summarizes the implications, from each of the various perspectives, for public administration incorporating more imaginative creativity. The second refers to Step 2. It offers a synthesis. The third section asks two questions about imagination and imaginization. Why does public administration need more imagination? What more should be asked about the nature of the imaginative?

Summarizing in a Context of Complexity

Here are implications—from each of the selected perspectives (from Question 10 in each chapter)—for adopting a strategy to seek the imaginatively creative in both public administration theorizing and practice.

The complexities for imaginative creativity include the fact that imagination is neither an unadulterated good nor the only capability that is needed in an organization. A way to think of imagination-in-governance is in terms of a range of options, showing the differing extents of the relative primacy of imagination and rationalization. At the unimaginative end, rationalization completely dominates imagination—and at the other, vice versa. The optimal point is at neither extreme. The amount of imagination that is optimal may be expected to depend on the level and kind of function. A rule of thumb might be that more imagination is required at higher, rather than lower, levels.

Complexities also exist in specifying the nature of imagination—extraordinary or ordinary—that is optimal. Some hold a trivial view of the nature of the imaginative; others (e.g., Carl Jung) have a profound view.

The suggested implications are as follows.

From a Business Perspective

Public administration requires imaginative creativity in identifying and adapting business approaches and techniques to the public sector. Clearly, other qualities are also required, like intelligence and energy. For instance, aren't these "other qualities"—in addition to imaginative creativity—required to act on what Osborne and Gaebler (1992) called catalytic government and anticipatory government? Public administration also requires imaginative creativity in identifying unhelpful assumptions that can be imported unconsciously when useful techniques (e.g., those from Peters and Waterman 2004) are adapted from business administration. Examples of such assumptions could be a belief in the primacy of consumerism, and a belief that government is always incompetent. As another example, deficiencies in the economic framework (e.g., those described by Barber 2007 and Reich 2007) may tend to be covered over, hindering understanding of how public administration and the state should relate to business. For commentary on these claims, see chapter 3 (a business perspective).

From an Economic Perspective

Public administration requires imaginative creativity in adequately applying some economic theory to the public administration situation. (Again, other qualities are no less desirable, e.g., intelligence; and yet other qualities are undesirable, e.g., anti-intellectualism.) For instance, imagination is required to act on the fact that Kenneth Arrow's possibility theorem is useful for understanding and designing citizen participation arrangements. Again, some in public administration can attempt to emulate economists who have displayed extraordinary creativity in shifting paradigms in economics, for example, John Maynard Keynes and the creation of macroeconomics. For more on the possibility theorem, see chapter 4 (an economic perspective).

From a Political Perspective

Political theorist Harold Lasswell emphasized the importance of cultivating creativity in the study and teaching of political science. He held that the absence of static certainties in politics and political science make it important to cultivate imagination and other qualities. To the extent that it also faces a similar absence of static certainties, public administration should also adopt the same priority. For example, don't the features recommended by Janet and Robert Denhardt (2003, "think strategically, act democratically" and "value people, not just productivity") also require imaginative creativity from both public administration theorists and practitioners? On another point, public administration also requires imaginative creativity in applying insights from political theory, from political philosophy. Again, other qualities are also required; Plato said, for example, that the practitioner and the thinker should exhibit excellence in wisdom, courage, self-control (or temperance), and a balance (justice) between these qualities. For more, see chapter 5 (a political perspective).

From a Critical Theory Perspective

Public administration should seek imaginative creativity in order to emancipate its theory and practice in at least two respects. First, it requires imagination (and other qualities, like wisdom) to see through what we currently count as commonsense truths. Second, it requires imaginative creativity to switch bureaucracy from inward discourse and action to outward discourse and action. Inward is what contributes to the internal benefit of the bureaucracy or program; outward is what benefits beyond the bureaucracy or program, such as the primary concern with the human-in-society. It requires imagination (and other excellences) to shift from primary concern with the systems world to a privileging of the lifeworld. For more, see chapter 6 (a critical theory perspective).

From a Post-Structural Perspective

Public administration should now aim for imaginization (as noted in the opening of this chapter) to have a parallel and pervasive effect on public administration and on society, as rationalization did during the Enlightenment and later. In the Enlightenment, the idea was that more and more rationality (rationalization) results in more and more happiness and more and more moral behavior. Under a regime of imagination (where rationality is not abandoned), the idea is that more and more imaginative creativity (imaginization) will result in more and more happiness and more and more moral behavior. Public managers should encourage imagination. For such claims, see chapter 7 (a post-structural perspective).

From a Psychoanalytic Perspective

Public administration requires imaginative creativity (and other qualities) to seek to upgrade bureaucratic creativity through psychologically informed analysis. The psychoanalytic emphasis on free association suggests the value for public administration of thinking as play and the talking cure. For more, see chapter 8 (a psychoanalytic perspective).

From a Neuroscientific Perspective

Public administration should use neuroscientific findings in promoting extraordinary creativity, at both the macro and micro levels. Neuroscientist Nancy Andreasen (2005) distinguishes between extraordinary creativity and ordinary creativity. Extraordinary creativity, as mentioned above and in my view, can be understood as what is required for paradigm shifting. On the macro level, Andrew Modell (2003) uses neuroscience to indicate how trauma can foreclose on the imaginative. This raises the macro question as to whether public administration has been traumatized, for example, by any questioning of its intellectualism by political science specialists. On the micro level, public administration theorists and practitioners should practice imagining, using the exercises recommended by Andreasen and described in chapter 18. For more, see chapter 9 (from a neuroscientific perspective).

From a Feminist Perspective

Public administration should recognize that the range and role of imagination in public administration and in society are socially constructed—in the "same" way that gender (in some feminist theorizing) is socially constructed. Public administration should school its imagination to be sensitive to, and to understand, not only the other but also the extent to which the public administration context is male dominated in such terms as fostering heroic leadership. For more, see chapter 10 (a feminist perspective).

From an Ethical Perspective

Public administration requires extraordinary imaginative creativity to adapt and use what Robert Fogel calls the spiritual. It also requires imagination to correct the insularity of the subtopic of public administration ethics. Fogel 2000, a Nobel Prize winner in economics, describes what he means by spirituality in terms of self-realization. (Let me repeat that spirituality in this case is intended neither to include, nor to exclude, religion.) Fogel holds that self-realization should be understood in terms of fifteen spiritual resources—a sense of purpose, a vision of opportunity, a sense of mainstream life and work, a capacity to engage with diverse groups, and so on. For more description, see chapter 11 (an ethical perspective).

From a Data Perspective

Public administration should pay attention to ways of triggering and fostering creativity. Real though the total world is, for example, discursive practices can limit us to perceiving as real only a certain portion of that total reality. Insofar as they foster creativity, the life-transforming books listed in chapter 12 can be triggers. Public administration creativity can be fostered by exposure to a wide variety of perspectives. This brings us to epistemic pluralism. For more on these claims, see chapter 12 (a data perspective).

From a Traditional Perspective

Traditional public administration thinking and practice, to the extent that imagination is a concern, tends to utilize an unduly constricted view of imaginative creativity. This was reflected in the view of imagination adopted by the 9/11 Commission on Terrorist Attacks upon the United States. The 9/11 National Commission is good support for belief in the relevance of privileging imagination in governance and bureaucracy, because people take terrorism very seriously. The commission identified failures in imagination as the first problem. Yet the commission celebrated and emphasized an unduly narrow view of imagination. For more, see chapter 2 (a traditional perspective).

Synthesizing

Imagine. Five claims synthesize implications for imaginative creativity in public administration. The reader is encouraged to substitute her own synthesis, using the suggested claims as a point of departure.

Complexity is reflected in the ways already noted. The synthesizing should incorporate not only the implications just summarized but also implications indicated for the other public administration elements; for example, imaginative creativity is interconnected with what lies underneath public administration. Complexity, again, extends to avoiding being led by our own prejudices.

Here are the suggested five syntheses:

1. For public administration thinking and action, imagine. Public administration should emphasize extraordinary imaginative creativity and ordinary imaginative creativity. It should aim for imaginization to have a parallel and pervasive effect in public administration and on society, as rationalization did during the Enlightenment and later.
2. Public administration should seek imaginative creativity in order to see through what counts as commonsense truths. To put it another way, public administration theory and practice should seek the capability of bursting the "bubble" within which public administration thinks and acts. It is a "bubble" that can constrain and harm thinking and action—and even the capacity to imagine.
3. Public administration requires imaginative creativity in adapting helpful understandings from other disciplines (like from business administration, economics, and political science), without swallowing associated unhelpful assumptions.
4. Public administration should develop the imaginative capability to permit it to switch bureaucracy from inward to outward discourse and action, and to extend public administration ethics to include what Fogel describes as the spiritual. It should recognize that the range and role of imagination in public administration is socially constructed, for example, in relation to sensitivity to the other. In recognizing this, PA should pay attention to the dynamic unconscious, using psychologically and culturally informed analysis (including contemplation and free association).
5. Public administration theorists and practitioners should perform Andreasen's (2005) neuroscience-based "extraordinary" creativity exercises regularly (see chapter 18).

Imagine

Why and what? First, why does public administration need more imaginative creativity? Second, what more should be asked about the nature of the imaginative?

Here are thoughts about point 1, with the aim of facilitating synthesizing. Point 1 urges, "For public administration thinking and action, imagine. Public administration should emphasize extraordinary imaginative creativity and ordinary imaginative creativity. It should aim for imaginization to have a parallel and pervasive effect in public administration and on society, as rationalization did during the Enlightenment and later."

The Need for More Imaginative Creativity

Turn to myths and contexts, underscoring the need for more imaginative creativity. Let's preface this by recalling that there are good and bad, and in-between, uses for imagination. Even the Nazis could have imaginative war plans, for instance. Also, let's repeat that imagination is not the only capacity needed in an organization. "Imagination only" is unimaginative.

Turn to myths and to President John F. Kennedy. It is hard for public administration specialists to acknowledge that our subject and our practice is beset with belief and misbelief systems, with myths. It is not that others are free of myths; but public administration certainly has its share. If you doubt this, read these beautiful words from President John F. Kennedy: "For the great enemy of the truth is very often not the lie—deliberate, contrived, and dishonest— but the myth, persistent, persuasive, and unrealistic. Too often we hold fast to the clichés of our forebears. We subject all facts to a prefabricated set of interpretations. . . . Mythology distracts us everywhere—in government as in business, in politics as in economics" (Kennedy 1962). Imaginative creativity is needed to cope.

Turn to new contexts. Public administration needs extraordinary imaginative creativity in responding successfully to new and changing features in the administrative context. As instances, note the new contexts of hyper-lobbying, of communication technology, and of untruths. On hyper-lobbying dominated by business interests, William Greider (1992, p. 321) writes that the increasing political activity of business "is the centerpiece in the breakdown of contemporary democracy." Charles Lindblom (1977, p. 356) judged that the "large corporation fits oddly into democratic theory and vision. Indeed, it does not fit." On communications technology, the world of BlackBerry and Facebook is different from its predecessor; will a world of new brand names be long in coming?

What More Should Be Asked About the Nature of Imagination?

Four more questions, at least, should be asked about the nature of imagination.

1. Can imagination be schooled and reschooled? Ivan Illich gives his view of some results of how imaginations are "schooled," and this leads us to recognize how the schooling of the imagination in organizations can lead to public administration misconceptions. Illich (1970, p. 1) claims that "Medical treatment is mistaken for health care, social work for the improvement of community life, police protection for safety, military poise for national security, the rat race for productive work. Health, learning, dignity, independence, and creative endeavor are defined as little more than the performance of the institutions which claim to serve these ends." His view is that mistaking what the institution does (e.g., what the military or the police do) for what they are intended to achieve (e.g., national security or safety) results from imaginations schooled and disciplined to believe such harmful misconceptions. Let's hope that imaginations can be reschooled, because these misconceptions within organizations shape (in Karl Weick's words) "things that are forgotten in the heat of battle, values that get pushed aside in the rough-and-tumble of everyday living, the goals we ought to be thinking about and

never do, the facts we don't like to face, and the questions we lack the courage to ask" (Weick 2002, p. 57).

2. Are different degrees of imaginative capacity merely qualitative, or quantitative, differences? Imagine a range extending from the utterly unimaginative to the utterly imaginative—a range from supreme clerk to supreme poet. Recall the biting judgment from Thomas Macauley (1828) about John Dryden. "Dryden's imagination resembled the wings of an ostrich. It enabled him to run, but not to soar." Some might think that the ostrich level of imagination is essentially the same, except in degree, as the eagle level. However, the vast imaginations of great scientists like Einstein (or of great philosophers like Plato) exhibit a quantum difference from, say, valet Jeeves's imagination.

3. Are there different "psychic" components in some different levels of imagination? Consider intelligence, and then fancy. At first sight, it seems as though there must be a positive relationship between intelligence and imagination; but the evidence is against it (e.g., see Andreasen 2005). The fact is that we have all encountered highly intelligent people who are imagination-dead. Think of characters in Kafkaesque insurance offices, managers not at all stupid but entirely high-level clerks. But we have to be careful because the clericalia may be a cover for, or a cause of, sadomasochism or some other condition.

Even more interesting is the relationship between fancy and imagination. Some will rush to point out that, while we want imagination, we don't want any off-the-wall fancy. Yet, like conjoined twins, I think it is hard surgically to separate imagination from fancy without one or both babies dying. Consider John Keats, who spoke of invention being the polar star of poetry, "as fancy is the sails, and imagination is the rudder" (Keats 1935). Consider the case of George Carlin. He was more than a mere comedian; he was an imaginative social critic who let fancy fill his sails. He was not merely negative; rather, he could clear space for his readers and listeners. A number of Carlinisms are relevant to governance and bureaucracy. Here's only one from *When Will Jesus Bring the Pork Chops?* "As you know, people no longer have problems in this country, they have issues. This shift grows out of our increasingly desperate need to shade the truth and see things as more positive than they really are . . . Poor . . . [person]. He has problems. I have . . . issues!" Carlin doesn't have a problem with this. He says that he has a concern (Carlin 2004, p. 293). Yes, imagination is not the same as "mere" fancy, although I don't imagine that it excludes fancy.

4. Is it possible to be relatively imaginative in one faculty (or even field) and relatively unimaginative in another? Yes. In terms of a faculty, for example, isn't it possible to be relatively imaginative in (say) the logic of discovery and relatively unimaginative in the logic of justification—or vice versa? In terms of a field, isn't it possible to be relatively imaginative as, say, a cook but relatively unimaginative outside the kitchen? I would add other examples. I can imagine Schopenhauer being princely imaginative in his metaphysics and utterly unimaginative (some say that his dog was his only friend) in his daily life.

Epilogue

Can the character of imagination in bureaucracy be considered independently of the context of imagination in society?

Suggested Readings

Farmer, David John. 2005. *To Kill the King: Post-Traditional Governance and Bureaucracy.* Armonk, NY: M.E. Sharpe.
Huizinga, Johan. 1971. *Homo ludens: A Study of the Play-Element in Culture.* Boston, MA: Beacon.
Illich, Ivan. 1970. *Deschooling Society.* New York: Harper & Row.
Morgan, Gareth. 1997. *Imaginization: New Mindsets for Seeing, Organizing, Managing.* Thousand Oaks, CA: Sage.

Part III
Public Administration as a Whole

18

Contemplating:
Public Administration on a Treadmill?

"Finally, there is this possibility: after I tell you something, you just can't believe it. You can't accept it. You don't like it. A little screen comes down and you don't listen anymore." So writes Richard Feynman (1985, p. 10), a 1965 Nobel Prize winner in physics. "I'm going to describe to you how Nature is—and if you don't like it, that's going to get in the way of your understanding. It's a problem that physicists have learned to deal with. They've learned to realize that whether they like a theory or don't like a theory is not the essential question. . . . It's not a question of whether a theory is philosophically delightful, or easy to understand, or perfectly reasonable from the point of view of common sense."

Feynman (1985, p. 10) continues, writing in *QED: The Strange Theory of Light and Matter*, "The theory of quantum electrodynamics describes Nature as absurd from the point of view of common sense." He adds, "I hope you can accept Nature as She is—absurd. I'm going to have fun telling you about this absurdity, because I find it delightful. Please don't turn yourself off because you can't believe Nature is so strange."

The little screen (to borrow Feynman's phrase) is even more likely to come down in public administration. It is not just that public administration theory is less advanced and less dramatic and less beautiful, as contrasted with physics; it is not just that physicists are more familiar with universe-upsetting innovations. It is true that most of us don't expect such in public administration. But also, public administration thinkers and practitioners do not focus enough on cultivating their consciousness. In public administration (whether or not in physics), we have to work not just on understanding things out there. We have to work also on our own consciousness, which processes the understandings—which admits or blocks. We need to prepare ourselves to escape our commonsense delusions and to nourish counterintuitive ideas—both agencies and serious public administration thinkers and practitioners.

A four-part contemplation exercise is suggested, adapting neuroscientist Nancy Andreasen's (2005) mental exercises for fostering extraordinary creativity. This is exercise 3 noted in chapter 1. For readers who are students, this chapter also includes suggestions for written exercises, if that is preferred.

The chapter is divided into four sections. The first section discusses contemplation of the public administration syntheses worked out in chapters 13–17. The second speaks of reflecting on the syntheses in terms of one's own public administration work and lived experience. The third concerns contemplating the application of syntheses to public administration programs and situations. The fourth section relates to public administration and the unfamiliar.

Contemplating the Public Administration Syntheses

Public administration theorists and practitioners should spend time on a regular basis contemplating the syntheses. Andreasen (2005) advises cultivating extraordinary creativity by spending some time each day practicing meditation or just thinking. This is the same Andreasen mentioned in chapters 9 and 17. As she is a neuroscientist, her explanation (briefly summarized here) may seem technical. Apparently, meditation—as, say, in Tibetan Buddhism—has a beneficial effect on gamma synchrony (with gamma waves being high-frequency oscillations in the brain). The effect is greatest in the frontal, temporal, and parietal regions. Andreasen also emphasizes (as noted in chapter 9) that brain plasticity research indicates that the brain is continually changing in response to cultural and other inputs until the moment of death.

PA on a treadmill? So this meditation exercise has the beneficial side effect that it will slow senile decay, which starts when the brain is twenty years old. It is a side effect that can be increased if done on a treadmill, as physical exercise also helps neurons grow and slows down the brain's slowing up.

Writes Andreasen, "The essence of my mental exercises to enhance your own creativity is to set aside some time in your daily life that is devoted exclusively to learning to think and perceive in novel ways. Develop your own 'creativity workout,' just as you might develop a physical workout" (2005, p. 161). Andreasen explains that when you first start such an exercise program, it is hard—just like a physical exercise program. We have so little time; we are tired; it is easier to watch TV. But as you persist and build up the "mental muscles," the exercises might become easier. "You might find you get a thinker's high that is comparable to a runner's high. And just imagine that gray matter slowly expanding in your brain as you increase those synapses" (p. 161).

The public administration participant should reflect on the meaning of the syntheses. She should do this on a one-per-session basis.

Reflecting on the meaning of a selected synthesis adapts Andreasen's preference for letting her brain focus on any object and wander where it wants. The public administration participant in this case can let her mind wander when thinking of the item's meaning. The aim of contemplation is to meditate on (just think about) a selected synthesis for about ten or fifteen minutes on the selected day. Focus on the meaning of the synthesis on the first day. On a later day, this focus could be extended to thinking about what the synthesis means for public administration, that is, what the synthesis amounts to, how it would be done, what difference it would make, and so on.

Imagine that the reader has chosen the fifth of the five planning syntheses, for example. This is the synthesis that states, "When advising political superiors and when planning independently, public administration thinkers and practitioners should aim to exceed a regulative ideal confined to mere efficiency; alternatives include, for instance, caring and loving. This should include aiming to overcome *othering* by seeking administrative action that recognizes the whole person-in-herself in-her-difference." In reflecting about the meaning, the public administration participant could let her brain wonder (wander) about what precisely is (1) a regulative ideal, (2) an ideal of efficiency, (3) caring, (4) love, and (5) *othering*. What could such concepts mean? What are the different kinds of each concept? (Aren't there different kinds of each? Of regulative ideal, of efficiency, of caring, of love, and of *othering*?) The reader should go slowly and let the brain do the work by itself. So she might find it better to think about only one or two of these sub-items, such as regulative ideal and an ideal of efficiency. In that case, it would be better to hold another session the next day on the next sub-item, such as caring.

How many contemplation sessions should be held? Should the sessions be held every day of every week? These are matters of preference. If one synthesis were completed each day (too much, too fast), it would be a 25-day chore to go through all of the 25 syntheses. Yet sessions will probably vary, as when pounding on a treadmill: the treader may find that several days of contemplating syntheses alters her attitude toward today's contemplation—or not.

For students wanting to write a paper, the same exercise is suggested—except that it would culminate in writing. The essence of any paper, as indicated in chapter 1, should be analytical in at least three respects. It should be informed about what is relevant to the topic in the public administration literature. It should be creative in the sense that it should aim to say something interesting. It should go beyond being a position statement, beyond being like a newspaper editorial.

The 25 items in the synthesis are as follows.

On Planning: Uncover More of What Is Hidden

1. When advising political superiors and when conducting their own independent planning, public administration thinkers and practitioners should excel in uncovering more of what is hidden. They should include uncovering relevant scientific and hermeneutic results, including those about forces that underlie public administration. Policy, program, and administrative

planning in public administration should include uncovering more of the longer run and the macro.

2. The public administration discipline should develop its own strategic plan for good governance.

3. The public administration plan should use epistemic pluralism in order to reflect more on public administration as a discipline. This reflection should include the aim of reflection for its own sake, critical reflection, and seeking what is just and right. It should include putting administration and policy and programs on the analytic couch, as it were.

4. Public administration thinkers and practitioners should aim to advocate (both when advising political superiors on planning and when conducting their own independent planning) policies, and programs and administrative arrangements that would seek societal emancipation toward the lifeworld.

5. When advising political superiors and when planning independently, public administration thinkers and practitioners should aim to exceed a regulative ideal confined to mere efficiency; alternatives include, for instance, caring and loving. This should include aiming to overcome *othering* by seeking administrative action that recognizes the whole person-in-herself in-her-difference.

On Managing: More Visioning, Less Othering

6. Embrace a visionary management style that seeks to avoid *othering*. This style seeks to avoid *othering* perspectives, employees, and clients.

7. Seek nonhierarchical management arrangements and practices. Manage in ways consistent with nonhierarchical democracy, honest transparency (rather than mainly public relations agency-justifying talk), genuine citizen participation (rather than mainly "sham" participation). Adopt a less hierarchical regulative ideal than mere efficiency.

8. Aim to administer anti-administratively, seeking the ethical.

9. Develop deeper understandings of the administrative self (e.g., through more extensive use of psychoanalytic and neuroscientific insights). Pursue deeper understandings of the agency (e.g., storying and restorying, with such aims as deconstructing what is socially constructed yet what appears given).

10. Emphasize understanding managing at the macro and longer-run levels, without neglecting the micro and shorter run.

On What Underlies Public Administration: Even More Conscious of the Unconscious

11. Become more conscious of the unconscious workings of symbolic systems

and rhetoric in shaping surface public administration. Recognize that this goes deep into culture, for example, into beliefs like those in the American dream and in American exceptionalism.

12. Become more conscious of the dynamic unconscious, as elucidated in Freudian, Jungian, and Lacanian psychoanalysis. Recognize the significance of the unconscious in shaping human and public administration action and thinking.

13. Steer away from one-dimensionality. Also include understanding of new public administration insights, for example, those of Jean Baudrillard.

14. Public administration should be concerned not only with mechanical things "out there." It should also focus on our own consciousness.

15. Adapt the play of analysis (informed by accounts of the dynamic unconscious), emphasizing thinking in the form of contemplative play and free association.

On the Public Administration Field: Deterritorialize

16. Deterritorialize. Public administration should recognize that it limits its effectiveness by its narrow boundaries, excluding insights available from subjects and perspectives currently excluded or marginalized.

17. Public administration should expand to establish a sophisticated macro public administration subject, on the general pattern of the macro-micro split in economics.

18. Public administration should expand to emphasize and incorporate the kind of reflection contemplated in feminine language.

19. Public administration should expand to obviate its artificial boundary demarcations. Even within the public sector area, its exclusions are arbitrary, such as that of the military—and subspecialties are eating farther away at the public administration body. Within the management area, excluding activities like business is arbitrary.

20. Public administration should expand to diminish its emphasis on the mechanics of administrative systems and to augment its emphasis on the lifeworld.

On Imaginative Creativity: Imagine

21. For public administration thinking and action, imagine. Public administration should emphasize extraordinary imaginative creativity and ordinary imaginative creativity. It should aim for imaginization to have a parallel and pervasive effect in public administration and on society, as rationalization did during the Enlightenment and later.

22. Public administration should seek imaginative creativity in order to see

through what counts as commonsense truths. To put it another way, public administration theory and practice should seek the capability of bursting the "bubble" within which public administration thinks and acts. It is a "bubble" that can constrain and harm thinking and action—and even the capacity to imagine.

23. Public administration requires imaginative creativity in adapting helpful understandings from other disciplines (like from business administration, economics, and political science), without swallowing associated unhelpful assumptions.

24. Public administration should develop the imaginative capability to permit it to switch bureaucracy from *inward* to *outward* discourse and action, and to extend public administration ethics to include what Fogel describes as the spiritual. It should recognize that the range and role of imagination in public administration is socially constructed, for example, in relation to sensitivity to the other. In recognizing this, public administration should pay attention to the dynamic unconscious, using psychologically informed and culturally informed analysis (including contemplation and free association).

25. Public administration theorists and practitioners should do Andreasen's neuroscience-based "extraordinary" creativity exercises regularly.

As Strange as Physics?

Let's agree that one of the reasons that Feynman's little screen comes down in public administration is that the prescriptions in the syntheses do appear strange and difficult—and neither strangeness nor difficulty is typically appreciated in public administration.

The syntheses, taking some at random and adapted, do prescribe public administration moving away from the traditional and comfortable to the more strange and difficult polar visions. Let's acknowledge the strangeness and difficulty, considering the effects of some of the prescriptions (selected from the list and reformulated). Consider two polar visions of public administration. The visions can be conceptualized as being at the extreme poles of a range of consciousness of public administration, with the intermediate positions on ranges populated by types that share in varying degrees characteristics from both of the extremes. These extremes provide alternative visions of the human (PA "who"), alternative visions of institutions (PA "how"), alternative visions of levels of administration (PA "what"), and alternative visions of the direction of inquiry (PA "where").

Public Administration Who?

Who am I? What is the nature of the humans that administer and that are administered? What is it to be fully human? Let's identify two alternative stereotypes that serve as *competing bases for structuring and doing public administration*. The traditional extreme can be described in terms of a person's sense of identity and the relationship of that identity to the person's group. One icon for this understanding of what it is to be fully human is economic man and his derivative, administrative man, as well as other derivatives like welfare woman, contractor, and budget analyst. At the other extreme is the whole person-in-herself in-her-difference. Such a human doesn't exhibit the kind of unity and linearity that looks so coherent in such publications as *Who's Who in America*. This conceptualization of the human does not center on systems, but on the life-affirming and libidinal force of the individual human, in Max Weber's phrase—in her full and beautiful humanity.

Public Administration How?

Turn now to another set of competing bases for structuring and doing public administration. How should public administration organize its policy making, programming, and administering? That is, what basic principle should be used? At the traditional extreme, the basic principle is hierarchical. Policy making and programming should be unhesitant, for example, and administering is viewed as most efficient when it is directed, coordinated, and controlled by the leader and his leadership team. At this traditional extreme, the aim is to give direction through nonhesitant or assertive policies and prescriptions (e.g., "don't ask, don't tell" for this person, and "life in prison without the possibility of parole" for that person). At the opposite extreme, the basic principle is the banishment of hierarchy. There is a shift away from top-down policy, programmatic, and administrative action, with the aim of greater openness to the self and the other. The shift is toward authentic hesitation—not mere hesitation but a reticence to enforce the judgments of one's own or the power group.

Public Administration What?

Yet another set of competing bases for structuring and doing public administration. What should be the focus of public administration theory, research, and education? At the traditional extreme, attention is limited to the short-term and to the micro; it is also limited to the mid-level manager. There are exceptions, of course; but they *are* exceptions. At the other extreme, attention is also given to the longer-term and to the macro—and to higher public administration levels. The big picture enters.

Public Administration Where?

A last set of competing bases for structuring and doing public administration. Where can we find an optimal and neglected level of analysis—an optimal place—for achieving public administration changes? At the traditional end of the range, attention is devoted almost exclusively to things, such as public administration and economic things. I am genuinely impressed by the capability of commonsense systems analysis and commonsense rules of thumb to ameliorate surface-level hurts in administrative agencies, typically for short periods. At the opposite pole, attention is devoted mainly to matters of the unconscious. What we see depends on how we see, as we have seen before. We live—also—in a world of the dynamic unconscious and of the symbolic.

Contemplating in View of Lived Experience

Public administration thinkers and practitioners should reflect on the syntheses—one selected synthesis at a time—in terms of work and lived experience. One element is to describe a synthesis in terms of our *unexamined* lived experience. The other is to examine the selected synthesis in terms of our *examined* lived experiences.

On the one hand, lived experience—unexamined—in public administration provides insights that seem beyond the reach of those who have never been there. To feel and to know what it is like to be in public employment seems to increase appreciation of what is and what should be in public administration. There can be joy in the lived and practical experience of managing, of doing. For most of us, the "facts" that we learn from such experience are powerful. So are the attitudes and the frameworks that we use to process such facts. Other "facts" are meshed into that experience and into those frameworks. Work and lived experience seem to equip us with a basis for greater understanding.

On the other hand, reflect on and examine our lived and work experience so that we can escape the limits of what counts as public administration traditional common sense—something we can distinguish from good sense or good judgment. In his essay "Dreams and Facts," Bertrand Russell (1928, pp. 14–22) tells us about the flies that constitute our epistemological context—a context for knowing that an enlightened public administration thinking requires cutting through. Russell begins his essay by explaining that it is dull to suppose that our beliefs are derived rationally, only occasionally disturbed by desire. On the contrary, his view is that the mass of beliefs that support our daily life (and for the public administration thinker, isn't public administration her daily life?) is merely the "bodying forth of desire, corrected here and there." Claims Russell, "man is essentially a dreamer wakened sometimes for a moment by some peculiarly obtrusive element in the order of the world, but lapsing quickly." And we return to the "day-dreams that we call beliefs." It is then that Russell unloads his fly metaphor. "Every man, wherever he goes, is encompassed by a cloud of comforting convictions which move with him like flies on a summer day." Some of these convictions or beliefs are personal, for example, a person's belief about the rosy prospect of his career, or about his sexual prowess. Some concern the worth of his family, or the excellence of his school, or the accomplishments of his group, the distinctiveness of mankind in general compared against brute animals, or the Number 1 nature and uniqueness of his nation. "Concerning his nation, almost every man cherishes comfortable delusions," writes Russell. If he had written about public administration, Russell would have reiterated that the problem with public administration is not entirely "out there"; it is also "in here"—inside the defenses and limitations of what in our own brains counts as public administration common sense.

Start with lived experience, first unexamined and then examined.

Lived Experience

Public administration rightly recognizes (and so do I) the invaluable learning benefit in lived experience. But there are negative side effects to the extent that mislearning occurs. For many of us, our lived and work input is a profound learning (and mislearning) experience, with a lasting impact on the receptivity of our consciousness and on our public administration imaginative creativity. What I learned (and mislearned) as a manager in (say) the U.S. federal government and in the city of New York and elsewhere is burned into my psyche; the learning was in the field of action, where the rubber hit the road and where there was the excitement of real uncertainty and real consequences. Does the combination of learning and mislearning have a long-lasting and almost traumatic impact, often foreclosing later and competing understandings and often eliminating creative possibilities? For many, what is a public administration book compared with daily action in the field of public administration?

The nature of lived and work experience is often misunderstood. It can be underestimated; or, if it is too limited to a particular function or level, it can be overestimated. More importantly, it can be misinterpreted if it is not recognized as being shaped by taking place within a specific context. As our experiences and lives are inevitably limited (even for the most widely experienced), it is misguided to suppose that unexamined lived experience can be trumps. Lived experience is misinterpreted if it is supposed that that experience does not require contemplation and supplementation.

Lived experience is also more complicated than is commonly supposed. Ursula Franklin distinguishes between vernacular, constructed (or reconstructed) and projected realities, for example. Vernacular reality is "bread and butter, soup, work, clothing and shelter, the reality of everyday life" (Franklin 1999, p. 26). In public administration terms, is it what we think of as *really, really happening* in an agency? Constructed or reconstructed reality is what comes to us, as I would put it. Franklin adds that such reality "encompasses situations and interpretations of these situations that are considered archetypal rather than representative. These descriptions furnish us with patterns of behavior" that we consider "real" (p. 27). In public administration terms, is it how we look at the job, even when we know that that is not how it is? Projected reality is "the vernacular reality of the future" (p. 27). In public administration terms, is that what we suppose that (say) managing will be when the context has changed?

We need imaginative creativity to begin to transcend our own myths and our own deafness to the discourse of others. Much that we suppose is public administration vernacular reality is, in fact, public administration constructed reality. Consider this practice example. Recall ex–chief judge of the New York State Court of Appeals Sol Wachtler, describing his life in prison. "I have learned by being commanded to strip, bend, spread, lift and do a sort of naked and public pirouette that is beyond embarrassment" (Wachtler 1997, p. 71). The judge was sentenced in 1993 to 15 months. I write with appropriate respect for ex-Judge Wachtler. But shouldn't judges be able to imagine the degradation of prison life *before* sentencing others and *before* being sentenced themselves? Shouldn't they imagine the discourse of the other?

Appropriate receptivity to counterintuitive public administration ideas depends not only on the power of perspectives from outside public administration but also on the degree of sensitivity of our own public administration consciousness. The success, or failure, of epistemic pluralism depends on a sensitized public administration consciousness. As public administration professionals, we should reflect on the features and character of our own public administration consciousness. We should turn to more thorough and greater self-awareness, requiring professional attention to our individual and to our social unconscious. "Know yourself" was the motto written on the forecourt of the Temple of Apollo at Delphi in ancient Greece. We should move toward that.

Examined Lived Experience

Practice imagining, Andreasen advises. She recommends getting outside yourself. If you are like Einstein, you can imagine riding on a photon. If you like cars, you can imagine yourself as being a carburetor. If you like neuroscience, you can imagine yourself as a single neuron among the 100 billion neurons in a typical human brain. Readers may, or may not, want to do the imagining on a treadmill. For students wanting to write a paper, a parallel written analysis is suggested.

The creativity workout you design could start by making use of any one of the 25 items in the synthesis. Let's say that you have decided (again) that this exercise week will be "planning" week. Day 1 would be handling point 1 of the five syntheses, day 2 handling point 2, and so on. Let's imagine that it is day 5, and you have reached point 5—the synthesis selected as the example in the previous section.

For each of the points, the creativity exercise could consist of reflecting on three questions. Does this synthesized point conflict with my lived and work experience? Is my lived and work experience vernacular reality or constructed reality? Is an alternative lived and work experience feasible?

In raising these questions, however, I don't mean to suggest that the work and lived experience is always the complete loser. But neither is my experience always the complete winner. In terms of my own lived experience in managing, how do such elements of synthesis fit in—or not—with my learned feeling that much good management seems to be associated with gut feeling? How do they fit in—or not—with my learned feeling that much management seems to require decision making in conditions of uncertainty and a pragmatic back and forth. Why should I swallow my own conditioning feelings, sans examination?

Turn to point 5 of the Planning Week, and consider the subpoint about shifting the regulative ideal from mere efficiency to loving or caring. If I worked in a Department of Economics and Development (as I once did), I can stand on my treadmill and readily imagine how loving (as a regulative ideal) conflicts with the way that we operated; I could count the ways. Yet I can also reflect on the reasons why I conclude that that lived and work experience was entirely constructed. Then, I could turn to the question of whether I could get outside myself and suppose that an alternative lived experience is feasible—or not. I could reflect on my experience in an intensive-care department of a hospital after major surgery, and I might well reflect that mere efficiency is inadequate there as a regulative ideal for the staff. I could reflect whether a kind of love (or a kind of caring) is a better regulative ideal. And so on.

Again, focus on point 5 in planning. Consider the subpoint about overcoming *othering*, and imagine that this conflicts with my work and lived experience. Can I get outside myself and contemplate an alternative lived experience—or not? Can I imagine an alternative where I am deaf to the discourse of others? Can I imagine where that would make a difference? Adding emphasis to this, Bruce Wexler (2006, p. 183) quotes O'Henry's *Cabbages and Kings*: "In all the scorched and exotic places of the earth, Caucasians meet when the day's work is done to preserve the fullness of their heritage by aspersion of alien things."

Contemplating the Application

Reflect on the application of the syntheses from chapters 13–17 to a particular program. Take as your focus the example at the beginning of this book (question 1 of chapter 1), speaking of the relevance of epistemic pluralism to planning a national homeland security, or a police, program. Or, if you are familiar with planning homeland security in Miami, take the planning program in Miami as your focus. Or, if you are employed as a planner of A or B program in community X or Y, take planning that program as your focus. The more bosses you include, the less freedom of action—albeit not less freedom of contemplation—you will have.

This reflection bears some resemblance to Andreasen's third mental exercise, which prescribes observing or describing. Andreasen recommends exercising the emotional and intuitive parts of the brain. She advises observing or describing, starting with the gestalt and then doing so analytically.

Re-reflect on point 5 of the planning syntheses, especially the subpoints about the regulative ideal and shifting toward caring or loving. How could that be implemented in the selected program? Contemplate on the treadmill.

Contemplating in View of the Unfamiliar

> One of the best ways to get a new perspective on things—an important resource for thinking creatively—is to tackle a new field that you know little or nothing about. If your college major was biology or physics, try studying poetry or painting. If you spend your life thinking about computer architecture, try studying history or reading biographies. If you have spent your life in the business world, try learning about geography, earth science, or oceanography. . . . Churchill and Eisenhower painted . . . Einstein played the violin. . . . (Andreasen 2005, pp. 162–163)

This is the fourth extraordinary creativity exercise prescribed by Andreasen.

For the public administration reader, it cannot all be done on a treadmill; it also includes pounding the library shelves before sitting in an armchair. Andreasen favors reflective reading because she wants a complex neurological process, implicating multiple brain regions. This is also what is desirable for public administration, rather than dabbling (which perhaps is more fun).

For public administration specialists, choose among the unfamiliar disciplines discussed in this book—from the business, economic, political, critical theory, post-structural, pscyhoanalytic, neuroscientific, feminist, and other perspectives. And there are others. Consider evolutionary biology, for instance. Do you recall the comment in chapter 9 that a leading view in evolutionary psychology is that the brain/mind consists of many specific-purpose modules, rather than a general-purpose problem-solving program? Having evolved by natural selection, these programs are designed to solve a particular adaptive problem, for example, reading other people's minds, selecting mates, eating nonpoisonous food. Isn't that relevant in reflecting, for example, on point 5 of planning—about efficiency, love, and caring? For public administration significance, it is hard to think of an irrelevant discipline, a dry well.

For those wanting to write an analytical paper, students can be invited to write about public administration theory and practice from a selected unfamiliar perspective.

Epilogue

Why should public administration theory and practice be put in perspective? First, public administration is too important to fail: institutionalization pervades human action. Second, public-administration-out-of-perspective is too weak to succeed. Third, we have the medicine: epistemic pluralism.

Suggested Readings

For both specialists and students, consider including in your contemplation of the unfamiliar one of the suggested readings:

Feynman, Richard. 1985. *QED: The Strange Theory of Light and Matter.* Princeton, NJ: Princeton University Press.
Andreasen, Nancy C. 2005. *The Creating Brain: The Neuroscience of Genius.* New York: Dana Press.

References

Ackerman, Diane. 1995. *A Natural History of Love*. New York: Vintage Books.

Alford, J.R. 2006. "Neuroscientific Advances in the Study of Political Science." Conference panel. Philadelphia, PA: American Political Science Association. September 1.

Andreasen, Nancy C. 2005. *The Creating Brain: The Neuroscience of Genius*. New York: Dana Press.

Ansermet, Francois, and Pierre Magistretti. 2007. *Biology of Freedom: Neural Plasticity, Experience and the Unconscious*. Trans. S. Fairfield. New York: Other Press.

Appleby, P. 1949. *Policy and Administration*. Tuscaloosa, Alabama: University of Alabama Press.

Argyris, Chris. 1973. "Organization Man: Rational and Self-Actualizing." *Public Administration Review* 33 (4): 356.

Arrow, Kenneth J. 1963. *Social Choice and Individual Values*. Rev. ed. New York: John Wiley.

Atkins, K. 1996. "Of Sensory Systems and the 'Aboutness' of Mental States." *Journal of Philosophy* 93: 337–372.

Axelrod, Robert. 2007. "Political Science and Beyond: Presidential Address to the American Political Science Association." ASPA Presidential Addresses: ASPA.

Ayers, J. 2001. *Handbook of Supply Chain Management*. Boca Raton, FL: St. Lucie Press.

Baer, Mark, Barry Connors, and Michael Paradiso. 2007. *Neuroscience: Exploring the Brain*. 3rd ed. New York: Lippincortt, Williams, and Wilkins.

Balkwell, Fran, and Mic Rolph. 2003. *Gene Machines*. Cold Spring Harbor, NY: Cold Spring Harbor Laboratory Press.

Ball, Terence, and Richard Dagger. 2002. *Political Ideologies and the Democratic Ideal*. 4th ed. New York: Longman.

Barber, Benjamin R. 2007. *Consumed: How Markets Corrupt Children, Infantilize Adults, and Swallow Citizens Whole*. New York: W.W. Norton.

Baudrillard, Jean. 1984. "Game with Vestiges." *On the Beach* 5 (1).

———. 1994. *Simulacra and Simulation*. Trans. Sheila Glaser. Ann Arbor: University of Michigan Press.

Beauvoir, Simone de. 1993 (1952). *The Second Sex*. Trans. H.M. Parshley. New York: Alfred A. Knopf.

Bell, Dan. 2006. "They Deserve It." *The Nation* 283 (2): 18–24.

Bernardete, Seth, ed. 2001. *Leo Strauss: On Plato's Symposium*. Chicago: University of Chicago Press.

Berry, Jeffrey M. 1997. *The Interest Group Society.* New York: Longman.

Berzoff, Joan, Laura Melano Flanagan, and Patricia Hertz. 2008. "Inside Out, Outside In: An Introduction." In *Inside Out and Outside In: Psychodynamic Clinical Theory and Psychopathology in Contemporary Multicultural Contexts*, ed. Joan Berzoff, Laura Melano Flanagan, and Patricia Hertz, pp. 1–15. New York: Jason Aronson.

Bhabha, Homi. 1994. *The Location of Culture.* London: Routledge.

Biddle, C.R., ed. 1855. *Jean-Baptiste Say, A Treatise on Political Economy.* Trans. C.R. Prinsep. 55th ed. (1st published in French, 1803.) Philadelphia: Lippincott, Grambo and Co.

Bieck, William. 1977. *Response Time Analysis* (Summary, Vol. 1 "Methodology," Vol. 2, "Analysis"). Kansas City, MO: Kansas City Police Department.

———. 1979. *Response Time Analysis* (Vol. 3, Part 2, "Crime Analysis"). Kansas City, MO: Kansas City Police Department.

———. 1980. *Response Time Analysis* (Vol. 4, "Non-Crime Analysis"). Kansas City, MO: Kansas City Police Department.

Blais, Andre, and Stephane Dion. 2007. "Are Bureaucrats Budget Maximizers? The Niskanen Model and Its Critics." In *Readings in Public Choice Economics*, ed. Jac C. Heckelman, pp. 126–145. Ann Arbor: University of Michigan Press.

Blau, Peter M. 1970. "A Formal Theory of Differentiation in Organizations." *American Sociological Review* 35 (2): 201–218.

Bloom, Harold. 2003. *Hamlet: Poem Unlimited.* New York: Penguin Putnam.

Bochal, Hugh, and Sue Duncan. 2007. *Making Policy in Theory and Practice.* Bristol, England: The Polity Press.

Bove, Jose, and F. Dufour. 2000. *Le monde n'est pas une marchandise: Des paysans contre le malbouffe.* Paris: La Decouverte.

Box, Richard C. 2001. "Private Lives and Anti-Administration." *Administrative Theory and Praxis* 23 (4): 541–558.

———. 2003. "Contradiction, Utopia, and Public Administration." *Administrative Theory and Praxis* 25 (2): 243–260.

———. 2005. *Critical Social Theory in Public Administration.* Armonk, NY: M.E. Sharpe.

Brownlow, Louis, Charles Merriam, and Luther Gulick. 1937. *Administrative Management in the Government of the United States.* Washington, DC: Government Printing Office.

Burke, Kenneth. 1966. *Language as Symbolic Action.* Berkeley: University of California Press.

———. 1969. *A Rhetoric of Motives.* Berkeley: University of California Press.

Burke, P. 2000. *A Social History of Knowledge: From Gutenberg to Diderot.* Malden, MA: Blackwell.

Butler, Michael, and Carl Senior. 2007. "Toward an Organizational Cognitive Neuroscience." In *The Social Cognitive Neuroscience of Organizations. Annals of the New York Academy of Sciences*, ed. Carl Senior and Michael Butler, pp. 1–17. Boston, MA: Blackwell on behalf of the New York Academy of Sciences.

Cabinet Office 1999. *Modernizing Government.* London, England: The Stationary Office.

Caldicott, Helen. 2002. *The New Nuclear Danger: George W. Bush's Military-Industrial Complex.* New York: New Press.

Camerer, Colin, George Loewenstein, and Drazen Prelec. 2005. "Neuroeconomics: How Neuroscience Can Inform Economics." *Journal of Economic Literature* 43 (March): 9–64.

Camfield, D. 2005. "Neurobiology of Creativity." In *Neurobiology of Exceptionality*, ed. C. Stough, pp. 53–72. New York: Kluwer Academic.

Campbell, R.H., and A.S. Skinner. 1976. *Adam Smith: An Inquiry into the Nature and the Causes of the Wealth of Nations.* Oxford: Clarendon Press.

Caputo, John D. 1993. *Against Ethics: Contributions to a Poetics of Obligation with Constant Reference to Deconstruction.* Bloomington: Indiana University Press.

Carlin, George. 2004. *When Will Jesus Bring the Pork Chops?* New York: Hyperion.

Caro, Robert A. 1974. *The Power Broker: Robert Moses and the Fall of New York.* New York: Alfred A. Knopf.

Carroll, James. 2006. *House of War: The Pentagon and the Disastrous Rise of American Power.* Boston: Houghton Mifflin.

Castoriadis, Cornelius. 1997. *World in Fragments: Writing on Politics, Society, Psychoanalysis, and the Imagination.* ed. and trans. David Ames Curtis, Stanford, CA: Stanford University Press.

Catlaw, Thomas. 2006. "The Death of the Practitioner." *Administrative Theory and Praxis* 28 (2): 190–207.

———. 2009. "Kill the King, Love Your Neighbor." *Public Administration Quarterly* 33 (3): 318–332.

Center for Public Integrity. 2005. "Lobbyists Double Spending in Six Years." Lobby Watch, April 7. www.publicintegrity.org/pns/default.aspx?act=summary (accessed April 15, 2006).

Chen, Chung-An. 2009. "Antecedents of Contracting-Back-In." *Administration and Society* 41 (1): 101–126.

Chessick, Richard. 1993. *Dictionary for Psychotherapists: Dynamic Concepts in Psychotherapy.* Northvale, NJ: Jason Aronson.

Churchland, Patricia. 2002. *Brain-wise: Studies in Neurophilosophy.* Cambridge, MA: MIT Press.

Cixous, Hélène. 1980. "The Laugh of the Medusa." In *New French Feminisms: An Anthology*, ed. Elaine Marks and Isabelle de Coutivron, pp. 245–264. Amherst: University of Massachusetts Press.

———. 2004. *Against All Enemies: Inside America's War on Terror.* New York: Free Press.

Clarke, Richard. 2008. *Your Government Failed you: Breaking the Cycle of National Security Disasters.* New York: Harper Perennial.

Cochran, Charles L., and Eloise F. Malone. 1999. *Public Policy: Perspectives and Choices.* New York: McGraw-Hill.

Cohen, Stephen F. 2006. "The New American Cold War." *The Nation* 283 (2): 9–17.

Coles, Robert. 1998. "Psychoanalysis: The American Experience." In *Freud: Conflict and Culture*, ed. Michael S. Roth, pp. 140–151. New York: Alfred A. Knopf.

Congressional Quarterly Service. 1968. *Legislators and Lobbyists.* Washington, DC: Congressional Quarterly Service.

Cornell, Drucilla. 1998. *At the Heart of Freedom: Feminism, Sex, and Equality.* Princeton, NJ: Princeton University Press.

Cornell, Drucilla, Michel Rosenfeld, and David Gray Carlson. 1992. *Deconstruction and the Possibility of Justice.* New York: Routledge.

Creighton, James L. 2005. *The Public Participation Handbook: Making Better Decisions Through Citizen Involvement.* San Francisco: Jossey-Bass.

Cudd, Ann E., and Robin O. Andreasen, eds. 2005. *Feminist Theory: A Philosophical Anthology.* Malden, MA: Blackwell.

Culler, J. 1983. *On Deconstruction: Theory and Criticism After Structuralism.* London: Routledge.

Cunningham, Robert. 2009. "Review Symposium: To Kill the King by David John Farmer." *Public Administration Quarterly* 33 (3): 300–302.

Cunningham, Robert, and Robert Schneider. 2001. "Anti-Administration: Redeeming Bureaucracy by Witnessing and Gifting." *Administrative Theory and Praxis* 23 (4): 573–588.

Dahl, Robert A. 1947. "The Science of Public Administration." *Public Administration Review* 7: 1–11.

———. 1998. *On Democracy*. New Haven, CT: Yale University Press.

Damasio, Antonio. 2003. *Looking for Spinoza: Joy, Sorrow, and the Feeling Brain*. New York: Harcourt.

Dawkins, Richard. 1989. *The Selfish Gene*. Oxford: Oxford University Press.

Decety, J., and J.P. Keenan. 2006. "Social Neuroscience: A New Journal." www.social-neuroscience.com/introduction.asp (accessed July 23, 2006).

Deleuze, Gilles, and Félix Guattari. 1977. *Anti-Oedipus: Capitalism and Schizophrenia*. Minneapolis: University of Minnesota Press.

———. 1987. *A Thousand Plateaus*. Minneapolis: University of Minnesota Press.

Denhardt, Janet V., and Robert B. Denhardt. 2003. *The New Public Service: Serving, Not Steering*. Armonk, NY: M.E. Sharpe.

Denhardt, Robert B. 2004. *Theories of Public Organization*. 4th ed. Belmont, CA: Wadsworth.

Derrida, Jacques. 1978. *Writing and Difference*. Trans. Alan Bass. Chicago: University of Chicago Press.

Descartes, Rene. 1984. "Second Meditation." In *Philosophical Writings of Descartes*, II, ed. and trans. J. Cottingham and D. Murdock. New York: Cambridge University Press.

Diamond, Marion, and Arnold Scheibel. 1985. *The Human Brain Coloring Book*. New York: HarperCollins.

Diamond, Michael A. 1993. *The Unconscious Life of Organizations: Interpreting Organizational Identity*. Westport, CT: Quorum.

Diesing, Paul. 1991. *How Does Social Science Work? Reflections on Practice*. Pittsburgh, PA: University of Pittsburgh.

Dimock, Marshall E. 1936. "Criteria and Objectives of Public Administration." In *The Frontiers of Public Administration*, ed. J.M. Gauss, L.D. White, and M.E. Dimock, pp. 278–297. Chicago: University of Chicago Press.

Donaldson, Lex. 1996. *For Positivist Organization Theory: Proving the Hard Core*. Thousand Oaks, CA: Sage.

Drucker, Peter F. 1993. *Innovation and Entrepreneurship*. New York: HarperCollins.

Duncan, David Ewing. 2005. *The Geneticist Who Played Hoops with My DNA . . . and Other Masterminds from the Frontiers of Biotech*. New York: HarperCollins.

Dupont, J., ed. 1988. *The Clinical Diary of Sandor Ferenczi*. Cambridge: Harvard University Press.

Echols, Alice. 1989. *Daring to Be Bad: Radical Feminism in America 1967–1975*. Minneapolis: University of Minnesota.

Edelman, Murray J. 1971. *Politics as Symbolic Action*. New York: Academic Press.

Ehrenreich, Barbara. 2001. *Nickel and Dimed: On (Not) Getting By in America*. New York: Metropolitan Books.

Evans, Dylan. 1996. *An Introductory Dictionary of Lacanian Psychoanalysis*. London: Routledge.

Evans, Dylan, and Oscar Zarate. 2005. *Introducing Evolutionary Psychology*. Cambridge, UK: Icon.

Faludi, Susan. 2007. *The Terror Dream: Fear and Fantasy in Post-9/11 America*. New York: Metropolitan.

Farmer, David John. 1968. *Civil Disorder Control: A Planning Program of Municipal Coordination and Cooperation*. Chicago, Illinois: Public Administration Service.

———. 1981. "Thinking About Research: The Contribution of Social Science Research to Contemporary Policing." *Police Studies* 3 (4): 22–40.

———. 1995. *The Language of Public Administration: Bureaucracy, Modernity, and Postmodernity*. Tuscaloosa: University of Alabama Press.

———. 1997. "Derrida, Deconstruction, and Public Administration." *American Behavioral Scientist* 41 (1): 12–27.

———, ed. 1998a. *Papers on the Art of Anti-Administration.* Burke, VA: Chatelaine.

———. 1998b. "Public Administration as Play with a Purpose." In *Papers on the Art of Anti-Administration*, ed. D.J. Farmer, pp. 37–56. Burke, VA: Chatelaine.

———. 2000. "The Ladder of Organization-Think: Beyond Flatland." *Administrative Theory and Praxis* 22 (1): 66–88.

———. 2001. "Mapping Anti-Administration: Introduction to the Symposium." *Administrative Theory and Praxis* 23 (4): 475–492.

———. 2002. "The Discourses of Anti-Administration." In *Rethinking Administrative Theory: The Challenge of the New Century*, ed. Jong S. Jun, pp. 271–288. Westport, CT: Praeger.

———. 2003. "The Allure of Rhetoric and the Truancy of Poetry." *Administrative Theory and Praxis* 25 (1): 9–36.

———. 2005a. *To Kill the King: Post-Traditional Governance and Bureaucracy.* Armonk, NY: M.E. Sharpe.

———. 2005b. "The Moral First, the Technical Second!" *Administrative Theory and Praxis* 27 (3): 581–594.

———. 2006. "Neuro-Gov: Neuroscience and Governance." *Administrative Theory and Praxis* 28 (4): 653–662.

———. 2007a. "Five Great Issues in the Profession of Public Administration." In *Handbook of Public Administration*, ed. J. Rabin, W.B. Hildreth, and G.J. Miller, pp. 1205–1219. 3rd ed. New York: Taylor and Francis.

———. 2007b. "Neuro-Gov: Neuroscience as Catalyst." *Annals of the New York Academy of Sciences* 1118: 74–89. New York: New York Academy of Sciences.

———. 2007c. "Change the Course, Neurons." *Administrative Theory and Praxis* 29 (1): 182–192.

———. (2009). Is the King Dead? *Public Administration Quarterly* 33(3): 373–396.

Farmer, David John, and Patricia Patterson. 2003. "The Reflective Practitioner and the Uses of Rhetoric." *Public Administration Review* 63: 65–71.

Farmer, Rosemary L. 1998. "Recognizing the Right Brain in Organizations." In David John Farmer (ed.), *Papers on the Art of Anti-Administration*, ed. David John Farmer, pp. 71–86. Burke, VA: Chatelaine.

———. 2009. *Neuroscience and Social Work Practice: The Missing Link.* Thousand Oaks, CA: Sage.

Farmer, Rosemary L., and Ananda K. Pandurangi (1997). *Diversity in schizophrenia: Toward a richer biopsychosocial understanding for social work practice.* Health and Social Work 22(2): 109–116.

Feinberg, Todd, and Julian Keenan. 2005. *The Lost Self: Pathologies of the Brain and Identity.* New York: Oxford University Press.

Feynman, Richard. 1985. *QED: The Strange Theory of Light and Matter.* Princeton, NJ: Princeton University Press.

Firestone, Shulamith. 1979. *The Dialectic of Sex: The Case for Feminist Revolution.* New York: The Woman's Press.

Flexner, Hans. 1979. The Curriculum, the Disciplines, and Interdisciplinarity in Higher Education. Pennsylvania State University: University Press.

Fogel, Robert. 2000. *The Fourth Great Awakening and the Future of Egalitarianism.* Chicago: University of Chicago Press.

Foucault, Michel. 1972. *Archaeology of Knowledge.* New York: Pantheon.

———.1977a. *Discipline and Punish: The Birth of the Prison.* Trans. Alan Sheridan. New York: Pantheon.

———. 1977b. "Preface." In *Anti-Oedipus: Capitalism and schizophrenia*, ed. Gilles Deleuze and Felix Guattari, pp. xiii–xiv. Trans. Robert Hurley, Mark Seem, and Helen Lane. New York: Viking Press.

————. 1980. "Power/Knowledge: Selected Interviews and Other Writings 1972–1977." Brighton, UK: Harvester Press.

Franklin, Ursula M. 1990. *The Real World of Technology*. Toronto: Anansi.

Freeman, Lucy. 1972. *The Story of Anna O*. New York: Walker.

Freud, Sigmund. 1932 (1899). *The Interpretation of Dreams*. London: Allen and Unwin.

————. 1986. *The Essentials of Psycho-analysis*. Trans. James Strachey. London: Hogarth Press.

Friedan, Betty. 1997 (1963). *The Feminine Mystique*. New York: W.W. Norton.

Friedman, Milton. 1953. "The Methodology of Positive Economics." In *Essays in Positive Economics*, ed. Milton Friedman, pp. 3–43. Chicago: University of Chicago.

————. 1994. "Introduction to the Fiftieth Anniversary Edition." In F.A. Hayek, *The Road to Serfdom*, pp. ix–xx. Chicago: University of Chicago.

Frye, Marilyn. 1983. "Oppression." In *The Politics of Reality*, pp. 1–16. Freedom, CA: The Crossing Press.

Gaddis, John Lewis. 2005. *The Cold War: A New History*. New York: Penguin.

Gildin, Hilail, ed. 1989. *An Introduction to Political Philosophy: Ten Essays by Leo Strauss*. Detroit: Wayne State University Press.

Gilligan, Carol. 1982. *In a Different Voice: Psychological Theory and Women's Development*. Cambridge: Harvard University Press.

Gladden, Edgar Norman. 1972. *A History of Public Administration*. London: Frank Cass and Co.

Glimcher, Paul, Colin Camerer, Ernst Fehr, and Russell Poldrack. 2008. *Neuroeconomics: Decision Making and the Brain*. New York: Elsevier Academic Press.

Gluck, F.W. 1986. "Strategic Management: An Overview." In *Handbook of Strategic Planning*, ed. J.R. Gardner, R. Rachlin, and H.W.A. Sweeney, pp. 1.1–1.26. New York: John Wiley & Sons.

Gold, Steven Jay. 1993. *Paradigms in Political Theory*. Ames: Iowa State University Press.

Goldenberg, G. 2005. "Body Image and the Self." In *The Lost Self: Pathologies of the Brain and Identity*, ed. T.E. Feinberg and J.P. Keenan, pp. 81–99. New York: Oxford University Press.

Graham, Angus. 1992. *Unreason Within Reason: Essays on the Outskirts of Rationality*. La Salle, IL: Open Court.

Greenspan, Alan. 2007. *The Age of Turbulence: Adventures in a New World*. New York: Penguin.

Greider, William. 1992. *Who Will Tell the People? The Betrayal of American Democracy*. New York: Simon & Schuster.

Griffin, Susan. 1978. *Woman and Nature: The Roaring Inside Her*. New York: Harper & Row.

Grunbaum, Adolf. 1998. "A Century of Psychoanalysis: Critical Retrospect and Prospect." In *Freud: Conflict and Culture*, ed. Michael S. Roth, pp. 183–195. New York: Alfred A. Knopf.

Gulick, Luther. 1948. *Administrative Reflections from World War II*. Westport, CT: Greenwood.

————. 1984. "Introduction." In *Biology and Bureaucracy: Public Administration and Public Policy from the Perspective of Evolutionary, Genetic and Neurobiological Theory*, ed. E. White and J. Losco, pp. xii–xvi. Lanham, MD: University Press of America.

Gunnell, John G. 1983. "Political Theory: The Evolution of a Sub-Field." In *Political Science: The State of the Discipline*, ed. Adad W. Finifter. Washington, DC: American Political Science Association.

Habermas, Jurgen. 1983. "Modernity: An Incomplete Project." In *The Anti-Aesthetic: Essays on Postmodern Culture*, ed. Hal Foster, pp. 3–15. Port Townsend, WA: Bay Press

————. 1987. *Theory of communicative action.* Boston, MA: Beacon Press.

————. 1989. *The Structural Transformation of the Public Sphere: An Inquiry into a Category of Bourgeois Society.* Trans. Thomas Burger and Frederick Lawrence. Cambridge: MIT Press.

————. 1996. *Between Facts and Norms: Contributions to a Discourse Theory of Law and Democracy.* Cambridge: MIT Press.

Haines, S.G. 2000. *The Systems Thinking Approach to Strategic Planning and Management.* Boca Raton, FL: CRC Press.

Hall, Calvin S., and Gardner Lindzey. 1957. *Theories of Personality.* New York: John Wiley.

Harmon, Michael M., and Richard T. Mayer. 1994. *Organization Theory for Public Administration.* Burke, VA: Chatelaine.

Harvey, D. 2005. *A Brief History of Neoliberalism.* New York: Oxford University Press.

Haworth, Alan. 1994. *Anti-Libertarianism: Markets, Philosophy and Myth.* New York: Routledge.

Hayek, Friedrich A. 1944. *The Road to Serfdom.* Chicago: University of Chicago.

————. 1982. *Law, Legislation, and Liberty.* London: Routledge.

Heady, Ferral, Bruce Perlman, and Mario Rivera. 2007. "Issues in Comparative and International Administration." In *Handbook of Public Administration*, ed. Jack Rabin, W. Bartley Hildreth, and Gerald J. Miller, pp. 605–631. 3rd ed. New York: Taylor and Francis.

Heckelman, Jac C. 2004. *Readings in Public Choice Economics.* Ann Arbor: University of Michigan Press.

Heilbroner, Robert L. 1999. *The Worldly Philosophers: The Lives, Times, and Ideas of the Great Economic Thinkers.* 7th ed. New York: Simon & Schuster.

Heineman, Robert A., William T. Bluhm, Steven A. Peterson, and Edward N. Karny. 2002. *The World of the Policy Analyst.* New York: Seven Bridges.

Held, David. 1980. *Introduction to Critical Theory: Horkheimer to Habermas.* London: Hutchinson.

Henry, Nicholas, Charles T. Goodsell, Laurence E. Lynn, Camilla Stivers, and Gary L. Wamsley. 2008. *Understanding Excellence in Public Administration. Report of the Task Force on Educating for Excellence in the Master of Public Administration Degree.* February, 20. Washington, DC: American Society for Public Administration.

Hill, Philip. 1997. *Lacan for Beginners.* London: Writers and Readers Publishing.

Hollis, Martin. 1994. *The Philosophy of Social Science: An Introduction.* New York: Cambridge University Press.

Holzer, Marc, Vache Gabrielyan, and Kaifeng Yang. 2007. "Five Great Ideas in American Public Administration." In *Handbook of Public Administration*, ed. Jack Rabin, W. Bartley Hildreth, and Gerald J. Miller, pp. 49–101. 3rd ed. New York: Taylor and Francis.

Honneth, Axel. 2004. "A Social Pathology of Reason: On the Intellectual Legacy of Critical Theory." In *The Cambridge Companion to Critical Theory*, ed. Fred Rush, pp. 336–360. New York: Cambridge University Press.

hooks, bell. 1984. "Black Women: Shaping Feminist Theory." In *Feminist Theory: From Margin to Center*, pp. 1–15. Boston: South End Press.

————. 2002. *Communion: The Female Search for Love.* New York: HarperCollins.

Hoover Commission. 1949. The Hoover Commission report on organization of the executive branch of government. New York: McGraw-Hill.

Hoover, K.R. 2003. *Economics as Ideology: Keynes, Laski, Hayek, and the Creation of Contemporary Politics.* New York: Rowman & Littlefield.

Horkheimer, Max, and Theodor W. Adorno. 2002. *Dialectic of Enlightenment.* Stanford, CA: Stanford University Press.

Howe, Louis E. 2003. "Ontology and Refusal in Subaltern Ethics." *Administrative Theory and Praxis* 25 (2): 277–298.

Hutchinson, Janet. 2001. "Multigendering PA: Anti-Administration and Anti-Blues." *Administrative Theory and Praxis* 23 (4): 589–604.

Illich, Ivan. 1970. *Deschooling Society.* New York: Harper & Row.

Ito, T.A., G.R. Urland, E. Willardsen-Jensen, and J. Correll. 2006. "The Social Neuroscience of Stereotyping and Prejudice: Using Event-related Brain Potentials to Study Social Perception." In *Social Neuroscience: People Thinking About Thinking People*, ed. John Cacioppa, Penny Visser, and Cynthia Pickett, pp. 189–208. Cambridge: MIT Press.

Jacobs, Debra. 2001. "Alterity and the Environment: Making the Case for Anti-Administration." *Administrative Theory and Praxis* 23 (4): 605–620.

Jenkins, Mark, and Veroniqu Ambrosini 2007. *Strategic Management: A Multi-Perspective Approach.* New York: Palgrave.

Journal of Homeland Security and Emergency Management (May 2008) www.bepress.com/jhsem.

Jun, Jong S., ed. 2006. *Rethinking Administrative Theory: The Challenge of the New Century.* Westport, CT: Praeger.

Jung, Carl G. 1953. *Collected Works.* Vol. 7: *Two Essays on Analytical Psychology.* New York: Pantheon.

———. 1980. "The Archetypes and the Collective Unconscious." In *Collected Works of C.G. Jung*, vol. 9, part 1. Trans R.F.C. Hull. Princeton, NJ: Princeton University Press.

Katznelson, Ira. 2006. "At the Court of Chaos: Political Science in an Age of Perpetual Fear." ASPA Presidential Address. www.aspnet,org/imgtest/2006AddrKatznelson.pdf.

Kaufman, Walter. 1960. *From Shakespeare to Existentialism.* Garden City, NY: Doubleday.

———. 1980. *Discovering the Mind.* Vol. 3: *Freud Versus Adler and Jung.* New York: McGraw-Hill.

Keller, Lawrence L. 2007. *Public Administration and the American Republic: The Continuing Saga and Management and Administration in Politics.* In Jack Rabin, W. Bartley Hildreth and Gerald J. Miller, pp. 3–48. *Handbook of Public Administration.* New York: Taylor and Francis.

Kelling, George. 1974. *The Kansas City Preventive Patrol Experiment: A Technical Report.* Washington, DC: The Police Foundation.

Kellner, Douglas. 1989. *Critical Theory, Marxism, and Modernity.* Baltimore, MD: The John Hopkins University Press.

Kennedy, Emmet. 1979. "'Ideology' from Destutt de Tracy to Marx." *Journal of the History of Ideas* 40 (3): 353–368.

Kennedy, John Fitzgerald. 1962. Commencement address at Yale University, June 11. www.jfklibrary.org/Historical+Resources/Archives/Reference+Desk/Speeches/JFK/003POF03YYale06111962.htm (accessed December 11, 2006).

Kettl, Donald F. 2004. *System Under Stress: Homeland Security and American Politics.* Washington, DC: CQ Press.

Key, Valdimer Orlando. 1940. "The Lack of a Budgetary Theory." *American Political Science Review* 34 (December).

Keynes, John Maynard. 1936. *The General Theory and Employment, Interest and Money.* New York: Harcourt Brace.

Khilnani, Sunil. 1999. *The Idea of India.* New York: Farrar, Straus and Giroux.

Klein, Julie Thompson. 1990. *Interdisciplinarity: History, Theory and Practice.* Detroit: Wayne State University.

Knapp, Whitman. 1973. *Report on Police Corruption.* New York: Brazilier.

Kouzmin, Alexander, Matthew Witt, and Kim Thorne. 2009. "Killing the King in Public Administration: From Critical Epistemology to Fractured Ontology and Limited Agency." *Public Administration Quarterly* 33 (3): 341–372.

Koven, Steven G. 1988. *Ideological Budgeting: The Influence of Political Philosophy on Public Policy*. New York: Praeger.

Kuhn, Thomas. 1970. *The Structure of Scientific Revolutions*. 2nd ed. Chicago: University of Chicago Press.

Lacan, Jacques. 1966. *Ecrits*. Paris: Seuil.

———. 1988. *The Seminar*. Book I. *Freud's Papers on Technique, 1953–54*. Trans. John Forrester. New York: W.W. Norton.

———. 1992. *The Seminar*. Book II. *The Ethics of Psychoanalysis, 1959–60*. Trans. Dennis Porter. London: Routledge.

———. 1993. *The Seminar*. Book III. *The Psychoses, 1955–56*. Trans. Russell Grigg. London: Routledge.

Laing, Ronald D. 1970. *Knots*. London: Tavistock.

Landau, Martin. 1969. "Redundancy, Rationality, and the Problem of Duplication and Overlap." *Public Administration Review* 29 (4): 346–358.

Lanham, R.A. 1991. *A Handlist of Rhetorical Terms*. Berkeley: University of California Press.

Laplanche, Jean, and Jean-Baptiste Pontalis. 1973. *The Language of Psycho-Analysis*. New York: W.W. Norton.

La Porte, Todd R. 1971. "The Recovery of Relevance in the Study of Public Organization." In *Toward a New Public Administration: The Minnowbrook Perspective*, ed. Frank Marini, pp. 17–48. Scranton, PA: Chandler.

Lasch, Christopher. 1979. *Culture of Narcissism: American Life in an Age of Diminishing Expectations*. New York: W.W. Norton.

Lasswell, Harold D. 1963. *The Future of Political Science*. New York: Prentice-Hall.

Lecours, Andre. 2005. *New Institutionalism: Theory and Analysis*. Toronto: University of Toronto Press.

LeDoux, Joseph. 1996. *The Emotional Brain: The Mysterious Underpinnings of Emotional Life*. New York: Simon & Schuster.

Leopold, David, and Marc Stears. 2008. *Political Theory: Methods and Approaches*. New York: Oxford University Press.

Levi, Margaret. 2005. "Why We Need a New Theory of Government." ASPA Presidential Speech. www.aspanet.org/imgtest/2005AddrLev.pdf.

Levy, Bernard-Henri. 2008. *Left in Dark Times: A Stand Against the New Barbarism*. Trans. Benjamin Moser. New York: Random House.

Lindblom, Charles E. 1977. *Politics and Markets*. New York: Basic Books.

Lipset, Seymour Martin. 1996. *American Exceptionalism: A Double-Edged Sword*. New York: W.W. Norton.

Loh, Michael. 1997. *Re-engineering at Work*. Aldershot, UK: Gower.

Luffman, George, Edward Lea, Stuart Sanderson, and Brian Kenny. 1996. *Strategic Management: An Analytic Introduction*. New York: Blackwell.

Lukacs, John. 2005. *Democracy and Populism*. New Haven, CT: Yale University Press.

Lyotard, Jean-Francois. 1984. *The Postmodern Condition: A Report on Knowledge*. Trans. G. Bennington and B. Massumi. Minneapolis: University of Minnesota Press.

Macauley, Thomas. 1828. "On John Dryden." *Edinburgh Review*, January.

Machiavelli, Niccolo. 2008. *The Prince*. Jackson Hole, WY: Akasha.

Malpas, Simon, and Paul Wake, eds. 2006. *The Routledge Companion to Critical Theory*. New York: Routledge.

Marcuse, Herbert. 1955. *Eros and Civilization*. Boston: Beacon Press.

———. 1991 (1964). *One-Dimensional Man: Studies in the Ideology of Advanced Industrial Society*. Boston: Beacon Press.

Martin, Daniel W. (1987) "Deja Vu: French Antecedents of American Public Administration." *Public Administration Review* 47 (4): 298–301.

Marini, F. 1971. *Toward a New Public Administration: The Minnowbrook Perspective.* San Francisco: Chandler.

Marshall, Alfred. 1920 (1890). *Principles of Economics.* 8th ed. London: Macmillan.

McClosky, Deidre. 1985. *The Rhetoric of Economics.* Madison: University of Wisconsin Press.

McCurdy, Howard E. 1972. *Public Administration: A Bibliography.* Washington, D.C: American University.

McDermott, R., J. Alford, T. Brader, J. Hibbing, G. Marcus, D. Schreiber, and R. Wilson. 2006. "What Neuroscience Has to Offer Political Science." Short course #4. APSA Annual Meeting. Philadelphia, PA: American Political Science Association.

McGinn, Colin. 2003. "Fear Factor." *New York Times Book Review*, February 23, p. 13.

McGinn, Kathy, and Patricia M. Patterson. 2005. "A Long Way to What? Sex, Gender, Feminism, and the Study of Public Administration." *International Journal of Public Administration* 28: 929–942.

McIntyre, Alastair. 2007. *After Virtue: A Study in Moral Theory.* Notre Dame, IN: University of Notre Dame Press.

McLean, I. 1987. *Public Choice: An Introduction.* New York: Basil Blackwell.

McSwite, O.C. 1997a. "Jacques Lacan and the Theory of the Human Subject: How Psychoanalysis Can Help Public Administration." *American Behavioral Scientist* 41 (1): 43–63.

———. 1997b. *Legitimacy in Public Administration: A Discourse Analysis.* Thousand Oaks, CA: Sage.

———. 2000. "On the Discourse Movement: A Self Interview." *Administrative Theory and Praxis* 22 (1): 49–65.

———. 2001. "The Psychoanalytic Rationale for Anti-Administration." *Administrative Theory and Praxis* 23 (4): 493–506.

———. 2002. *Invitation to Public Administration.* Armonk, NY: M.E. Sharpe.

———. 2003. "Now More Than Ever—Refusal as Redemption." *Administrative Theory and Praxis* 25 (2): 183–204.

———. 2006. "Public Administration as the Carrier of the New Social Bond." *Administrative Theory and Praxis* 28 (2): 176–189.

———. 2009. "Socrates Redux: A Roundabout Exegesis of Farmer's *To Kill the King.*" *Public Administration Quarterly* 33 (3): 303–317.

Migue, Jean-Luc, and Gerard Belanger. 1974. "Toward a General Theory of Managerial Discretion." *Public Choice* 17 (2): 27–43.

Mill, John Stuart. 1978. *On Liberty.* Indianapolis, IN: Hackett.

Modell, Arnold H. 2003. *Imagination and the Meaningful Brain.* Cambridge: MIT Press.

Mollen, M. 1994. *The City of New York Commission to Investigate Allegations of Police Corruption and the Anti-Corruption Systems of the Police Department.* New York: City of New York.

Morgan, Gareth. 1980. "Paradigms, Metaphors and Puzzle Solving in Organization Theory." *Administrative Science Quarterly* 25: 605–622.

Mueller, Dennis C. 1989. *Public Choice II: A Revised Edition of Public Choice.* New York: Cambridge University Press.

Nelson, John S. 1998. *Tropes of Politics: Science, Theory, Rhetoric, Action.* Madison: University of Wisconsin Press.

Nelson, Randy, ed. 2006. *Handbook of Biology of Aggression.* New York: Oxford University Press.

New, S., and R. Westbrook. 2004. *Understanding Supply Chains: Concepts, Critiques, and Futures.* New York: Oxford University Press.

Nigro, Felix A. 1970. *Modern Public Administration.* New York: Harper & Row.

Nigro, Felix A. and Lloyd G. Nigro. 1973. *Modern Public Administration.* 2nd ed. New York: Harper & Row.

9/11 Commission on Terrorist Attacks upon the United States. 2004. *Final Report of the National Commission on Terrorist Attacks upon the United States.* New York: W.W. Norton.

Nisbett, Richard E. 2005. *The Geography of Thought.* Boston: Nicholas Brealey.

Niskanen, William. 1971. *Bureaucracy and Representative Government.* Chicago: Aldine-Atherton.

———. 1974. "Comment." *Public Choice* 17 (2): 43.

Osborne, D., and T. Gaebler. 1992. *Reinventing Government: How the Entrepreneurial Spirit Is Transforming the Public Sector.* New York: Addison-Wesley.

Ostrom, Elinor, Roger Parks, and Gordon Whitaker. 1977. *Patterns of Metropolitan Policing.* Cambridge, MA: Ballinger.

Ostrom, Vincent. 2008 (1973). *The Intellectual Crisis in American Public Administration.* Tuscaloosa: University of Alabama Press.

Ostrom, Vincent, and Elinor Ostrom. 1965. "A Behavioral Approach to the Study of Intergovernmental Relations." *Annals of the American Academy of Political and Social Sciences* (May), pp. 1–139.

Patterson, Patricia M. 1999. "On Behalf of, But with Regard for, Persons: Toward the Alternative Possibility That Bureaucrats Might Care." Annual Conference, Public Administration Theory Network. Portland, Oregon.

———. 2001. "Imagining Anti-Administration's Anti-Hero (Antagonist? Protagonist? Agonist?)." *Administrative Theory and Praxis* 23 (4): 529–540.

———. 2003. "Interpretation, Contradiction and Refusal: The Best Lack All Conviction." *Administrative Theory and Praxis* 25 (2): 233–242.

Peters, B. Guy, and Jon Pierre. 2006. *Handbook of Public Policy.* Thousand Oaks, CA: Sage.

Peters, Thomas, and Robert Waterman. 2004. *In Search of Excellence: Lessons from America's Best-Run Companies.* New York: HarperBusiness.

Philbrick, Nathaniel. 2006. *Mayflower: A Story of Courage, Community, and War.* New York: Viking.

Pinker, Steven. 1998. *How the Mind Works.* New York: W.W. Norton.

———. 2002. *The Blank Slate: The Modern Denial of Human Nature.* New York: Penguin.

Pugh, D.S., D.J. Hickson, and C.R. Hinings. 1969. "An Empirical Taxonomy of Organization Structures." *Administrative Science Quarterly* 14 (1): 91–114.

Raadschelders, Jos C.N. 1999. "A Coherent Framework for the Study of Public Administration." *Journal of Public Administration Research and Theory* 9 (2): 281–304.

Rabin, Jack, and James S. Bowman, eds. 1984. *Politics and Administration: Woodrow Wilson and American Public Administration.* New York: Marcel Dekker.

Rabin, Jack, W. Bartley, and Gerald L. Miller. 2007. *Handbook of Public Administration.* New York: Taylor and Francis.

Rabin, Jack, Gerald J. Miller, and W.B. Hildreth. 1989. *Handbook of Strategic Management.* New York: Marcel Dekker.

Redford, Emmette S. 1969. *Democracy in the Administrative State.* New York: Oxford University Press. www.aspanet.org/imgtest/2005AddrRudolph.pdf.

Reich, Robert. 2007. *Supercapitalism: The Transformation of Business, Democracy, and Everyday Life.* New York: Alfred Knopf.

Restak, Richard. 2006. *The Naked Brain: How the Emerging Neurosociety Is Changing How We Live, Work, and Love.* New York: Harmon Books.

Ricoeur, Paul. 1970. *Freud and Philosophy: An Essay on Interpretation.* New Haven, CT: Yale University Press.

Rifkin, Jeremy. 2004. *The European Dream: How Europe's Vision of the Future Is Quietly Eclipsing the American Dream.* New York: Tarcher/Penguin.

Riggs, Fred W. 1998. "Public Administration in America: Why Our Uniqueness Is Exceptional and Important." *Public Administration Review* 58: 22–31.

Rivlin, Alice M. 1971. *Systematic Thinking for Social Action.* Washington, DC: The Brookings Institution.

Robbins, Lionel. 1945. *An Essay on the Nature and Significance of Economic Science.* 2nd ed. London: Macmillan.

Robertson, Lynn. 2004. *Space, Objects, Minds, and Brains.* New York: Psychology Press.

Rorty, Richard. 1980. *Philosophy and the Mirror of Nature.* Princeton, New Jersey: Princeton University Press.

Rubin, Irene S. 1990. *The Politics of Public Budgeting: Getting and Spending, Borrowing and Balancing.* Chatham, New Jersey: Chatham House.

———. 2006. *Public Budgeting: Policy, Process and Politics.* Armonk, New York: M.E. Sharpe.

Rudolph, Suzanne. 2004. "The Imperialism of Categories: Situating Knowledge in a Globalizing World." Presidential address to the American Political Science Association, ASPA Presidential Addresses; ASPA.

Russell, Bertrand. 1928. *Dreams and Facts: Sceptical Essays.* London: George Allen and Unwin.

Sadock, Benjamin James, and Virginia Alcott Sadock. 2003. *Kaplan and Sadock's Synopsis of Psychiatry: Behavioral Sciences/Clinical Psychiatry.* 9th ed. Philadelphia: Lippincourt, Williams and Wilkins.

Saltzstein, Alan, Yuan Ting, and Grace Hall Saltzstein. 2001. "Work-Family Balance and Job Satisfaction." *Public Administration Review* 61 (4): 452–467.

Samuelson, Paul. 1948. *Economics.* New York: McGraw-Hill.

Samuelson, Paul, and William Norhaus. 2004. *Economics: An Introductory Analysis.* New York: McGraw-Hill.

Sapolsky, Robert. 2005. *Biology and Human Behavior: The Neural Origins of Individuality.* Chantilly, VA: The Teaching Company.

Sarap, Madan. 1993. *An Introductory Guide to Post-Structuralism and Postmodernism.* 2nd ed. Athens: University of Georgia Press.

Sardar, Ziauddin, and Boris Van Loon. 1997. *Introducing Cultural Studies.* New York: Totem Books.

Savage, Leonard J. 1972. *The Foundations of Statistics.* New York: Dover.

Scott, James C. 1990. *Domination and the Arts of Resistance: Hidden Transcripts.* New Haven, CT: Yale University Press.

Searle, John. 1964. "How to Derive an 'Ought' from an 'Is.'" *Philosophical Review* 73: 43–58.

Sen, Amartya. 2003. "Democracy and Its Global Roots." *New Republic*, November.

———. 2005. *The Argumentative Indian: Writings on Indian History, Culture and Identity.* New York: Farrar, Straus and Giroux.

Shafritz, Jay M., Albert C. Hyde, and Sandra Brooks. 2004. *Classics of Public Administration.* Belmont, CA: Wadsworth/Thomson.

Sifrey, Micah, and Nancy Watzman. 2004. *Is That a Politician in Your Pocket? Washington on $2 Million a Day.* Hoboken, New Jersey: John Wiley.

Sim, Stuart, ed. 1999. *Critical Dictionary of Postmodern Thought.* New York: Routledge.

Simchi-Levi, D., P. Kaninsky, and E. Simchi-Levi. 2000. *Designing and Managing the Supply Chain: Concepts, Strategies and Case Studies.* New York: Irwin McGraw-Hill.

Simon, Christopher. 2007. *Public Policy: Preferences and Outcomes.* New York: Pearson Longman.

Simon, Herbert A. 1946. "The Proverbs of Administration." *Public Administration Review* 6 (1) (Winter): 53–67.

———. 1976. *Administrative Behavior: A Study in Decision Making Processes in Administrative Organization.* New York: Free Press.

———. 1991. *Models of My Life.* Oshkosh, WI: Basic Books.

Skocpol, Theda. 2003. "Voice and Inequality: The Transformational of American Civic Democracy." ASPA presidential address. www.aspanet.org./imgtest/2003AddrSKOCPOL. pdf.

Soros, George. 2008. *The New Paradigm for Financial Markets: The Credit Crisis of 2008 and What It Means.* Philadelphia, PA: Penguin.

Spicer, Michael. 2001. "Value Pluralism and Its Implications for American Public Administration." *Administrative Theory and Praxis* 23 (4): 507–528.

Spiker, Paul. 2006. *Policy Analysis for Practice: Applying Social Policy.* Bristol, England: The Policy Press.

Stigler, Stephen M. 1986. *The History of Statistics: The Measurement of Uncertainty Before 1900.* Cambridge: Harvard University Press.

Stillman, Richard J. 1991. *Preface to Public Administration: A Search for Themes and Direction.* New York: St. Martin's Press.

Stone, Deborah. 2001. *Public Paradox and Political Reason.* New York: HarperCollins.

Strauss, Leo. 1989. "What Is Political Philosophy?" In *An Introduction to Political Philosophy: Ten Essays by Leo Strauss*, ed. Hilail Gildin, pp. 3–57. Detroit: Wayne State University Press.

Swanson, Larry. 2003. *Brain Architecture: Understanding the Basic Plan.* New York: Oxford University Press.

Tancredi, L. 2005. *Hardwired Behavior: What Neuroscience Reveals About Morality.* New York: Cambridge University Press.

Tanner, Robert. 2006. "States Signing on to Deadly Force Law." May 24. www.comcast. net/includes/article/print?fn=/data/news/html/2006/05/24/399485 (accessed May 25, 2006).

Taylor, Charles. 1989. *Sources of the Self: The Making of the Modern Identity.* Cambridge: Harvard University Press.

Tien, James M., and Michael Cahn. 1980. "Management of Demand: A Productivity-oriented Approach to Meeting the Demand for Public Services." Cambridge, MA: IEEE Conference on Systems, Man and Cybernetics.

Tien, James M., James W. Simon, and Richard C. Larson. 1979. *An Alternative Approach in Police Patrol: The Wilmington Split-Force Experiment.* Cambridge, MA: Public Systems Evaluation.

Tiller, R. Mark. 1997. *Big Ideas: An Introduction to Ideologies in American Politics.* New York: St. Martin's Press.

Tronto, Joan. 1993. *Moral Boundaries: A Political Argument for an Ethic of Care.* New York: Routledge.

Turner, Francis J. 1986 (1974). *Social Work Treatment: Interlocking Theoretical Approaches.* New York: The Free Press.

Turse, Nick. 2008. *The Complex: How the Military Invades our Everyday Lives.* New York: Henry Holt.

Wachtler, Sol. 1997. *After the Madness: A Judge's Own Prison Memoir.* New York: Random House.

Waldo, Dwight. 1955. *The Study of Public Administration.* New York: Doubleday.

———. 1956. *Perspectives on Administration.* Tuscaloosa: University of Alabama Press.

———. 1980. *The Enterprise of Public Administration.* Novato, CA: Chandler and Sharp.

———. 1984. *The Administrative State: The Study of the Political Theory of American Public Administration.* 2nd ed. New York: Holmes and Meier.

Walker, Alice. 1983. *In Search of Our Mothers' Gardens: Womanist Prose.* Orlando, FL: Harcourt.

Warnock, G.J. 1971. *The Object of Morality.* London: Methuen.

Weber, Max. 1958. *The Protestant Ethic and the Spirit of Capitalism*. New York: Scribner's.

Weick, K.E. 2002. "Puzzles in Organizational Learning: An Exercise in Disciplined Imagination." *British Journal of Management* 13, S7–S15.

Weimer, David L., and Aidan R. Vining. 1992. *Policy Analysis: Concepts and Practice*. Englewood Cliffs, NJ: Prentice Hall.

Weston, Anthony. 2001. *A Rulebook for Arguments*. Indianapolis, IN: Hackett.

Wexler, Bruce. 2006. *Brain and Culture*. Cambridge: MIT Press.

White, Leonard D. 1954. *The Jacksonians: A Study in Administrative History 1829–1861*. New York: Macmillan.

White, Orion. 2003. "Reason as a Homosocial Construct." *Administration and Society* 35 (2): 238–240.

Wildavsky, Aaron. 1987. *Speaking Truth to Power: The Art and Craft of Policy Analysis*. New Brunswick, NJ: Transaction.

Wilson, E.O. 1998. *Consilience: The Unity of Knowledge*. New York: Alfred Knopf.

Wilson, Woodrow. 1887. "The Study of Administration." *Political Science Quarterly* 2: 197–222.

Wisdom, John. 1987. *Challengeability in Modern Science*. Aldershot, UK: Avebury.

Wittgenstein, Ludwig. 1953. *Philosophical Investigations*. New York: Macmillan.

Wittmer, D.P., and R.P. McGowan. 2007. "Five Conceptual Tools for Decision Making." In *Handbook of Public Administration*, ed. J. Rabin, W.B. Hildreth, and G.J. Miller, pp. 315–342. 3rd ed. New York: Marcel Dekker.

Wollstonecraft, Mary. 1792. *A Vindication of the Rights of Women*. London: Joseph Johnson.

Woodruff, Paul. 2005. *First Democracy: Challenge of an Ancient Idea*. New York: Oxford University Press.

Woodson, L. 1979. *A Handbook of Modern Rhetorical Terms*. Urbana, IL: National Council of Teachers of English.

Wordsworth, William. 1986. *The Prelude*. New York: Chelsea House.

Zanetti, Lisa A. 2003. "Holding Contradictions: Marcuse and the Idea of Refusal." *Administrative Theory and Praxis* 25 (2): 261–276.

Zinn, Howard. 1999. *A People's History of the United States*. New York: HarperCollins.

Index

About the Author

David John Farmer is professor of political science and public administration, School of Government and Public Affairs, Virginia Commonwealth University. He received his bachelor of science degree from the London School of Economics and Political Science, University of London; master's degrees from the University of Toronto and from the University of Virginia; a PhD in economics from the University of London, and a PhD in philosophy from the University of Virginia.

Dr. Farmer was employed by the city of New York and by the U.S. Department of Justice. He has provided management consulting services to some forty states and local governments, including the states of Illinois and Pennsylvania and the cities of Los Angeles, Atlanta, Northampton, Galesburg, Reading, Salt Lake, New Hope, Durham, Oklahoma City, Plymouth, Moberly, Tacoma, Kansas City, and Milwaukee. He is the author of *Crime Control: The Use and Misuse of Police Resources* (1984); *Being in Time: The Nature of Time in Light of McTaggart's Paradox* (1990); *The Language of Public Administration: Bureaucracy, Modernity, and Postmodernity* (1995); and *To Kill the King: Post-Traditional Governance and Bureaucracy* (2005). He is the editor of *The Art of Anti-Administration* (1998).